Empiricism, Perceptual Knowledge,
Normativity, and Realism

MIND ASSOCIATION OCCASIONAL SERIES

This series consists of occasional volumes of original papers on predefined themes. The Mind Association nominates an editor or editors for each collection, and may cooperate with other bodies in promoting conferences or other scholarly activities in connection with the preparation of particular volumes.

Publications Officer: M. A. Stewart
Secretary: R. D. Hopkins

Empiricism, Perceptual Knowledge, Normativity, and Realism

Essays on Wilfrid Sellars

EDITED BY

Willem A. deVries

OXFORD
UNIVERSITY PRESS

OXFORD
UNIVERSITY PRESS

Great Clarendon Street, Oxford OX2 6DP

Oxford University Press is a department of the University of Oxford.
It furthers the University's objective of excellence in research, scholarship,
and education by publishing worldwide in

Oxford New York

Auckland Cape Town Dar es Salaam Hong Kong Karachi
Kuala Lumpur Madrid Melbourne Mexico City Nairobi
New Delhi Shanghai Taipei Toronto

With offices in

Argentina Austria Brazil Chile Czech Republic France Greece
Guatemala Hungary Italy Japan Poland Portugal Singapore
South Korea Switzerland Thailand Turkey Ukraine Vietnam

Oxford is a registered trademark of Oxford University Press
in the UK and in certain other countries

Published in the United States
by Oxford University Press Inc., New York

© The several contributors 2009

The moral rights of the authors have been asserted
Database right Oxford University Press (maker)

First published 2009

British Library Cataloguing in Publication Data
Data available

Library of Congress Cataloging in Publication Data
Data available

Typeset by Laserwords Private Limited, Chennai, India
Printed in Great Britain
on acid-free paper by the
MPG Books Group, Bodmin and King's Lynn

ISBN 978-0-19-957330-1

10 9 8 7 6 5 4 3 2

1006084985

In memory of Jay F. Rosenberg

Contents

List of Contributors

JOHN MCDOWELL is University Professor of Philosophy at the University of Pittsburgh. Before moving to Pittsburgh in 1986, he taught at University College, Oxford. He has visited at Harvard, the University of Michigan, UCLA, and Princeton University. His major interests are Greek philosophy, philosophy of language, philosophy of mind, metaphysics and epistemology, and ethics. He is a fellow of the British Academy and a fellow of the American Academy of Arts and Sciences.

ROBERT B. BRANDOM is Distinguished Service Professor of Philosophy at the University of Pittsburgh, a fellow of the Center for the Philosophy of Science there, and a Fellow of the American Academy of Arts and Sciences. His interests center on philosophy of language, philosophy of mind, and the philosophy of logic.

PAUL COATES is Professor of Philosophy at the University of Hertfordshire. He served as President of the Mind Association in 1998–9. He has published in leading journals on topics connected with Perception, Philosophy of Mind, and Meaning and Normativity.

PAUL SNOWDON is Grote Professor of Mind and Logic at University College London. Professor Snowdon's research and publications relate to three main areas: the problem of personal identity (on which he is completing a book manuscript), the philosophy of perception, and the mind–body problem.

MICHAEL WILLIAMS is a Krieger-Eisenhower Professor and Chair of the Department of Philosophy. Before moving to Johns Hopkins, he taught at Yale, the University of Maryland, and Northwestern. He has visited at several universities including Chicago, Michigan, Pennsylvania, and MIT. His main areas of interest are epistemology (with special reference to skepticism), philosophy of language, and the history of modern philosophy.

JAMES R. O'SHEA is Senior Lecturer at University College Dublin. He serves as reviews editor for the *International Journal of Philosophical Studies*.

His interests include Kant, Hume, Sellars, Pragmatism, Epistemology, and Philosophy of Mind.

WILLEM A. DEVRIES is Professor of Philosophy at the University of New Hampshire. He has also taught at Amherst College, Harvard, Tufts University, and the University of Vienna. His interests include Philosophy of Mind, M&E, and the history of philosophy, especially German Idealism.

JOHANNA SEIBT is Associate Professor of Philosophy at Aarhus University, Denmark. She has also taught at the University of Texas. Her principal interests are in Ontology, Metaphysics, and Process Philosophy.

JAY F. ROSENBERG was Taylor Grandy Professor of Philosophy at the University of North Carolina, Chapel Hill. His interests included Metaphysics and Epistemology, the Philosophy of Language, and Kant. He was arguably the most authoritative interpreter of Sellars's philosophy. Regrettably, Professor Rosenberg died in February 2008.

References for Sellars's Works

A Note on Citations

An effort has been made to use a common system of citation for all references to Sellars's works. A standard set of abbreviations for Sellars's books and articles has been developed, thanks to the efforts of Jeff Sicha at Ridgeview Publishing and Andrew Chrucky at the "Problems from Wilfrid Sellars" website. These abbreviations have been used throughout, and, where available, chapter and/or paragraph numbers, followed by the page numbers in the relevant source. Collections of Sellars's essays are proliferating, and this citation format offers sufficient information to facilitate locating the citation in any version. In particular, EPM is itself now available in four different locations, including its original venue in the *Minnesota Studies in the Philosophy of Science*. References to EPM include the section number and page references in *Science, Perception and Reality* *[SPR]*; *Knowledge, Mind, and the Given: a Reading of Wilfrid Sellars's "Empiricism and the Philosophy of Mind"* *[KMG]*; and Harvard University Press's publication of the essay, edited by R. Brandom [B].

AR   1975. "Autobiographical Reflections: (February, 1973)". In *Action, Knowledge and Reality: Studies in Honor of Wilfrid Sellars*, H.-N. Castañeda (ed.), 277–93. New York: Bobbs-Merrill.

BBK   1960. "Being and Being Known". *Proceedings of the American Catholic Philosophical Association* (1960), 28–49. [Reprinted in SPR, ISR.]

BD   1977. "Berkeley and Descartes: Reflections on the 'New Way of Ideas'". In *Studies in Perception: Interpretations in the History of Philosophy and Science*, P. K. Machamer and R. G. Turnbull (eds.), 259–311.

Columbus, OH: Ohio State University Press.
[Reprinted in KTM.]

CDCM   1957. "Counterfactuals, Dispositions, and the Causal
Modalities". In *Minnesota Studies in the Philosophy of
Science*, vol. II, H. Feigl, M. Scriven, and
G. Maxwell (eds.), 225–308. Minneapolis, MN:
University of Minnesota Press.

CE   1956. "The Concept of Emergence" (with Paul
Meehl). In *Minnesota Studies in the Philosophy of
Science*, vol. I, H. Feigl and M. Scriven (eds.),
239–52. Minneapolis, MN: University of
Minnesota Press.

CIL   1948. "Concepts as Involving Laws and
Inconceivable without Them". *Philosophy of Science*
15: 287–315. [Reprinted in PPPW.]

ENWW   1947. "Epistemology and the New Way of Words".
Journal of Philosophy 44: 645–60. [Reprinted in
PPPW.]

EPM   1956. "Empiricism and the Philosophy of Mind". In
Minnesota Studies in the Philosophy of Science, vol. I,
H. Feigl and M. Scriven (eds.), 253–329.
Minneapolis, MN: University of Minnesota Press.
[Originally presented at the University of London
Special Lectures in Philosophy for 1956 as "The
Myth of the Given: Three Lectures on Empiricism
and the Philosophy of Mind". Reprinted in SPR
with additional footnotes. Published separately as
*Empiricism and the Philosophy of Mind: with an
Introduction by Richard Rorty and a Study Guide by
Robert Brandom*, R. Brandom (ed.) (Cambridge,
MA: Harvard University Press, 1997). [B] Also
reprinted in W. deVries and T. Triplett,
*Knowledge, Mind, and the Given: A Reading of
Sellars' "Empiricism and the Philosophy of Mind"*
(Indianapolis, IN: Hackett, 2000) [KMG].]

FMPP   1981. "Foundations for a Metaphysics of Pure Process" [The Carus Lectures]. *The Monist* 64: 3–90.

I   1972. "... this I or he or it (the thing) which thinks". Presidential address 1970, American Philosophical Association (Eastern Division). *Proceedings of the American Philosophical Association* 44: 5–31. [Reprinted in EPH, ISR.]

IIOR   1963. "Imperatives, Intentions, and the Logic of 'Ought'". In *Morality and the Language of Conduct*, H.-N. Castañeda and G. Nakhnikian (eds.), 159–214. Detroit, MI: Wayne State University Press. [A radically revised and enlarged version of IIO.]

IKTE   1978. "The Role of Imagination in Kant's Theory of Experience". The Dotterer Lecture 1978. In *Categories: A Colloquium*, H. W. Johnstone, Jr. (ed.), 231–45. University Park, PA: Pennsylvania State University Press.

IM   1953. "Inference and Meaning". *Mind* 62: 313–38. [Reprinted in PPPW, ISR.]

IM   1957. "Intentionality and the Mental". A symposium by correspondence with Roderick Chisholm. In *Minnesota Studies in the Philosophy of Science*, vol. II, H. Feigl, M. Scriven, and G. Maxwell (eds.), 507–39. Minneapolis, MN: University of Minnesota Press.

ISR   2007. *In the Space of Reasons*, Kevin Scharp and Robert Brandom (eds.). Cambridge, MA: Harvard University Press.

KTM   2002. *Kant's Transcendental Metaphysics: Sellars' Cassirer Lectures and Other Essays*, J. F. Sicha (ed.). Atascadero, CA: Ridgeview Publishing.

LRB   1949. "Language, Rules and Behavior". In *John Dewey: Philosopher of Science and Freedom*, S. Hook (ed.), 289–315. New York: Dial Press. [Reprinted in PPPW.]

MEV   1981. "Mental Events". *Philosophical Studies* 39: 325–45.

MFC   1974. "Meaning as Functional Classification (A Perspective on the Relation of Syntax to Semantics)", *Synthese* 27 (special issue Intentionality, Language and Translation, J. G. Troyer and S. C. Wheeler, III (eds.)): 417–37. [Reprinted in ISR.]

MGEC   1979. "More on Givenness and Explanatory Coherence". In *Justification and Knowledge*, G. Pappas (ed.), 169–82. Dordrecht: D. Reidel. [Reprinted in *Perceptual Knowledge*, J. Dancy (ed.), 177–91 (Oxford: Oxford University Press, 1988).]

NAO   1980. *Naturalism and Ontology* [The John Dewey Lectures for 1973–74]. Atascadero, CA: Ridgeview Publishing. [Reprinted with corrections in 1997.]

NS   1962. "Naming and Saying". *Philosophy of Science* 29: 7–26. [Reprinted in SPR, ISR.]

OMR   1952. "Obligation and Motivation". In *Readings in Ethical Theory*, W. Sellars and J. Hospers (eds.), 511–17. New York: Appleton-Century-Crofts. [A revised and expanded version of OM.]

PHM   1963. "Phenomenalism". In *Science, Perception and Reality*, 60–105. London: Routledge & Kegan Paul. [Reprinted in ISR.]

PP   1967. *Philosophical Perspectives*. Springfield, IL: Charles C. Thomas. [Reprinted in two volumes, PPME and PPHP (Atascadero, CA: Ridgeview Publishing, 1977).]

PPHP   1977. *Philosophical Perspectives: History of Philosophy*. Atascadero, CA: Ridgeview Publishing. [A reprint of Part I of Philosophical Perspectives.]

PPME   1977. *Philosophical Perspectives: Metaphysics and
          Epistemology.* Atascadero, CA: Ridgeview
          Publishing. [A reprint of Part II of Philosophical
          Perspectives.]

PPPW   1980. *Pure Pragmatics and Possible Worlds: The Early
          Essays of Wilfrid Sellars,* J. F. Sicha (ed.).
          Atascadero, CA: Ridgeview Publishing.

PR   1955. "Physical Realism". *Philosophy and
          Phenomenological Research* 15: 13–32. [Reprinted in
          PP and PPME.]

PSIM   1962. "Philosophy and the Scientific Image of Man".
          In *Frontiers of Science and Philosophy,* R. Colodny
          (ed.), 35–78. Pittsburgh, PA: University of
          Pittsburgh Press. [Reprinted in SPR, ISR.]

RET   1952. *Readings in Ethical Theory,* W. Sellars and
          J. Hospers (eds.). New York: Appleton-
          Century-Crofts.

RNWW   1948. "Realism and the New Way of Words".
          Philosophy and Phenomenological Research 8: 601–34.
          [Reprinted in *Readings in Philosophical Analysis,*
          H. Feigl and W. Sellars (eds.) (New York:
          Appleton-Century-Crofts, 1949) and in PPPW.]

SK   1975. "The Structure of Knowledge: (I) Perception;
          (II) Minds; (III) Epistemic Principles". In *Action,
          Knowledge and Reality: Studies in Honor of Wilfrid
          Sellars,* H.-N. Castañeda (ed.), 295–347. New
          York: Bobbs-Merrill.

SM   1967. *Science and Metaphysics: Variations on Kantian
          Themes,* The John Locke Lectures for 1965–66.
          London: Routledge & Kegan Paul. [Reissued
          (Atascadero, CA: Ridgeview Publishing, 1992).]

SPR   1963. *Science, Perception and Reality.* London:
          Routledge & Kegan Paul. [Reissued (Atascadero,
          CA: Ridgeview Publishing, 1991).]

SRI   1965. "Scientific Realism or Irenic Instrumentalism:
               A Critique of Nagel and Feyerabend on
               Theoretical Explanation". *Boston Studies in the
               Philosophy of Science*, vol. 2, R. Cohen and
               M. Wartofsky (eds.), 171–204. Dordrecht:
               D. Reidel. [Reprinted in PP and PPME.]

SRLG   1954. "Some Reflections on Language Games".
               Philosophy of Science 21: 204–28. [Reprinted in
               ISR; reprinted with extensive revisions in SPR.]

SRPC   1978. "Some Reflections on Perceptual
               Consciousness". In *Crosscurrents in Philosophy:
               Selected Studies in Phenomenology and Existential
               Philosophy* 7, R. Bruzina and B. Wilshire (eds.),
               169–85. The Hague: Martinus Nijhoff.

SSIS   1971. "Science, Sense Impressions, and Sensa: A
               Reply to Cornman". *Review of Metaphysics* 25:
               391–447.

SSMB   1953. "A Semantic Solution of the Mind–Body
               Problem". *Methodos* 5: 45–82. [Reprinted in
               PPPW.]

SSOP   1982. "Sensa or Sensings: Reflections on the
               Ontology of Perception". *Philosophical Studies* 41
               (Essays in Honor of James Cornman): 83–111.

TC   1962. "Truth and Correspondence". *Journal of
               Philosophy* 59: 29–56. [Reprinted in SPR.]

TTP   1983. "Towards a Theory of Predication". In *How
               Things Are*, J. Bogen and J. McGuire (eds.),
               281–318. Dordrecht: D. Reidel.

Introduction

In 1956, Wilfrid Sellars, an American philosopher from the University of Minnesota, returned to England (he'd been a Rhodes Scholar at Oxford twenty years earlier) to deliver a set of lectures at the University of London titled "The Myth of the Given: Three Lectures on Empiricism and the Philosophy of Mind." Published soon afterward as "Empiricism and the Philosophy of Mind" [EPM] in the first volume of the Minnesota Studies in the Philosophy of Science, it went on to become one of the most influential articles of the century. The critique of the "Myth of the Given" it contained was credited with being one of the final nails in the coffin of positivism and logical empiricism and set an anti-foundationalist agenda in epistemology for the rest of the century. But the essay went far beyond simply criticizing the notion of epistemological foundations. Sellars also presciently anticipated the argument between epistemological internalism and externalism and produced a positive epistemological theory that combined elements of both. The essay was also a landmark achievement in the philosophy of mind, overthrowing long-standing Cartesian orthodoxy, in part via the introduction of Sellars's own myth, the myth of Jones. This story rejects the idea that mental states are self-intimating; instead, it proposes that our mentalistic concepts can be fruitfully compared to theoretical concepts in the sciences. One of the earliest clear functionalist treatments of intentionality, it also recognized the inadequacy of functionalist solutions to the "hard problem" of sensory consciousness. Sellars's essay challenged almost every philosophical school, and became widely known and referred to. But it was challenging in other ways as well, and also acquired a reputation for being complex and difficult to read.

This ground-breaking essay was, in fact, just the tip of a rather substantial iceberg, for Sellars developed a complex, systematic philosophy that worked out in significant detail many of the themes that were only adumbrated in EPM. But for many years, EPM was the canonical work by Sellars, the work everyone knew one was supposed to read. A more complete view of Sellars's thought has taken longer to make its mark. One cannot deny that Sellars's work is difficult: each of his essays is a perspectival glimpse of a multi-dimensional structure and is hard to understand entirely on its own. Some overview of Sellars's larger plan is called for, and that calls for patiently working through his essays individually, usually several times.[1] Sellars's essays and books take a substantial investment of time to master, but they articulate an unusually comprehensive and coherent philosophical view of the world and the place of humanity in it.

In 2006, to celebrate the fiftieth anniversary of Sellars's original London lectures, the Institute of Philosophy in the School of Advanced Studies at the University of London, with the financial assistance of the Mind Association, sponsored a conference bringing together a number of philosophers deeply influenced by Sellars. This volume collects the papers delivered there, supplemented by several other contributions. Though the conference celebrated the anniversary of EPM, the papers do not all focus on that essay, by any means. And this is as it should be. EPM contains pieces of, hints about, and allusions to most of the major themes in Sellars's philosophy, but much of it is still *in nuce*. Many themes are developed further in other papers, and in pursuing those issues, it is natural to look towards the more thorough exposition they receive elsewhere. Some of the papers included here are critical of Sellars's doctrines and arguments, some defend Sellars's positions,

---

[1] For the impatient, there are now several books that seek to draw a more easily comprehensible picture of the Sellarsian whole. Willem A. deVries, *Wilfrid Sellars*. Philosophy Now Series (Chesham, Bucks: Acumen Publishing and Montreal and Kingston: McGill-Queen's University Press, 2005) and James R. O'Shea, *Wilfrid Sellars: Naturalism with a Normative Turn*. Key Contemporary Thinkers. (Cambridge, UK, and Malden, MA: Polity Press, 2007).

but all attest to the richness of insight and the ongoing relevance and fecundity of Sellars's philosophy.

The opening essay in this collection also served as the keynote address at the conference. In it, John McDowell engages a long-running argument he has had with his colleague, Robert Brandom. Brandom has claimed that the intent and effect of Sellars's argument in EPM is to "dismantle empiricism," which Brandom, with decided rationalist leanings, counts as a Good Thing. McDowell, however, argues that Sellars's intent (and effect) is not to dismantle, abandon, or kill off empiricism, but to *revise* it, and revise it in the direction of greater coherence and consistency. In McDowell's eyes, it is precisely this revised empiricism that we should welcome. "To avoid the myth of the given in the form it takes in traditional empiricism, what we need is an empiricism that keeps faith with the nominalism only imperfectly conformed to by traditional empiricism" (p. 30). Sellars's intent in EPM is to work out a more rigorous empiricism, not to abandon empiricism altogether.

In his essay, Robert Brandom continues this argument, though only indirectly. The basic lesson Brandom wants to teach us here is that empiricism's traditional skepticism about the modalities is faulty and, ultimately, incompatible with the constructive project empiricism promises its proponents. Brandom traces this argument through several of Sellars's essays contemporaneous with EPM and pinpoints the crucial move, which he calls the 'Kant–Sellars thesis about modality,' "that in being able to use non-modal, empirical-descriptive vocabulary, one already knows how to do everything one needs to know how to do in order to deploy modal vocabulary, which accordingly can be understood as making explicit structural features that are always already implicit in what one *does* in describing" (p. 58). Is Sellars's rejection of the traditional empiricist skepticism concerning modality tantamount to a rejection of empiricism, or is his attempt to carve out a nominalistically acceptable interpretation of the modalities another way in which Sellars would revise empiricism?

Paul Coates defends a slightly modified version of Sellars's Critical Realist theory of perception. According to Critical Realism, perceptual experience is complex, consisting of both an inner, sensory episode, and a conceptual episode. Perceptual states are epistemically direct in the sense that their semantic or conceptual reference is to the distal object that, if they are veridical, they are perceptions of. But they are causally mediated by the sensory state, which is the proximal stimulus for the conceptual episode. Coates gives us a fine-grained analysis of Sellars's theory, emphasizing the role in perception Sellars attributes to the imagination. The revision Coates proposes is centered on the question of how the imagination enriches the sensory experience at the heart of perception. Sellars talks mostly of the involvement of images in such states, but Coates proposes that a more plausible treatment would emphasize instead the role of anticipations and expectations of future sensory experience. Coates then argues that Critical Realism gives a better account of demonstrative reference in perception than any of the available alternatives.

Paul Snowdon examines a number of Sellars's arguments concerning the nature and status of perception, and finds in them a curious mix of insight and illusion. Richard Rorty attributes to Sellars the discrediting of sense-datum theory, at least on the western side of the Atlantic, but Snowdon argues that this is not justified. Snowdon examines the arguments against sense-datum theories to be found in EPM and concludes that while they raise significant problems for such theories, they are not conclusive. Furthermore, Sellars ends EPM by engaging in a *rapprochement* with sense-data that makes him hardly a critic of the theory at all. Snowdon also examines Sellars's own myth, the Myth of Jones, and declares it to be doubly a myth: that is, it so misconstrues the logic of ordinary talk about sensations and impressions that it cannot do the job of helping us understand the nature of our concepts of sensory states.

Coates and deVries, in their short joint contribution, argue that Robert Brandom's discussion of Sellars's two-ply account of observation in his *Tales of the Mighty Dead* makes several crucial errors that would make Sellars's analysis of "looks"-sentences incoherent. Brandom does not recognize the difference in "level" between observation reports concerning physical objects and "looks"-statements, and he denies that "looks"-statements are reports or even make claims. They argue that a careful reading of "Empiricism and the Philosophy of Mind" does not support Brandom's interpretation, and show how to read Sellars properly on the analysis of such sentences, including the way they intimate inner, sensory states.

James O'Shea focuses on the relationship in Sellars's thought between the normative and the natural. This relationship poses a significant interpretive challenge in Sellars's works, for Sellars defends two theses that are not clearly compatible: (1) He is a scientific realist who accords ontological priority to entities in the causal network of space–time. In the culminating Scientific Image of the world, anything real in our world will be reducible to such entities and their relations. (2) Sellars defends the irreducibility of the "logical space of reasons" to the logical space of causes and claims that the normative vocabulary of the Manifest Image will have to be "joined" to the vocabulary of the Scientific Image, and neither eliminated nor reduced away. O'Shea distinguishes *conceptual* from *causal* reducibility, and then argues that Sellars attempts to knit the natural and the normative together via the principle that the "Espousal of principles is reflected in uniformities of performance" (TC 216).

Michael Williams begins his paper by noting that, though Sellars was well known as a critic of foundationalism, he also clearly rejects classical coherentism in EPM. How can one chart a course between these two camps? The key to Sellars's solution, which Williams thinks is a right-spirited effort, is tied to appreciating Sellars's radical fallibilism. After taking some time to explain what he takes the Myth of the Given to amount to (and why he thinks McDowell's construal is overly narrow), Williams further distinguishes the semantic holism that Sellars espouses (against the semantic atomism of the empiricists) from the epistemic holism that traditional coherentists have defended. Such a distinction would enable Sellars to privilege observational knowledge without falling prey to the myth of the given, but, according to Williams, this cannot be the whole story behind Sellars's attempt to avoid both foundationalism and coherentism, for Sellars is a kind of epistemic holist. In Sellars's view, our observation vocabulary is subject to conceptual change, even radical revision, and, perhaps even more crucially, Sellars insists on the epistemic reflexivity of knowledge. That is, observational knowledge presupposes knowledge of some general truths about the reliability of our cognitive capacities and our current circumstances. Rather, Williams argues, Sellars offers us a picture in which there are two dimensions of epistemic priority. "Epistemic principles are basic in the order of fundamental epistemic warrant. But IPM judgments [introspective, perceptual, or memory judgments] are epistemically prior to explanations of why epistemic principles hold" (p. 172). Sellars's emphasis on the dynamic default-and-challenge structure of the justification of empirical claims can evade both classical opponents: foundationalism and coherentism.

A number of notable philosophers influenced by Sellars have flirted (or more) with idealism. Rorty, for instance, has been accused of a version of linguistic idealism, and the current fascination with Hegel in Pittsburgh also speaks of the attraction of idealistic modes of thought for Sellars's successors. Sellars himself certainly proclaimed his own realism vociferously, though. Willem A. deVries's paper investigates the complex attitude towards idealism actually to be found in Sellars's thought. Distinguishing the epistemologically-based arguments that led many empiricists to a form of idealism from a different set of more purely metaphysical arguments that came to dominate in German idealisms, deVries shows that Sellars resolutely rejects all of the epistemologically-based arguments for idealism. The arguments of Kant and Hegel centered on the autonomy of reason, however, are much more attractive to Sellars, who, deVries claims, ends up introducing his controversial conception of *picturing* in order to avoid falling into such a version of idealism.

Sellars's conception of picturing has not garnered a great deal of attention in the literature, and Johanna Seibt offers a set of reflections to situate it more clearly both in Sellars's work and in a broader philosophical/scientific context. Picturing, Seibt contends, is Sellars's account of a "dimension of givenness ... that is not in dispute," namely that dimension of givenness that ensures that when we change our concepts "we do not change that to which we are responding" (FMPP I §87). Seibt seeks to go beyond Sellars's fairly abstract characterizations of picturing by arguing that picturing is "a certain type of non-linear causal processing" (p. 249) and that combining this view of picturing with contemporary accounts of natural functions affords us an understanding of how Sellars intends to use picturing to introduce and ground the normativity of linguistic representations and thought in the "low-grade normativity" present in certain forms of causal representational systems.

Jay Rosenberg's contribution to the EPM conference was published separately in his book *Wilfrid Sellars: Fusing the Images*, but for this volume, Jay has contributed an essay in which he reviews Sellars's arguments for the ultimate ontological primacy of the "scientific image" over the "manifest image," despite the fact that the manifest image is essential to the constitution of humanity. Rosenberg's essay begins by playing off an earlier essay by Bruce Aune on Sellars's two images in which Aune compares the distinction to David Hume's distinction between two "systems of ideas" for explaining the world. In order to better understand the relation Sellars takes to hold between the objects of the manifest image and "theoretical" postulates of the sciences, Rosenberg considers the fundamental conception of scientific explanation in Sellars's philosophy. Rosenberg finds that "already within the manifest image, the epistemology of natural science is arguably best understood in Sellarsian terms as a systematic working out of an ontological dialectic of appearance vs. reality" (p. 288). In Sellars's view, then, the ontological primacy of the scientific image is simply a consequence of commitments already present in the manifest image.

Acknowledgments

This volume owes much to many people. Initial thanks must go to Tim Crane, then head of the Institute of Philosophy in the School of Advanced Studies at the University of London for undertaking to sponsor and organize the conference celebrating the anniversary of Sellars's original presentation of EPM. Sharar Ali, the administrator of the Institute, ensured that everything happened like clockwork and with style. The Mind Association also deserves thanks for financial support of the conference and for accepting this volume into its publications series. Professor M. A. Stewart and an anonymous referee are to be thanked for their helpful involvement in bringing this volume to press.

One of our authors, Jay F. Rosenberg, passed on before this volume could see the light of day. Besides being one of Sellars's most sensitive exponents, Jay was a friend and an exemplar to many philosophers. We would like to dedicate this volume to his memory.

1

Why Is Sellars's Essay Called "*Empiricism* and the Philosophy of Mind"?

John McDowell

I.

I take my question from Robert Brandom, who remarks in his Study Guide (B: 167): "The title of this essay is '*Empiricism* and the Philosophy of Mind,' but Sellars never comes right out and tells us what his attitude toward empiricism is."[1] Brandom goes on to discuss a passage that might seem to indicate a sympathy for empiricism on Sellars's part, but he dismisses any such reading of it. (I shall come back to this.) He concludes: "Indeed, we can see at this point [he has reached §45] that one of the major tasks of the whole essay is to dismantle empiricism" (B: 168).

I am going to argue that this claim is quite wrong.

To do Brandom justice, I should note that when he defends his claim, what he mentions is, specifically, *traditional* empiricism. But he nowhere contemplates a possibility left open by this more detailed (and correct) specification of Sellars's target—the possibility that Sellars might be aiming to rescue a *non-traditional*

---

[1] Robert Brandom, "Study Guide" in Wilfrid Sellars, *Empiricism and the Philosophy of Mind, with an Introduction by Richard Rorty and a Study Guide by Robert Brandom*, ed. Robert Brandom (Cambridge, MA: Harvard University Press, 1997) [B].

empiricism from the wreckage of traditional empiricism, so that he can show us how to be good empiricists. I think that is exactly what Sellars aims to do in this essay.

2.

Traditional empiricism, explicitly so described, is in Sellars's sights in the pivotal part VIII of "Empiricism and the Philosophy of Mind" (henceforth EPM).

Traditional empiricism answers the question "Does empirical knowledge have a foundation?", which is the title of part VIII, with an unqualified "Yes". Traditional empiricism is foundationalist in a sense that Sellars spells out like this (§32):

One of the forms taken by the Myth of the Given is the idea that there is, indeed *must be*, a structure of particular matter of fact such that (a) each fact can not only be noninferentially known to be the case, but presupposes no other knowledge either of particular matter of fact, or of general truths; and (b) ... the noninferential knowledge of facts belonging to this structure constitutes the ultimate court of appeals for all factual claims—particular and general—about the world.

(EPM: §32, in SPR: 164; in KMG: 243; in B: 68–9)

This formulation is in abstract structural terms. It does not mention experience. But from the way part VIII flows, it is clear that what Sellars is rejecting when he rejects this form of the myth is what he labels "traditional empiricism" at the part's conclusion (§38). To make the connection, all we need is the obvious point that according to traditional empiricism, *experience* is our way of acquiring the knowledge that is supposed to be foundational in the sense Sellars explains in §32. In traditional empiricism, experience is taken to yield noninferential knowledge in a way that presupposes no knowledge of anything else.

Sellars takes pains to draw our attention to this supposed freedom from presuppositions, the second sub-clause of clause (a) in his formulation of an unqualified foundationalism. §32 continues like this:

It is important to note that I characterized the knowledge of fact belonging to this stratum as not only noninferential, but as presupposing no knowledge of other matters of fact, whether particular or general. It might be thought that this is a redundancy, that knowledge (not belief or conviction, but knowledge) which logically presupposes knowledge of other facts *must* be inferential. This, however, as I hope to show, is itself an episode in the Myth.

(EPM: §32, in SPR: 164; in KMG: 243–4; in B: 69)

When he rejects traditional empiricism at the end of part VIII, he is rejecting that sub-clause in particular. The rest of the affirmative answer to the question about foundations can stand. In §38 he says:

If I reject the framework of traditional empiricism, it is not because I want to say that empirical knowledge has *no* foundation. For to put it in this way is to suggest that it is really "empirical knowledge so-called," and to put it in a box with rumors and hoaxes. There is clearly *some* point to the picture of human knowledge as resting on a level of propositions—observation reports—which do not rest on other propositions in the same way as other propositions rest on them. On the other hand, I do wish to insist that the metaphor of "foundation" is misleading in that it keeps us from seeing that if there is a logical dimension in which other empirical propositions rest on observation reports, there is another logical dimension in which the latter rest on the former.

(EPM: §38, in SPR: 170; in KMG: 250; in B: 78)

Dependence in this second dimension is the presupposing missed by traditional empiricism. To recognize the second dimension is to accept that what is now—just for this reason—only misleadingly conceived as foundational knowledge presupposes knowledge of other matters of fact, knowledge that would have to belong to the structure that can now only misleadingly be seen as built on those foundations. If we stayed with the metaphor of foundations, we would be implying that the foundations of a building can depend on the building.

This passage characterizes a non-traditional empiricism. To make that explicit, we only need to register that it is *experience* that yields the knowledge expressed in observation reports. Recognizing the second dimension puts us in a position to understand observation reports properly. The knowledge they express is not inferentially grounded on other knowledge of matters of fact, but—in the crucial departure from traditional empiricism—it presupposes other knowledge of matters of fact. It is knowledge on which Sellars continues to hold that other empirical knowledge rests in the first dimension. By introducing an explicit mention of experience, we made it possible to see part VIII as beginning with a formulation of traditional empiricism, as we needed to do in order to make sense of how part VIII ends. The same move enables us to see that the position Sellars recommends at the end of part VIII, as a replacement for traditional empiricism, is a reformed empiricism.

3.

That is still somewhat abstract. To fill out this specification of a reformed empiricism, we would need to give a detailed picture of experience, explaining how it can yield noninferential knowledge, but only in a way that presupposes other knowledge of matters of fact—in contrast with the presupposition-free knowledge-yielding powers that experience is credited with by traditional empiricism.

And that is just what Sellars offers, starting in part III, "The Logic of 'Looks'". Experiences, Sellars tells us, contain propositional claims (§16). That is an initially promissory way (as Sellars insists) of crediting experiences with intentional content. He delivers on the promissory note in the first phase of the myth of Jones (part XV). The topic there is "thoughts"—inner episodes with intentional content—in general. But Sellars reverts to the intentional character of experiences in particular in a retrospective remark at the beginning of the next part, in §60. There he indicates, in effect, that he has finally put the verbal currency he issued in §16 on the gold standard.

In §16 *bis*, Sellars says it is clear that a complete account of (visual) experience requires "something more", over and above intentional content, namely "what philosophers have in mind when they speak of 'visual impressions' or 'immediate visual experiences' ". (It can be questioned whether this *is* clear, or even correct, but since my aim is entirely exegetical I shall not consider that here.) When Sellars introduces this "something more", he remarks that its "logical status... is a problem which will be with us for the remainder of this argument" (EPM: §16 *bis*, in SPR: 145; in KMG: 223; in B: 40). His final treatment of this topic comes at the end of the essay, in the second phase of the myth of Jones (part XVI). The myth of Jones offers an account of the non-dispositional mental in general. But in EPM it clearly has a more specific purpose as well: to complete the account of *experience*, in particular, that Sellars begins in part III. The first phase vindicates his promissory talk of experiences as having intentional content, and the second deals with the "something more" he thinks is needed to accommodate their sensory character.

And already in part III, when the attribution of intentional content to experiences is still only promissory, and part VIII is yet to come, Sellars has his eye on ensuring that the capacity to yield noninferential knowledge that he is beginning to provide for, by attributing intentional content to experiences, is not as traditional empiricism conceives it. In part III Sellars is already insisting—to put things in the terms he will use in part VIII—that an experience's having as its intentional content that such-and-such is the case, and hence the possibility that such an experience might yield non-inferential knowledge that such-and-such is the case, presupposes knowledge other than that noninferential knowledge itself.

Part III is largely devoted to a telling example of this: visual experience of colour. Here it might be especially tempting to suppose experience can yield knowledge in self-standing chunks, without dependence on other knowledge. Experiences that, to speak in the promissory idiom, contain the claim that something in front of one is green are experiences in which it is at least true that it looks to one as if something in front of one is green. Some experiences that are non-committally describable in those terms are experiences in which one *sees*, and so is in a position to know noninferentially, that something in front of one is green. The ability to enjoy experiences in which it looks to one as if something in front of one is green is part of what it is to have the (visually applicable) *concept* of something's being green. And Sellars argues that having colour concepts "involves the ability to tell what colors things have by looking at them—which, in turn, involves knowing in what circumstances to place an object if one wishes to ascertain its color by looking at it" (EPM: §18, in SPR: 146; in KMG: 225; in B: 43). The possibility of having experiences in which it looks to one as if something is green, and hence the possibility of acquiring noninferential knowledge that something is green by having such an experience, depend—not inferentially, but in what is going to come into view as the second dimension—on knowledge about, for instance, the effects of different lighting conditions on colour appearances.

4.

Brandom conceives observational knowledge, the knowledge expressed in observation reports, as the upshot of a special kind of *reliable differential responsive disposition*—a kind that is special in that the responses its instances issue in are not *mere* responses, like an electric eye's opening a door when its beam is broken, but claims, moves in an *inferentially* articulated practice. Brandom attributes this picture of observational knowledge to Sellars; he calls it "Sellars's two-ply account of observation".[2]

In favourable circumstances, dispositions of this kind issue in expressions of observational knowledge. But a disposition of this

[2] See Robert Brandom, "The Centrality of Sellars's Two-Ply Account of Observation to the Arguments of 'Empiricism and the Philosophy of Mind' ", in *Tales of the Mighty Dead: Historical Essays in the Metaphysics of Intentionality* (Cambridge, MA: Harvard University Press, 2002).

kind can be triggered into operation in circumstances in which it would be risky to make the claim that is its primary output. Perhaps the claim would be false; certainly it would not express knowledge. Subjects learn to inhibit inclinations to make claims in such circumstances. For instance, subjects learn, in certain lighting conditions, to withhold the claims about colours that, if allowed free rein, their responsive dispositions would induce them to make. In such conditions "looks" statements serve as substitute outlets for the tendencies to make claims that the responsive dispositions embody. "Looks" statements *evince* responsive dispositions (of a specifically visual kind) whose primary output one is inhibiting.

If something appropriately conceivable as *sensory consciousness* figures in our acquisition of observational knowledge, Brandom thinks that is a mere detail about the mechanism by which the relevant responsive dispositions work in our case. There could perfectly well be responsive dispositions that issue in knowledge-expressing claims without mediation by sensory consciousness, or at any rate sensory consciousness with a content matching that of the knowledge yielded by the dispositions. Perhaps there are. (This is how it is with the chicken-sexers of epistemological folklore.) And Brandom thinks this possibility (or actuality, if that is what it is) lays bare the essential nature of observational knowledge. On this view, experience—a kind of shaping of sensory consciousness—is inessential to the epistemology of observational knowledge, and hence to the epistemology of empirical knowledge in general. If empiricism accords a special epistemological significance to experience, there is no room in this picture for empiricism, traditional or otherwise.

This is not the place to consider the prospects for this radical project of Brandom's, to dispense with experience in an account of empirical knowledge, and hence to leave no room for even a reformed empiricism. But given the question I have set out to address, I do need to consider Brandom's attempt to read the project into Sellars. I think this flies in the face of the plain sense of EPM—the whole essay, but to begin with part III in particular.

5.

In §16, where Sellars introduces the idea that experiences contain claims, he is not beginning to show us how to do without experience in our conception of empirical knowledge. On the contrary, he is beginning to *explain* experience, as a kind of inner episode that can figure in our understanding of empirical knowledge without entangling us in the myth of the given. Only beginning, because he needs the myth of Jones to vindicate the very idea of inner episodes, and in particular the idea of inner episodes with intentional content, before he can claim to have completed the task.

In the doctrine Brandom thinks Sellars is trying to expound in part III, claims figure only in the guise of overt linguistic performances—the primary outlet of responsive dispositions, what subjects evince an inhibited tendency towards when they say how things look to them. But Sellars uses the notion of claims in an avowedly promissory first shot at attributing intentional content *to experiences*, to be vindicated when Jones introduces concepts of inner episodes with intentional content on the model of overt linguistic performances with their semantical character. Claims figure in Brandom's picture only in the sense in which claims are Jones's *model*. What Sellars needs Jones to model on claims in the primary sense, to finish the task he begins in part III, is not on Brandom's scene at all.

Obviously looking forward to the myth of Jones, Sellars says, in §16, that justifying his promissory talk of experiences as containing propositional claims is "one of [his] major aims" (EPM: §16, in SPR: 144; in KMG: 223; in B: 39–40). When Jones starts work, his fellows already have the subjunctive conditional, hence the ability to speak of dispositions, and they can speak of overt linguistic behaviour with its semantical character. (Sellars adds that to the original "Rylean" resources in §49, before Jones begins.) To fulfil the major aim Sellars acknowledges in §16, he needs to follow Jones in going decisively beyond those pre-Jonesian resources. Only after the first phase of Jones's conceptual innovation does Sellars in effect declare that he has discharged his promissory note (§60). Brandom offers to account for "looks" statements in terms of dispositions, which can be inhibited, to make claims in the primary sense, overt linguistic performances of a certain sort. But this apparatus is all available before Jones's innovation. In implying that his apparatus suffices for Sellars's aims in part III, Brandom precludes himself from properly registering the promissory character Sellars stresses in his moves there.[3]

In §15, Sellars rejects the idea that a "looks" statement reports a minimal objective fact—objective in being "logically independent of the beliefs, the conceptual framework, of the perceiver", but minimal in being safer than a report of, say, the colour of an object in the perceiver's environment. He is certainly right to reject this; because of the sense in which these facts are supposed to be objective, this construal of "looks" statements is a version of the myth of the given.

But Brandom thinks "looks" statements, for Sellars, should not be reports at all—in particular, not reports of experiences, since Sellars is supposed to be showing us how to do without experiences in our picture of empirical knowledge. Thus, purporting to capture a point Sellars should be trying to make in §15, Brandom writes (B: 139): "it is a mistake to treat [statements to the effect that it looks to one as if something is *F*] as reports at all—since they *evince* a disposition to call something *F*, but may not happily be thought of

---

[3] In his *Science and Metaphysics: Variations on Kantian Themes* (London: Routledge & Kegan Paul, 1967; reissued Atascadero, CA: Ridgeview, 1992), Sellars allows for a version of "looks" statements in the pre-Jonesian language. He says : "This locution ['*x* looks red to me'] must ... be interpreted as having, roughly, the sense of '*x* causes me to be disposed to think-out-loud: Lo! This is red, or would cause me to have this disposition if it were not for such and such considerations" (SM: VI §22: 159). If one said that, one would be explicitly attributing a disposition to oneself, rather than evincing one, as in Brandom's picture. But what we have here is just a different way of exploiting the conceptual apparatus Brandom confines himself to. The passage brings out that the materials for Brandom's account of "looks" statements are available before Jones has done his work, and hence before Sellars has in hand the materials that he makes it clear he needs for *his* account of "looks" statements.

as *saying that* one has such a disposition." This general rejection of the idea that "looks" statements are reports does not fit what Sellars actually says, and Brandom tries to accommodate that by saying Sellars "wavers" on the point. But a glance at the text shows Sellars to be unwaveringly clear that "looks" statements *are* reports—not, certainly, of dispositions, the only candidate Brandom considers, but of *experiences*, and in particular of their intentional content. §15 ends like this:

Let me begin by noting that there certainly seems to be something in the idea that the sentence "This looks green to me now" has a reporting role. Indeed it would seem to be essentially a report. But if so, *what* does it report, if not a minimal objective fact, and if what it reports is not to be analyzed in terms of sense data?

(EPM: §15, in SPR: 144; in KMG: 222–3; in B: 39)

And a couple of pages later (in §16 *bis*), after he has introduced the two aspects he attributes to experiences, their intentionality and their sensory character, Sellars answers that question—he tells us what "looks" statements report:

Thus, when I say "X looks green to me now" I am *reporting* the fact that my experience is, so to speak, intrinsically, *as an experience*, indistinguishable from a veridical one of seeing that x is green. Included in the report is the ascription to my experience of the claim 'x is green'; and the fact that I make this report rather than the simple report "X is green" indicates that certain considerations have operated to raise, so to speak in a higher court, the question 'to endorse or not to endorse'.

(EPM: §16 *bis*, in SPR: 145; in KMG: 224; in B: 41)

This is not wavering. It is a straightforward, indeed emphatic, statement of something Brandom thinks Sellars should be denying, that "looks" statements are reports: not (to repeat) of dispositions, but of the intentional (claim-containing) and, implicitly, the sensory character of experiences. When Sellars discharges the promissory note of §16, the culminating move (in §59) is precisely to provide for a *reporting* role for self-attributions of "thoughts", which include experiences *qua* characterizable as having intentional content.

If one goes no further than reporting one's experience as containing the claim that things are thus and so, one still has to determine whether to endorse that claim oneself. If one endorses it, one claims to see that things are thus and so (if the experience is a visual experience). If not, one restricts oneself to saying it looks to one as if things are thus and so. In a "looks" statement, that is, one withholds one's endorsement of the claim one reports one's experience as containing.

Now Brandom seizes on this withholding of endorsement, and exploits it in an explanation, which he attributes to Sellars, for the incorrigibility of "looks" statements. Brandom writes, on Sellars's behalf (B: 142): "Since asserting 'X looks *F*' is not undertaking a propositional commitment—but only expressing an overrideable disposition to do so—there is no issue as to whether or not that commitment (which one?) is correct."

But this reflects Brandom's failure to register the Sellarsian idea I have been documenting, the idea that when one says something of the form "X looks *F*" one reports the claim-containing character of one's experience. That one's experience contains a certain claim—in Brandom's schematic example, the claim that X is *F*—is an assertoric commitment one *is* undertaking when one says how things look to one, even though one withholds commitment to the claim one reports one's experience as containing. Brandom's question "Which one?" is meant to be rhetorical, but it has an answer: commitment to the proposition that one's experience contains a certain claim. Brandom's explanation of the incorrigibility of "looks" statements is not Sellarsian at all. For an authentically Sellarsian account of first-person authority in saying how things look to one—"privileged access" to what one reports in such a performance—we have to wait until the culmination of the first phase of the myth of Jones; Sellars addresses the issue in §59.[4]

---

[4] In his enthusiasm for the explanatory power of the idea of withholding endorsement, Brandom is led into a clearly wrong characterization of Sellars's treatment of generic looks in §17. Brandom says (B: 145): "Sellars's account is in terms of scope of endorsement. One says that the plane figure looks 'many-sided' instead of '119-sided' just in case one

6.

Commenting on §§19 and 20, Brandom remarks (B: 147): "These sections do not present Sellars's argument in a perspicuous, or even linear, fashion." This reflects the fact that what he thinks Sellars *should* be doing in part III is expounding the "two-ply" picture of observational knowledge, in which observation reports are explained in terms of reliable differential responsive dispositions whose outputs are constituted as conceptually contentful by their position in an inferentially articulated practice.

But it is questionable exegetical practice to insist that a text contains something one wants to find in it, even though that requires one to criticize its perspicuity. One should pause to wonder whether it does something else, perhaps with complete perspicuity.

And that is how things are here. In part III, and in particular in §§19 and 20, Sellars is not unperspicuously presenting Brandom's "two-ply" picture. He is, quite perspicuously, giving a preliminary account of how the knowledge-yielding capacity of experience—even experience of something as simple as colour—presupposes knowledge of matters of fact other than those noninferentially knowable by enjoying experiences of the kind in question. The presupposed knowledge is exactly not inferentially related to the knowledge that presupposes it; that is Sellars's point in part VIII.

Brandom says "endorsement" is Sellars's term for the second element in the "two-ply" picture (B: 140). He thinks Sellars's talk of endorsement is directed at entitling him to talk of claims at all, by placing what he is only thereby permitted to conceive as

is willing only to endorse (be held responsible for justifying) the more general claim." (For a similar statement, see Brandom's *Making It Explicit: Reasoning, Representing, and Discursive Commitment* (Cambridge, MA: Harvard University Press, 1994), 293.) But on Sellars's account, if one says a plane figure looks many-sided, one exactly does *not* endorse the claim that it is many-sided. Sellars's account of generic looks is not in terms of scope of endorsement, but in terms of what is up for endorsement. The claims that experiences contain, like claims in general, can be indeterminate in content.

conceptually contentful commitments in an inferentially organized deontic structure.

But Sellars introduces the idea that experiences contain claims without any hint that he feels obliged to concern himself—here—with the question of what claims are. His initial account of "looks" statements is promissory because he needs Jones to extend the idea of claims from its primary application, which is to a certain sort of overt linguistic performance, before it can be used in attributing intentional content to inner episodes. For these purposes, the primary application is unproblematic. Sellars's talk of endorsement is not code for the idea of taking up what would otherwise be mere responses into a deontically structured practice, so that they can be understood to have conceptual content. "Endorsement" just means *endorsement*. Once we are working with the idea that experiences contain claims, it is routinely obvious that the subject of an experience faces the question whether to endorse the claim her experience contains. The idea that the outputs of some responsive dispositions are constituted as conceptually contentful by inferential articulation is not relevant to any point Sellars has occasion to make in this part of the essay.

Or, I believe, anywhere in EPM. I mentioned earlier that before he puts Jones to work, Sellars adds concepts of overt linguistic performances, with their conceptual content, to the "Rylean" resources that are already in place (§49). He does that quickly and without fanfare. In this essay Sellars is not in the business of giving an "inferentialist" account of what it is for overt performances to have conceptual content at all, the thesis that is the second element in Brandom's "two-ply" picture. Not that he offers some other kind of account. His purposes here generate no need to concern himself with the question to which "inferentialism" is a response.

After his remark that Sellars's presentation in §§19 and 20 is not perspicuous, Brandom says "the argument is repeated in a more satisfactory form in [§§33–7]" (B: 147). He means that those sections, the central sections of part VIII, give a better formulation of the "two-ply" picture. But this reflects the fact that he misreads those sections too.

Brandom thinks the point of §§33–7 is to expound the second element in the "two-ply" account, the idea that the outputs of the responsive dispositions that issue in observation reports are constituted as conceptually contentful by their position in an inferentially articulated practice. Against this background, he argues that those sections bring out a problem for Sellars's epistemological internalism.

Sellars holds that for a claim to express observational knowledge, two conditions must be met (§35, the two hurdles). First, the claim must issue from a capacity whose outputs are reliably correct. And second, the person who makes the claim must be aware that her pronouncements on such matters have that kind of authority. As Sellars notes, the idea of reliability can be explicated in terms of there being a good inference—what Brandom calls "the reliability inference"—from the person's making a claim (in the circumstances in which she makes it) to things being as she says they are.

Brandom thinks this puts Sellars's second condition in tension with the thesis that observational knowledge is noninferential. He thinks the condition would imply that one arrives at an observation report by persuading oneself, via the "reliability inference", that things are as one would be saying they are if one indulged an inclination one finds in oneself to make a certain claim. That would imply that the knowledge expressed in the report is inferential. So Brandom concludes that we must reject the second condition if we are to hold on to Sellars's own thought that observational knowledge is not inferential. To be better Sellarsians than Sellars himself, we should insist that an observational knower can invoke her own reliability at most *ex post facto*.[5] And it is a short step from

---

[5] For the idea of *ex post facto* inferential justifications of noninferential beliefs, see "Insights and Blind Spots of Reliabilism", in Robert Brandom's *Articulating Reasons: An Introduction to Inferentialism* (Cambridge, MA: Harvard University Press, 2000), especially at 103–4 and 211, n. 3.

there to claiming, as Brandom does, that there can be cases of observational knowledge in which the knower cannot invoke her own reliability even *ex post facto*. It is enough if someone else, a scorekeeper, can justify a belief as the conclusion of the "reliability inference", even if the believer herself cannot do that.[6]

But here Brandom misses what Sellars, in §32, signals as the central point of part VIII: to bring into view the second dimension of dependence. One bit of knowledge can depend on another in this dimension without any threat to the thesis that it is noninferential.

We have already considered the example of this that Sellars elaborates in part III. (He refers back to part III, in particular to §19, in §37.) Claims about the colours of things, made on the basis of experience, depend in the second dimension on knowledge about the effects of different kinds of illumination on colour appearances. I might support my entitlement to the claim that something is green by saying "This is a good light for telling what colour something is". The relevance of this to my observational authority about the thing's colour belongs in the second dimension, which is not to be spelled out in terms of inference. I do not cast what I say about the light as a premiss in an inferential grounding for what I claim to know about the colour of the thing.

Similarly with Sellars's second hurdle. I might support my entitlement to the claim that something is green by invoking—not just *ex post facto*, but at the time—my reliability on such matters. I might say "I can tell a green thing when I see one (at least in this kind of light)". I must be aware of my reliability, to be able to cite it like this, in support of the authority of my claim. And here too, the support is in the second dimension, which Sellars carefully separates from the dimension in which one bit of knowledge provides inferential grounding for another.

It is true that the concept of reliability can be explicated in terms of the goodness of the "reliability inference". But that is irrelevant

<hr/>

[6] See *Making It Explicit*, 217–21. The idea is hinted at in the Study Guide; see B: 157, 159.

to the present point. To say that a claim depends for its authority, in the second dimension, on the subject's reliability (in a way that requires her to be aware of her reliability) is not to say that it depends in the first dimension, the inferential dimension, on her inclination to make it via the "reliability inference".

In Brandom's treatment of part III, taking Sellars to be concerned to expound the "two-ply" picture of observation knowledge led to a baseless accusation of lack of perspicuity. Here it leads him to miss, nearly completely, what Sellars signals as the central point he wants to make in part VIII.

With his fixation on the "two-ply" picture, Brandom makes almost nothing of Sellars's point about the second dimension. He almost exclusively explains Sellars's moves in part VIII in terms of a requirement for *understanding* the forms of words that are uttered in observation reports, that one be able to use them not only in making observation reports but also as premises and conclusions of inferences. There surely is such a requirement, but there is nothing to indicate that it is Sellars's concern here (or, as I have urged, anywhere else in this essay). Sellars's concern is with a requirement for claims to be expressive of observational knowledge, with the distinctive *authority* that that implies. Understanding what it is that one is claiming—in this case with that distinctive authority—is not what is in question. The point of Sellars's second hurdle is not to cite the "reliability inference" as part of the inferentially articulated structure in which forms of words must stand if they are to have conceptual content at all. Sellars's thesis is that *observational authority* depends on the subject's own reliability in the second dimension, and this dependence requires that the subject be aware of her own reliability. He invokes the "reliability inference" only as a gloss on the idea of reliability. (That it is a good gloss is obvious. This is not a first move in giving a contentious "inferentialist" account of conceptual content *überhaupt*.) The second hurdle stands in no tension with the thesis that observational knowledge is noninferential.

At one place in the Study Guide (B: 162, expounding §38), Brandom—as it were in spite of himself—lets a glimpse of Sellars's real point emerge, when he says that observation reports "themselves rest (not inferentially but in the order of *understanding* and sometimes of justification) on other sorts of knowledge". But the stress on the order of understanding—by which Brandom means the inferential structure that forms of words must belong to if they are to be conceptually contentful at all—is, as I have been urging, irrelevant to Sellars's point. Sellars's case against traditional empiricism relates entirely to the order of justification, the order of responses to the Kantian question "*Quid iuris?*". His point is that observational knowledge *always* (not sometimes) rests in the order of justification—in the noninferential second dimension—on other sorts of knowledge. That is why it is not foundational in the sense envisaged by traditional empiricism.

I have put this in the terms Brandom uses. But we could express Sellars's central point in part VIII by saying that this talk of *the* order of justification is misleading. One way of placing an episode or state in the space of reasons—as Sellars says we do when we classify it as an episode or state of knowing (§36)—is to give grounds for accepting that its content is true, premises from which there is a sufficiently good inference to the truth of what the putative knower claims or would claim. Sellars's point in introducing the second dimension is that there is another way of responding to the question "*Quid iuris?*", in which what one says in response relates quite differently to the claim whose candidacy to be recognized as knowledgeable is under discussion. In a response of this second kind, one does not offer grounds for endorsing a claim that purports to express knowledge. What one addresses, in the first instance, is not the truth of the particular thing the subject says but her authority, in the circumstances, to say something—anything—of the relevant sort: for example, her authority, in the prevailing illumination, to make a claim about something's colour. Of course if we accept that she is in a position to speak with authority on the matters in question, that supplies us with material that could serve in an inferential grounding for the particular thing she says, using the fact that she says it, plus the consideration we have accepted as bearing on her authority in saying things of the relevant kind, as premises. But the consideration that bears on her authority is directly relevant to whether the claim she makes is knowledgeable, not by way of its capacity to figure in an inferential grounding for the claim, an argument to its truth. We convince ourselves that it is true on the ground that her saying it is expressive of knowledge; its truth does not figure in our route to the conviction that she is a knower.[7]

I have been insisting that Sellars's aim in introducing the second dimension is *epistemological*. The second dimension pertains to what is required for claims to have the authority that belongs to expressions of knowledge. But the point is not epistemological in a way that excludes *semantical* significance. Concepts of, say, colour—in their usual form, as opposed to the versions of them that might be available to the congenitally blind—can be employed in claims (or judgments) with the distinctive authority that attaches to observation reports, and that fact is partly constitutive of the kind of content the concepts have.

But this semantical significance is quite distinct from the "inferentialism" that is the second element of Brandom's "two-ply" account. The point does not concern an inferential dependence between *claimables*, constituted as such only by there being inferential relations between them, as in Brandom's picture. It concerns a noninferential dependence thanks to which certain *claimings* can have the authority of observational knowledge. As I said, there is

---

[7] In the context in which Sellars identifies the space of reasons as the space in which one places episodes or states when one classifies them as episodes or states of knowing, he describes it as the space "of justifying and being able to justify what one says" (EPM: §36, in SPR: 169; in KMG: 248; in B: 76). What I have said about the second dimension implies that this description is not completely felicitous. A second-dimension response to the question "*Quid iuris?*" justifies *what one says* only indirectly. Its direct aim is to characterize one's right to speak with authority on the topic one speaks on. It does that independently of what, in particular, one says.

a semantical aspect to this, because the forms of words uttered in these claimings would not have the distinctive kind of conceptual content they do if they were not able to figure in claimings with that distinctive authority. But this is not a first step into "inferentialism". The relevant dependence is, as I have followed Sellars in insisting, not inferential. And anyway, since the dependence is exemplified only by observation reports, not by claims in general, the semantical thought here is not, as in Brandom's "inferentialism", one about conceptual contentfulness *überhaupt*.

7.

As I said at the beginning, when Brandom argues that Sellars's aim is to dismantle empiricism, he considers and dismisses a passage that might seem to point in a different direction. I promised to come back to this.

The passage is §6, where Sellars embarrasses classical sense-datum theorists with commitment to an inconsistent triad, of which one element is the thesis that "the ability to know facts of the form *x is* ϕ is acquired". One could avoid the inconsistency by giving up that thesis. But against that option Sellars says it would "do violence to the predominantly nominalistic proclivities of the empiricist tradition" (EPM §6, in SPR: 132; in KMG: 210; in B: 21). As Brandom acknowledges, the thesis that the ability to have classificatory knowledge is acquired is part of the "psychological nominalism" Sellars is going to espouse in his own voice (see §§29, 30, 31). So it is tempting to suppose we are intended to recognize a convergence with that Sellarsian doctrine when, spelling out the nominalistic proclivities of the empiricist tradition, he says:

[M]ost empirically minded philosophers are strongly inclined to think that all classificatory consciousness, all knowledge *that something is thus-and-so,* or, in logicians' jargon, all subsumption of particulars under universals, involves learning, concept formation, even the use of symbols.

(EPM §6, in SPR: 131; in KMG: 210; in B: 20)

But Brandom insists that Sellars is not indicating any sympathy with the empiricist tradition. Brandom implies (B: 169) that part VI deals with some nominalistic proclivities, distinctive to the empiricist tradition, in which Sellars himself does not indulge, even though Sellars agrees with the empiricists that the ability to have classificatory knowledge is acquired.

There are two things that are unsatisfactory about this.

First, part VI does not depict the classical empiricists as having their thinking shaped by nominalistic proclivities not indulged in by Sellars. Sellars's point about the classical empiricists is that they take themselves to have a problem of universals only in connection with *determinable* repeatables. Where *determinate* repeatables are concerned, they proceed as if the ability to know facts of the form *x is ϕ* is a concomitant of mere sentience, not something that needs to be acquired. That is, the classical empiricists are only imperfectly faithful to the nominalism Sellars ascribes to their tradition in §6. As far as this goes, the nominalistic proclivities Sellars ascribes to the empiricist tradition can perfectly well be the nominalistic proclivities he is going to espouse for himself.

Second, on Brandom's account the argument Sellars deploys, to exclude that option for avoiding the inconsistent triad, is purely *ad hominem*. And this does not fit comfortably with the importance the argument has in the structure of the essay.

The nominalistic proclivities of the empiricist tradition are essential for justifying what Sellars says at the beginning of §7:

It certainly begins to look as though the classical concept of a sense datum were a mongrel resulting from a crossbreeding of two ideas:

(1) The idea that there are certain inner episodes—e.g. sensations of red or of C# which can occur to human beings (and brutes) without any prior process of learning or concept formation; and without which it would *in some sense* be impossible to *see*, for example, that the facing surface of a physical object is red and triangular, or *hear* that a certain physical sound is C#.

(2) The idea that there are certain inner episodes which are the non-inferential knowings that certain items are, for example, red or C#; and that these episodes are the necessary conditions of empirical knowledge as providing the evidence for all other empirical propositions.

(EPM §7, in SPR: 132; in KMG: 210–11; in B: 21–2)

Why must these two kinds of episodes be distinguished? Those described under (1) do not require a prior process of learning or concept formation. But those described under (2), noninferential knowings that..., do. And why should we accept that they do? The only ground so far on offer is that this is implied by the nominalism Sellars attributes to the empiricist tradition. His own nominalism, which Brandom says is different, has not yet been explicitly introduced.

Sellars repeats this diagnosis of classical sense-datum theory at the beginning of part III, in §10. And there he goes on as follows:

[A] reasonable next step would be to examine these two ideas and determine how that which survives criticism in each is properly to be combined with the other. Clearly we would have to come to grips with the idea of *inner episodes*, for this is common to both.

(EPM §10, in SPR: 140; in KMG: 218; in B: 33)

This sets the agenda for the rest of the essay. In §16 and §16 *bis* Sellars begins to explain experience as involving episodes of the two kinds conflated into a mongrel by classical sense-datum theory. And that continues to be his project until the end. The myth of Jones serves the purpose of coming to grips with the idea of inner episodes—episodes of those two kinds in particular.

Now it would be a structural weakness if this agenda-setting move were motivated by an argument that is purely *ad hominem*, an argument that should seem cogent only to adherents of the empiricist tradition, supposedly not including Sellars himself. The structure of the essay looks stronger if the argument in §6 is meant to be already, as formulated there, convincing to right-thinking people. It is true that the argument is explicitly directed *ad hominem*. It points out that a certain escape from the inconsistent triad is unavailable to classical sense-datum theorists, who belong to the empiricist tradition if anyone does. But the argument's role in motivating what becomes the programme for the rest of the essay recommends that we not understand it as exclusively *ad hominem*. We should take Sellars to be intending to exploit the convergence between the nominalism of §6 and his own nominalism, so as to indicate that he himself belongs to the empiricist tradition.

That fits with understanding EPM as aiming to recall empiricism to its better wisdom, in an argument that hinges on its nominalistic proclivities. As part VI points out, the canonical empiricists lapse from the nominalism of their tradition in their picture of our dealings with determinate observable qualities. To avoid the myth of the given in the form it takes in traditional empiricism, what we need is an empiricism that keeps faith with the nominalism only imperfectly conformed to by traditional empiricism. And that is just what Sellars provides.

8.

So far I have argued exclusively from the text of EPM. I shall end with a piece of evidence from elsewhere.

At one point in "Imperatives, Intentions, and the Logic of 'Ought' ",[8] Sellars considers a Jonesian account of intentions, in which "shall" thoughts are conceived as inner episodes modelled on certain overt utterances. He introduces the idea like this:

There is a consideration pertaining to intentions and their expression which, though not strictly a part of the argument of this paper, indicates

[8] IIOR In Hector-Neri Castañeda and George Nakhnikian, eds., *Morality and the Language of Conduct* (Detroit: Wayne State University Press, 1963): 159–218. Thanks to Joshua Stuchlik for drawing my attention to this passage.

how it might fit into the broader framework of an empiricist philosophy of mind.

(IIOR: 195)

And in an endnote he says:

For an elaboration of such a framework, see my "Empiricism and the Philosophy of Mind," ...

(IIOR: 217)

Here Sellars is explicit that EPM puts forward an empiricist philosophy of mind. He is talking about the Jonesian approach to the mental in general, rather than the epistemological and transcendental implications of the way EPM deals with perceptual experience in particular. But it is clear that the label "empiricist" is—to put it mildly—not one he is keen to disown. And it is natural to extend this to his discussion of experience itself.

This passage encourages me in answering my question in the way I have been urging. Why does "empiricism" figure in the title of EPM? Because a major purpose of the essay is to propound an empiricism free from the defects of traditional empiricism.

References

Robert Brandom, "The Centrality of Sellars's Two-Ply Account of Observation to the Arguments of 'Empiricism and the Philosophy of Mind' ", in Brandom, *Tales of the Mighty Dead: Historical Essays in the Metaphysics of Intentionality* (Cambridge, MA: Harvard University Press, 2002).

—— "Insights and Blind Spots of Reliabilism", in Brandom, *Articulating Reasons: An Introduction to Inferentialism* (Cambridge, MA: Harvard University Press, 2000).

—— *Making It Explicit: Reasoning, Representing, and Discursive Commitment* (Cambridge, MA: Harvard University Press, 1994).

Wilfrid Sellars, *Empiricism and the Philosophy of Mind, with an Introduction by Richard Rorty and a Study Guide by Robert Brandom* (Cambridge, MA: Harvard University Press, 1997). [EPM]

—— "Imperatives, Intentions, and the Logic of 'Ought' ", in Hector-Neri Castañeda and George Nakhnikian, eds., *Morality and the Language of Conduct* (Detroit: Wayne State University Press, 1963). [IIOR]

—— *Science and Metaphysics: Variations on Kantian Themes* (London: Routledge & Kegan Paul, 1967; reissued Atascadero, CA: Ridgeview, 1992). [SM]

2

Pragmatism, Inferentialism, and Modality in Sellars's Arguments against Empiricism

Robert B. Brandom

1. Introduction

In this essay I want to place the arguments of "Empiricism and the Philosophy of Mind" into a slightly less local context, by tracing further, into neighboring works, some strands of argumentation that intersect and are woven together in his critique of empiricism in its two principal then-extant forms: traditional, and twentieth-century logical empiricism. Sellars always accepted that observation reports resulting non-inferentially from the exercise of perceptual language-entry capacities play both the privileged epistemological role of being the ultimate court of appeal for the justification of empirical knowledge-claims and therefore (given his inferentialist semantics) an essential semantic role in determining the contents of the empirical concepts applied in such judgments. But in accord with his stated aspiration to "move analytic philosophy from its Humean into its Kantian phase," he was severely and in principle critical of empiricist ambitions and programs in epistemology and (especially) semantics that go beyond this minimal, carefully circumscribed characterization of the cognitive significance of sense experience. Indeed, I think the lasting philosophical interest of

Sellars's thought lies primarily in the battery of original considerations and arguments he brings to bear against all weightier forms of empiricism. Some, but not all, of these are deployed in the opening critical portions of "Empiricism and the Philosophy of Mind," where the ground is cleared and prepared for the constructive theorizing of the last half. But what is on offer there is only part of Sellars's overall critique of empiricism. We accordingly court misunderstanding of what is there if we do not appreciate the shape of the larger enterprise to which it contributes.

In an autobiographical sketch, Sellars dates his break with traditional empiricism to his Oxford days in the thirties. It was, he says, prompted by concern with understanding the sort of conceptual content that ought to be associated with "logical, causal, and deontological modalities." Already at that point he says that he had the idea that

> what was needed was a functional theory of concepts which would make their role in reasoning, rather than supposed origin in experience, their primary feature.

(AR: 285)[1]

This telling passage introduces two of the master ideas that shape Sellars's critique of empiricism. The first is that a key criterion of adequacy with respect to which its semantics will be found wanting concerns its treatment of *modal* concepts. The second is that the remedy for this inadequacy lies in an alternative broadly functional approach to the semantics of these concepts that focuses on their *inferential roles*—as it were, looking *downstream* to their *use*, as well as *upstream* to the circumstances that elicit their application.

This second, inferential-functionalist, semantic idea looms large in "Empiricism and the Philosophy of Mind." In fact, it provides the raw materials that are assembled and articulated into Sellars's positive account of the semantics of the concepts applied in reporting thoughts and sense-impressions. Concern with the significance

---

[1] In *Action, Knowledge, and Reality*, H. N. Castañeda (ed.) (Indianapolis: Bobbs-Merrill, 1975): 285.

of *modality* in the critique of empiricism, however, is almost wholly absent from that work (even though it is evident in articles Sellars wrote even earlier). I do not think that is because it was not, even then, an essential element of the larger picture of empiricism's failings that Sellars was seeking to convey, but rather because it was the result of a hard-won but successful divide-and-conquer expository strategy. That is, I conjecture that what made it possible for Sellars finally to write "Empiricism and the Philosophy of Mind" was figuring out a way to articulate the considerations he advances there *without* having also at the same time to explore the issues raised by empiricism's difficulties with modal concepts. Whether or not that conjecture about the intellectual-biographical significance of finding a narrative path that makes possible the separation of these aspects of his project is correct, I want to claim that it is important to understand what goes on in EPM in the light of the fuller picture of the expressive impoverishment of empiricism that becomes visible when we consider what Sellars says when he *does* turn his attention to the semantics of modality.

There is a third strand to the rope with which Sellars first binds and then strangles the excessive ambitions of empiricism. That is his methodological strategy of considering *semantic* relations among the meanings expressed by different sorts of vocabulary that result from *pragmatic* dependencies relating the practices one must engage in or the abilities one must exercise in order to count as using those bits of vocabulary to express those meanings. I will call this the 'pragmatist' element in Sellars's multi-front assault on empiricism. It makes a significant contribution to the early, critical portion of EPM, though Sellars does not overtly mark it, as he does the contribution of his inferential functionalism to the later, more constructive portion. The concern with what one must *do* in order to *say* various kinds of things remains implicit in what Sellars *does*, rather than explicit in what he *says about* what he *does*. As we will see, both the pragmatist and the inferentialist ideas are integral to his critique of empiricist approaches to modality and to his constructive suggestions for a more adequate treatment of modal vocabulary.

2. The Inferentialist and Pragmatist Critique of Empiricism in EPM

I think the classical project of analytic philosophy in the twentieth century was to explore how the meanings expressed by some target vocabularies can be exhibited as in some sense a logical elaboration of the meanings already expressed by some base vocabularies. The conception of the desired semantic relation between vocabularies (the sense of 'analysis') has varied significantly within this broadly defined semantic project, including definition, paraphrase, translation, reduction in various senses, supervenience, and truth-making, to name just a few prominent candidates. I take it to be integral to the analytic philosophical project during this period that, however that semantic relation is conceived, *logical* vocabulary is taken to play a special role in elaborating the base vocabulary into the target vocabulary. The distinctively twentieth-century form of *empiricism* should be understood as one of the *core programs* of this analytic project—not in the sense that every participant in the project endorsed some version of empiricism (Neurath, for instance, rejects empiricism where he sees it clashing with another core semantic program that was dearer to his heart, namely naturalism), but in the sense that even those who rejected it for some target vocabulary or other took the possibility of an empiricist analysis to be an important issue, to set a legitimate philosophical agenda.

Construed in these terms, twentieth-century empiricism can be thought of as having proposed three broad kinds of empiricist base vocabularies. The most restrictive kind comprises *phenomenalist* vocabularies: those that specify how things subjectively *appear* as opposed to how they objectively are, or the not-yet-conceptualized perceptual *experiences* subjects have, or the so-far-uninterpreted sensory *given* (the data of sensation: sense data). A somewhat less restrictive genus of empiricist base vocabularies limits them to those that express *secondary qualities*, thought of as what is *directly perceived* in some less demanding sense. And a still more relaxed version of empiricism restricts its base vocabulary to the *observational* vocabulary deployed in non-inferentially elicited perceptual reports of observable states of affairs. Typical target vocabularies for the first, phenomenalist, class of empiricist base vocabularies include those expressing empirical claims about how things really or *objectively* are—that is, those expressing the applicability of any objective empirical concepts. Typical target vocabularies for secondary-quality empiricism include any that specify *primary qualities* or the applicability of concepts that are not response-dependent. And typical target vocabularies for observational vocabulary empiricism include *theoretical* vocabulary. All species of empiricism are concerned with the possibility of underwriting the semantics of the modal vocabulary used to express laws of nature, probabilistic vocabulary, normative vocabulary, and other sophisticated vocabularies of independent philosophical interest. The standard empiricist alternatives are either to show how a given target vocabulary can be semantically elaborated from the favored empiricist base vocabulary, on the one hand, or to show how to live with a local skepticism about its ultimate semantic intelligibility, on the other.

At the center of Sellars's critique of empiricism in EPM is an argument against the weakest, least committive, observational, version of empiricism (a critique that then carries over, *mutatis mutandis*, to the more demanding versions). That argument depends on both his inferential-functionalist semantics and on his pragmatism. Its fundamental strategy is to show that the proposed empiricist base vocabulary is not pragmatically autonomous: that observational vocabulary is not a vocabulary one could use though one used no other. Non-inferential reports of the results of observation do not form an autonomous stratum of language. In particular, when we look at what one must *do* to count as making a non-inferential report, we see that that is not a practice one could engage in except in the context of *inferential* practices of using those observations as *premises* from which to draw inferential *conclusions*, as *reasons* for making judgments and undertaking commitments that are *not* themselves observations. The contribution to this argument of Sellars's inferential-functionalism about semantics lies in underwriting the claim that for *any* judgment, claim, or belief to be *cognitively, conceptually*, or *epistemically* significant, for it to be a potential bit of *knowledge* or *evidence*, to be a *sapient* state or status, it must be able to play a distinctive *role in reasoning*: it must be able to serve as a *reason for* further judgments, claims, or beliefs, hence as a *premise* from which they can be *inferred*. That role in reasoning, in particular, what those judgments, claims, or beliefs can serve as reasons or evidence *for*, is an essential, and not just an accidental component of their having the semantic content that they do. And that means that one cannot count as understanding, grasping, or applying concepts *non*-inferentially in observation unless one can also deploy them at least as premises in *inferences* to conclusions that do *not*, for that very reason, count as *non*-inferential applications of concepts. Nor, for the same reason, can any discursive practice consist entirely of non-inferentially acquiring *premises*, without any corresponding practice of drawing *conclusions*. So non-inferential, observational uses of concepts do not constitute an autonomous discursive practice: a language-game one could play though one played no other. And this conclusion about the pragmatic dependence of observational uses of vocabulary on inferential ones holds no matter what the subject-matter of those observations is: whether it is observable features of the external environment, how things merely appear to a subject, or the current contents of one's own mind.

Here the pragmatist concern with what one must *do* in order to be able to *say* (or think) something combines with semantic inferentialist-functionalism about conceptual content to argue that the proposed empiricist base vocabulary is not pragmatically autonomous—since one must be able to make claims inferentially in order to count as making any non-inferentially. If that is so, then potentially risky inferential moves cannot be seen as an in-principle optional superstructure erected on a semantically autonomous base of things directly known through observation.

Although this is his most general and most powerful argument, Sellars does not limit himself to it in arguing against the substantially more committive forms of empiricism that insist on phenomenalist base vocabularies. In addition, he develops a constructive account of the relations between (at least one principle species of) phenomenalist vocabulary and objective vocabulary that depends on pragmatic dependences between what one must *do* in order to deploy each kind, to argue once again that the proposed empiricist base vocabulary does not form a semantically autonomous stratum of the language. This is his account of the relation between 'looks'-talk and 'is'-talk.

It develops out of his positive account of what one must *do* in order to use vocabulary observationally. To apply the concept *green* non-inferentially one must be able to do at least two sorts of things. First, one must be able reliably to respond differentially to the visible presence of green things. This is what blind and color-blind language-users lack, but non-language-using pigeons and parrots possess. Second, one must be able to exercise that capacity by reliably responding differentially to the visible presence of green things by applying the *concept green*. So one must possess, grasp, or understand that concept. "Grasp of a concept is mastery of the use of a word," Sellars says, and his inferential-functionalism dictates that this must include the *inferential* use of the word: knowing at least something about what follows from and is evidence for or against something's being green. This the blind or color-blind language-user has, and the pigeon and parrot do not. Only the performances of the former can have the pragmatic significance of taking up a stand in the space of reasons, of committing themselves to something that has a *conceptual*, that is, inferentially articulated, content.

The point of Sellars's parable of John in the tie shop is to persuade us that the home language-game of the 'looks' or 'seems' vocabulary that expresses how things merely appear to us, without undertaking any commitment to how they actually are, is one that is pragmatically parasitic on the practice of making in-principle risky reports of how things objectively are. For what one must *do* in order to count as saying how things merely *look*, Sellars claims, is to *evince* the reliable differential disposition to respond to something by claiming that it is green, while *withholding* the endorsement of that claim (because of one's collateral beliefs about the situation and one's reliability in it). If that is what one is doing in making a 'looks'-claim, then one cannot be wrong about it in the same way one can about an 'is'-claim, because one has withheld the principal commitment rather than undertaking it. And it follows that phenomenalist 'looks'-talk, which expresses how things merely appear, without further commitment to how things actually are, is not an autonomous discursive practice—not a language-game one could play though one played no other—but is in fact pragmatically parasitic on objective 'is'-talk.

My point in rehearsing this familiar argument is to emphasize the role played both by Sellars's pragmatist emphasis on what one must be able to *do* in order to count as *saying* various kinds of thing—*using* vocabulary so as to express certain kinds of meanings—and by his inferentialist-functionalist insistence that the role some vocabulary plays in *reasoning* makes an essential contribution to its semantic content. Although Sellars does not go on to make this argument, the way these two lines of thought conspire to undermine the semantic autonomy of candidate empiricist base vocabularies provides a template for a parallel objection to secondary-quality empiricism. For at least a necessary condition on anything's being a secondary-quality concept is that it have an observational role that supports the introduction of corresponding 'looks'-talk, so that mastery of that 'looks'-talk can be taken to be essential to mastery of the concept—as 'looks-green' arguably is for mastery of the concept *green*, but 'looks'-square is *not* for mastery of the concept *square*. What would be needed to fill in the argument against secondary-quality empiricism via the non-autonomy of its proposed base vocabulary would be an argument that nothing could count as mastering a vocabulary consisting entirely of expressions of this sort, apart from all inferential connections to primary-quality concepts that did not have this structure.

3. A Tension within Empiricism about Modality

Thus far I have confined myself to offering a general characterization of anti-empiricist arguments that appear in "Empiricism and the Philosophy of Mind." None of them involve empiricism's treatment of modality. Now I want to put those arguments in a somewhat different frame, by conjoining them with one that is presented elsewhere, and which *does* turn on the significance of modal concepts. The previous arguments concerned the suitability of some vocabulary to serve as the *base* vocabulary of an empiricist analysis—since plausible motivations for caring about such an analysis typically require that it be semantically autonomous. This one turns on the criteria of adequacy of the analysis itself. My remarks in this section concern Sellars's arguments in his essay "Phenomenalism," which was written soon after EPM, and can be regarded as a kind of companion piece to it. (Later I will discuss another contemporary essay that I think should be thought of as yoked together with these two in a troika.) The first, modal, point is one that Sellars registers there, but does not linger on—his principal concern being rather with a second point, concerning another aspect of the vocabulary in which phenomenalist analyses would have to be couched. But given my purposes here, I want to make a bit more of the modal point than he does.

The basic idea of a phenomenalist–empiricist semantic analysis of ordinary objective vocabulary is that the expressive work done by talk of mind-independent objects and their properties and relations can be done by talk of *patterns* in, *regularities* of, or *generalizations* concerning sense experiences characterized in a phenomenalist vocabulary. Saying that the curved red surface I am experiencing is an experience *of* an apple that has parts I am *not* experiencing—a similarly bulgy, red back and a white interior, for instance—is properly understood as saying something about what I *would* experience if I turned it around or cut it open. That it continued to exist in the kitchen when I left the room is a matter of what I *would* have experienced *had* I returned. The first, obvious, observation is that an account of objective reality in terms of the *powers* of circumstances to *produce*, or my *dispositions* to *have*, sensations, experiences, beings-appeared-to and so on essentially involves *modal* concepts. The patterns, regularities, or generalizations in subjective appearances that are supposed to constitute objective realities are modally robust, counterfactual-supporting patterns, regularities, or generalizations. Talk of what I actually *do* experience will not by itself underwrite claims about unexperienced spatial or temporal parts of empirical objects. Twentieth-century logical empiricism promised to advance beyond traditional empiricism because it could call on the full expressive resources of *logical* vocabulary to use as the 'glue' sticking sensory experiences together so as to construct simulacra of external objects. But *extensional* logical vocabulary is not nearly expressively powerful enough for the phenomenalist version of the empiricist project. So the phenomenalist conditional 'terminating judgments' into an infinite set of which C. I. Lewis proposes (in his *Analysis of Knowledge and Valuation*) to translate the 'non-terminating judgments' of ordinary objective empirical discourse, have to use his modal notion of *strict* or necessary implication.[2] And similar points could be made about other phenomenalist reductionists such as Ayer. The consequence of this observation to which I want to draw attention is that one cannot use such a strategy in one's phenomenalist empiricist analysis, translation, or reduction of objective talk *and* at the same time be a Humean skeptic about what *modal* vocabulary expresses. Essential features of the only remotely plausible *constructive* strategy of phenomenalist empiricism are simply incompatible with the most prominent *skeptical* consequences characteristically drawn both by traditional and twentieth-century logicist empiricism.

---

[2] C. I. Lewis. *An Analysis of Knowledge and Valuation* (La Salle, IL: Open Court, 1946).

This is a powerful argument. Sellars's principal concern in his essay "Phenomenalism," however, is with a subsequent point. The conditionals that codify the patterns, regularities, or generalizations concerning sense experience corresponding to judgments about how things objectively are must not only be subjunctive, counterfactually robust conditionals, but in order to have any hope of being materially adequate (getting the truth-conditions even approximately correct) their *antecedents* must themselves be expressed in *objective* vocabulary, *not* in *phenomenalist* vocabulary. What is true (enough) is that if I were *actually* to turn the apple around, cut it open, or return to its vicinity in the kitchen I *would* have certain sense experiences. It is *not* in general true that if I merely *seem* to do those things I am guaranteed to have the corresponding experiences. For, phrased in such phenomenalist terms, the antecedent is satisfied in cases of imagination, visual illusion, dreaming, hallucination and so on that are precisely those *not* bound by the supposedly object-constituting rules and regularities. As Sellars summarizes the point:

To claim that the relationship between the framework of sense contents and that of physical objects can be construed on the [phenomenalist] model is to commit oneself to the idea that there are inductively confirmable generalizations about sense contents which are 'in principle' capable of being formulated without the use of the language of physical things.... [T]his idea is a mistake.

(PHM, in SPR: 87)

It is a mistake because:

[T]he very selection of the complex patterns of actual sense contents in our past experiences which are to serve as the antecedents of the generalizations in question presuppose our common sense knowledge of ourselves as perceivers, of the specific physical environment in which we do our perceiving and of the general principles which correlate the occurrence of sensations with bodily and environmental conditions. We select those patterns which go with our being in a certain perceptual relation to a particular object of a certain quality, where we know that being in this relation to an object of that quality normally eventuates in our having the sense content referred to in the consequent.

(PHM, in SPR: 84)

This argument then makes evident

the logical dependence of the framework of private sense contents on the public, inter-subjective, logical space of persons and physical things.

(PHM, in SPR: 84)

So the phenomenalist vocabulary is not autonomous. It is not a language-game one can play though one plays no other. In particular, the uses of it that might plausibly fulfill many of the same pragmatic functions as ordinary objective empirical talk themselves presuppose the ability to deploy such objective vocabulary.

As Sellars points out, the lessons learned from pressing on the phenomenalist version of empiricism apply more generally. In particular, they apply to the more liberal version of empiricism whose base vocabulary is observational, including observations of enduring empirical objects, and whose target vocabulary is theoretical vocabulary. To begin with, if talk of theoretical entities is to be translated into, or replaced by talk of patterns in, regularities of, or generalizations about observable entities, they must be *lawlike, counterfactual*-supporting regularities and generalizations. They must permit inferences to what one *would* observe if one *were* to find oneself in specified circumstances, or to prepare the apparatus in a certain way. For, once again, the patterns, regularities, or generalizations about observations the assertion of which an instrumentalist empiricist might with some initial plausibility take to have the same pragmatic effect as (to be doing the same thing one is doing in) deploying theoretical vocabulary must reach beyond the parochial, merely autobiographically significant contingencies of what subjects happen actually to observe. The theory is that electrical currents cause magnetic fields regardless of the presence of suitable measuring devices. And that can only be made out in terms of what is observ*able*, that is, *could* be observed, not just what *is* observed. And that is to say that the instrumentalist-observational form of empiricism is also incompatible with Humean–Quinean skepticism about the intelligibility of what is expressed by alethic modal vocabulary.

And an analogue of the second argument against phenomenalist forms of empiricism also applies to instrumentalist forms. For, once again, the *antecedents* of the counterfactual conditionals specifying what *could* or *would* have been observed *if* certain conditions *had* obtained or certain operations *were* performed cannot themselves be formulated in purely observational terms. The meter-needle *would* have been observably displaced if I had connected the terminals of a volt-ohmeter to the wire, but that something *is* a VOM is *not* itself a fact restatable in purely observational terms. Even leaving apart the fact that it is a *functional* characterization not equivalent to any specification in purely *physical* terms, a description of the construction of some particular kind of VOM is still going to help itself to notions such as being made of copper, or being an electrical insulator (another bit of vocabulary that is both functional and theoretical). To satisfy the semantic ambitions of the instrumentalist it is not enough to associate each theoretical claim with a set of jointly pragmatically equivalent counterfactual-supporting conditionals whose *consequents* are couched wholly in observational vocabulary. All the theoretical terms appearing in the *antecedents* of those conditionals must be similarly replaced. No instrumentalist reduction of any actual theoretical claim has ever been suggested that even attempts to satisfy this condition.

Though Sellars does not, and I will not, pursue the matter, one expects that corresponding arguments will go through, *mutatis mutandis*, also for the kind of empiricism that seeks to understand the use of primary-quality vocabulary wholly in terms of the use of secondary-quality vocabulary. What we mean by talk of primary qualities will have to be cashed out in terms of its *powers* to produce, or our *dispositions* to perceive, secondary qualities—that is, in terms of modally robust, counterfactual-supporting generalizations. And it will be a challenge to specify the antecedents of a materially adequate set of such conditionals wholly in the official secondary-quality vocabulary.

4. A Direct Argument Against Empiricist Skepticism about Modality

The arguments I have considered so far set limits to the semantic ambitions of phenomenalist and instrumentalist forms of analytic empiricism, first by focusing on the *pragmatic* preconditions of the required semantic autonomy of the proposed empiricist base vocabularies, and second by looking in more detail at the specific sorts of *inferential* patterns in the base vocabulary in terms of which it is proposed to reconstruct the circumstances and consequences of application of items in the various target vocabularies. Here it was observed that the material adequacy of such reconstructions seems to require the ineliminable involvement of terms from the target vocabulary, not only on the right side, but also on the left side of any such reconstruction—in the *definiens* as well as in the *definiendum*. Modality plays a role in these arguments only because the material adequacy of the reconstruction also turns out to require appeal to counterfactually robust inferences in the base vocabulary. Insofar as that is so, the *constructive* semantic projects of the phenomenalist, instrumentalist, and secondary-quality forms of empiricism are at odds with the local semantic skepticism about what is expressed by alethic modal vocabulary that has always been a characteristic cardinal *critical* consequence of empiricist approaches to semantics, as epitomized for its traditional phase by Hume and for its logicist phase by Quine.

In another massive, pathbreaking essay of this period, "Counterfactuals, Dispositions, and the Causal Modalities"[3] (completed in February of 1957), Sellars argues directly against this empiricist

---

[3] "Counterfactuals, Dispositions, and the Causal Modalities," in *Minnesota Studies in The Philosophy of Science*, vol. II, eds. Herbert Feigl, Michael Scriven, and Grover Maxwell (Minneapolis: University of Minnesota Press, 1957): 225–308. Henceforth CDCM.

treatment of modality, completing what then becomes visible as a two-pronged attack on the principle contentions and projects of empiricism, only the opening salvos of which were fired in "Empiricism and the Philosophy of Mind."[4] His principal target here is the "tendency to assimilate all discourse to describing," which he takes to be primarily "responsible for the prevalence in the empiricist tradition of 'nothing-but-ism' in its various forms (emotivism, philosophical behaviorism, phenomenalism)…" (CDCM §103: 303). The form Sellars addresses in this essay is the Humean one that one can find in statements of laws of nature, expressed in alethic modal vocabulary that lets us say what is necessary and what is and is not possible, "nothing but" expressions of matter-of-factual regularities or constant conjunctions (though he claims explicitly that considerations corresponding to those he raises for causal modalities are intended to apply to logical and deontological modalities as well) (CDCM §103: 302–3). His arguments are directed against the view that holds modal vocabulary semantically unintelligible, on grounds of inability to specify what it is saying about what the world is like, how it is describing things as being, insofar as by using it we are asserting something that goes beyond endorsing the existence of non-modally characterizable universal generalizations.

Hume found that even his best understanding of actual observable empirical *facts* did not yield an understanding of *rules* relating or otherwise governing them. Those facts did not settle which of

---

[4] As in EPM (and even, though to a lesser extent, in "Phenomenalism"), in this essay Sellars describes himself not as denying empiricism, but rather as correcting it, protecting its core insights from the damage done by their over-extension. But he also makes it clear that the result of such rectification is a Kantian view that gives equal weight to rationalist insights, when they are suitably reconstructed. So for instance he says:

It is my purpose to argue that the core truth of Hume's philosophy of causation is not only compatible with, but absurd without, *ungrudging* recognition of those features of causal discourse as a mode of rational discourse on which the "metaphysical rationalists" laid such stress, but also mis-assimilated to describing.

(CDCM, §82: 285)

And the final sentence of the essay invokes the "profound truth" of Kant's conception of reason, "which empiricism has tended to distort."

the things that *actually* happened *had* to happen (given others), that is, were (at least conditionally) *necessary*, and which of the things that did *not* happen nonetheless were *possible* (not ruled out by laws concerning what did happen). The issue here concerns the justifiability and intelligibility of a certain kind of *inference*: modally robust, counterfactual-supporting inferences, of the kind made explicit by the use of modal vocabulary. Hume (and, following him, Quine) took it that epistemologically and semantically fastidious philosophers face a stark choice: either show how to explain modal vocabulary—the circumstances of application that justify the distinctive counterfactual-supporting inferential consequences of application—in non-modal terms, or show how to live without it, to do what we need to do in science without making such arcane and occult supradescriptive commitments.

This demand was always the greatest source of tension between empiricism and naturalism, especially the scientific naturalism that Sellars epitomized in the slogan: "[S]cience is the measure of all things, of what is that it is, and of what is not that it is not" (EPM, §42, in SPR: 173; in KMG: 253; in B: 83). For modern mathematized natural science shorn of concern with laws, counterfactuals, and dispositions—in short of what is expressed by alethic modal vocabulary—is Hamlet without the prince, not just an impotent Samson but an inert, unrecognizable fragmentary remnant of a once-vital enterprise. Sellars's general recommendation for resolving this painful tension (felt particularly acutely by, and one of the principal issues dividing, the members of the Vienna circle) is to relax the exclusivism and rigorism he traces to empiricism's semantic descriptivism:

[O]nce the tautology 'The world is described by descriptive concepts' is freed from the idea that the business of all non-logical concepts is to describe, the way is clear to an *ungrudging* recognition that many expressions which empiricists have relegated to second-class citizenship in discourse are not *inferior*, just *different*.

(CDCM §79: 282)

Sensitized as we now are by Sellars's diagnoses of *semantic autonomy* claims as essential to various empiricist constructive and reconstructive projects, both in EPM and in the "Phenomenalism" essay, and familiar as we now are with his criticisms of them based on the inferentially articulated *doings* required to use or deploy various candidate base vocabularies, it should come as no surprise that his objections to critical empiricist suspicions of and hostility towards modality follow the same pattern. For the Humean–Quinean empiricist semantic challenge to the legitimacy of modal vocabulary is predicated on the idea of an independently and antecedently intelligible stratum of empirical discourse that is purely descriptive and involves no modal commitments, as a semantically autonomous background and model with which the credentials of modal discourse can then be invidiously compared.

In this case, as in the others, the argument turns both on the *pragmatism* that looks to what one is doing in deploying the candidate base vocabulary—here "purely descriptive" vocabulary—and on the nature of the *inferential* articulation of that vocabulary necessary for such uses to play the expressive role characteristic of that vocabulary. The argument in this case is subtler and more complex than the others however. For one thing, I take it that Sellars does *not* deny the intelligibility-in-principle of purely descriptive discourse that contains no explicitly modal vocabulary.[5] For another, there

---

[5] This conclusion requires some interpretation, as Sellars is, frustratingly but characteristically, not explicit on the point. He says:

The idea that the world can, in principle, be so described that the description contains no modal expression is of a piece with the idea that the world can, in principle, be so described that the description contains no prescriptive expression. For what is being called to mind is the ideal of statement of 'everything that is the case' which, however, serves *through and through only* the purpose of stating what is the case. And it is a logical truth that such a description, however many modal expressions might properly be used in *arriving at* it or in *justifying* it, or in showing the *relevance* of one of its components to another, could contain no modal expression.

(CDCM §80: 283)

Sellars's view about this ideal is complex: there is sense in which it is intelligible, and a sense in which it is not. Such a discourse would be unreflective and unself-conscious in a way ours is not. For reasons that will emerge, it would belong to what at the end of the essay

are special difficulties involved in, and corresponding delicacies required for, working out the general pragmatist-inferentialist strategy so as to apply it to this case, by specifying the relation between the expressive role distinctive of modal vocabulary, on the one hand, and what one is *doing* (in particular, the inferential commitments one is undertaking) in using ordinary, non-modal, descriptive vocabulary itself, on the other.

The pragmatic dependency relation that lies at the base of Sellars's argument is the fact that:

... although describing and explaining (predicting, retrodicting, understanding) are *distinguishable*, they are also, in an important sense, *inseparable*. It is only because the expressions in terms of which we describe objects, even such basic expressions as words for perceptible characteristics of molar objects, locate these objects in a space of implications, that they *describe* at all, rather than merely label. The descriptive and explanatory resources of language advance hand in hand....

(CDCM §108: 306–7)

Descriptive uses of vocabulary presuppose an inferentially articulated "space of implications," within which some descriptions show up as reasons for or explanations of others. Understanding those descriptions requires placing them in such a space. This pragmatist claim about what else one must be able to *do*—namely, *infer, explain*, treat one claim as a *reason* for another—in order for what one is doing to count as *describing* connects to the use of *modal* vocabulary via the principle that:

To make first hand use of these [modal] expressions is to be about the business of explaining a state of affairs, or justifying an assertion.

(CDCM §80: 283)

That is, what one is *doing* in *using* modal expressions is explaining, justifying, or endorsing an inference. So what one is doing in

---

he calls the stage of human language "when linguistic changes had *causes*, but not *reasons*, [before] man acquired the ability to reason about reasons" (CDCM §108: 307).

saying that As are *necessarily* Bs is endorsing the inference from anything's being an A to its being a B.

The first sort of difficulty I alluded to above stems from the fact that there are other ways of endorsing such a pattern of inference besides saying *that* all As are necessarily Bs. One's endorsement may be *implicit* in other things one *does*, the reasoning one engages in and approves, rather than *explicit* in what one *says*. So from the fact (assuming, as I shall, that it is a fact) that the activity of describing is part of an indissoluble pragmatic package that includes endorsing inferences and the fact that what one is doing in making a modal claim is endorsing an inference, it does not at all follow that there can be no use of descriptive vocabulary apart from the use of modal vocabulary. The second difficulty stems from the fact that although Sellars may be right that what one is *doing* in making a modal claim is endorsing a pattern of inference, it is clear that one is not thereby *saying* that an inference is good. When I say "Pure copper necessarily conducts electricity," and thereby unrestrictedly endorse inferences from anything's being pure copper to its conducting electricity, I have nevertheless *said* nothing about any inferences, explanations, justifications, or implications—indeed, have said something that could be true even if there had never been any inferences or inferrers to endorse them, hence no describers or discursive practitioners at all.[6] These two observations set the principal criteria of adequacy both for Sellars's positive working-out of the pragmatist-inferentialist treatment of modal vocabulary, and for his argument that the purely descriptive base vocabulary invoked by the empiricist critic of the semantic credentials of modal vocabulary lacks the sort of discursive autonomy the empiricist criticism presupposes and requires.

---

[6] Sellars connects this obvious fact with the observation that:

Idealism is notorious for the fallacy of concluding that because there must be minds in the world in order for *us* to have reason to make statements about the world, therefore there is no sense to the idea of a world which does not include minds.

(CDCM §101: 301)

Sellars's central rhetorical strategy in this essay is to address the issue of what is expressed by modal claims about necessary connections by offering:

… a sympathetic reconstruction of the controversy in the form of a debate between a Mr. C (for Constant Conjunction) and a Mr. E (for Entailment) who develop and qualify their views in such a way as to bring them to the growing edge of the problem.

(CDCM Introduction: 226)

Officially, he is even-handed in his treatment of the vices and virtues of the empiricist, who denies that the use of modal vocabulary can express any legitimate semantic content beyond that expressed by a descriptive, extensional universal generalization, and the rationalist, who understands that content in terms of entailments expressing rules of reasoning. In fact, however, as becomes clear when he launches into his own account, he is mainly concerned to develop a version of the rationalist account. As the second half of the essay develops, Sellars marks his abandonment of the disinterested pose by an uncharacteristically explicit expository shift:

It is now high time that I dropped the persona of Mr. E, and set about replying to the challenge with which Mr. C ended his first critique of the entailment theory.

(CDCM §85: 286)[7]

Doing that requires careful investigation of the differences between and relations among four different sorts of item:

---

[7] In fact, Sellars's 'defense' of Mr. C (see the passage from §82 quoted in note 3 above) consists of showing what concessions he needs to make to Mr. E. This proceeds first by Mr. C's qualification that "'A causes B' *says* that (x)[Ax → Bx] and *implies* that the latter is asserted on inductive grounds" (§62: 272), followed by the necessity of conceiving "of induction as establishing principles *in accordance with which* we reason, rather than as major premises *from which* we reason" (§83: 286). As will appear, the former concession, introducing the notion of what is *contextual implied* by contrast to what is explicitly said, is then dialectically made available to be pressed into service by Mr. E. This bit of dialectic is a pretty rhetorical flourish on Sellars's part, but I doubt that in the end it reflects any deep feature of the confrontation between the empiricist and rationalist approaches to modality.

- Practical endorsement of the propriety of an inference from things being A to their being B;
- The explicit statement that one may infer the applicability of 'B' from the applicability of 'A';
- The statement that A physically entails B;
- The statement that As are necessarily Bs.

The first is the sort of thing Sellars takes to be pragmatically presupposed by the activity of describing, that is, deploying descriptive vocabulary. The second fails to capture such practical endorsements, because of the possibility of asserting such statements regarding the *expressions* 'A' and 'B' without understanding what they express.[8]

The third sort of statement expresses Mr. E's initial stab at an analysis of the fourth. It is the answer to the question: what sort of entailment is it that modal statements are supposed to express?:

> Mr. E has a ready answer. ... it might ... be called 'natural' or 'physical' entailment, for while any entailment is a logical relation, we can distinguish within the broad class of entailments between those which are, and those which are not, a function of the specific empirical contents between which they obtain. The latter are investigated by general or formal logic (and pure mathematics). Empirical science, on the other hand, to the extent that it is a search for *laws*, is the search for entailments of the former kind. (Putative) success in this search finds its expression in statements of the form 'It is (inductively) probable that A physically entails B.'

(CDCM §56: 268)

The virtue of statements like "A physically entails B" is that they do plausibly codify the practical endorsement of an inference

---

[8] As Sellars says:

But one can know that Turks, for example, ought to withdraw '...' when they commit themselves to '- - -' without knowing the language, whereas the statement that '*p* entails *q*' contextually implies that the speaker not only knows the language to which 'p' and 'q' belong, but, in particular, knows how to use 'p' and 'q' themselves.

(CDCM §81: 284)

that is implicit in what one does in the form of something one can explicitly *say*, without bringing in irrelevant commitments concerning particular expressions, the activity of inferring, or discursive practitioners. The remaining difficulty is that they seem plainly not to have the same content, not to say the same thing, as explicitly modal statements of objective necessity.

Sellars's response to this problem is to acknowledge that modal statements do not *say that* some entailment holds, but to distinguish between what is *said* by using a bit of vocabulary and what is '*contextually implied*' by doing so. Sellars says very little about this latter notion, even though it bears the full weight of his proposed emendation of the rationalist account. It is recognizably the same distinction he had appealed to earlier, in "Inference and Meaning," as the distinction between what making a statement *says* and what it *conveys*. There his example is that in asserting "The weather is fine today," I *say* that the weather is fine today, but *convey* that I *believe* that it is fine.[9] That otherwise uninterpreted example suggests to me that what Sellars has in mind is the distinction between *semantic* and *pragmatic* inferences. That is the distinction between inferences underwritten by the *contents* of what is *said* or asserted, on the one hand, and inferences underwritten by what one is *doing* in saying them, on the other. The inference from "The weather is fine," to "It is not raining," is of the first sort; the inference from my asserting "The weather is fine," to "Brandom believes the weather is fine," is of the second sort. Inferences of these two kinds may generally be distinguished by the Frege–Geach embedding test: look to see whether those who make the inference in question also endorse the corresponding conditional. "If the weather is fine, then it is not raining," is generally true, while "If the weather is fine, then Brandom believes it is fine," is not generally true. (Compare the inference from my *saying* "That is an ugly tie you are wearing," to "Bob is annoyed with me.")

[9] Wilfrid Sellars, "Inference and Meaning" [IM] *Mind* 62 (1953): 332. Reprinted in J. Sicha (ed.) *Pure Pragmatics and Possible Worlds: The Early Essays of Wilfrid Sellars* (Reseda, CA: Ridgeview Publishing Company, 1980) [PPPW]: 280.

If that is in fact the distinction Sellars is after, then it seems to me that the view he is expounding and defending can be put less paradoxically if we don't take a detour through entailment statements, but concern ourselves directly with the relation between the endorsement of patterns of inference and modal statements. The underlying rationalist insight is a pragmatist-inferentialist one: what one is *doing* in making a modal claim is endorsing a pattern of inference. Modal vocabulary makes possible new kinds of *sayings* that have the *pragmatic effect* of endorsing inferences. To say that is not yet to say what they *say*, only what one is *doing by* saying them. But it does settle the *pragmatic significance* of such modal claims, in the sense of their appropriate circumstances and consequences of application.[10] If one practically endorses the pattern of inference that treats classifying anything at all as an A as sufficient grounds

---

[10] It is the attempt to specify this peculiar and distinctive sort of pragmatically mediated relation between vocabularies that leads Sellars to say things like:

It is sometimes thought that modal statements do not describe states of affairs in the world, because they are *really* metalinguistic. This won't do at all if it is meant that instead of describing states of affairs in the world, they describe linguistic habits. It is more plausible if it is meant that statements involving modal terms have the force of *prescriptive* statements about the use of certain expressions in the object language. Yet there is more than one way to '*have the force of*' a statement, and failure to distinguish between them may snowball into a serious confusion as wider implications are drawn.

(CDCM §81: 283)

and

Shall we say that modal expressions are metalinguistic? Neither a simple 'yes' nor a simple 'no' will do. As a matter of fact, once the above considerations are given their proper weight, it is possible to acknowledge that the idea that they are metalinguistic in character oversimplifies a fundamental insight. For our present purposes, it is sufficient to say that the claim that modal expressions are 'in the metalanguage' is not too misleading if the peculiar force of the expressions which occur alongside them (represented by the 'p' and the 'q' of our example) is recognized, in particular, that they have 'straightforward' translation into other languages, and if it is also recognized that they belong not only 'in the metalanguage', but in discourse about *thoughts* and *concepts* as well.

(CDCM §82: 284)

and

We must here, as elsewhere, draw a distinction between what we are committed to concerning the world by virtue of the fact that we have reason to make a certain assertion, and the force, in a narrower sense, of the assertion itself.

(CDCM §101: 301)

("all on its own," as Sellars says, in order to capture the way the pattern of inferences in question is counterfactually robust) for concluding that it is a B, then one is committed to the claim that all As are necessarily Bs. And commitment to that claim is commitment to practically ratify that pattern of inference. Assuming, as Sellars has claimed, that using ordinary, non-modal, descriptive vocabulary requires practically endorsing such patterns of inference ("situating descriptions in a space of implications"), that means that anyone who has the practical ability to deploy "purely descriptive" vocabulary already knows how to do everything he needs to know how to do to deploy modal vocabulary as well. He need not actually do so, since practically undertaking those inferential commitments does not require that one have available a language with vocabulary permitting one to *do* that by *saying* something. But *all* a practitioner lacks in such a circumstance is the *words* to hook up to discriminative and responsive abilities he already possesses. In this precise sense, the ability to deploy modal vocabulary is *practically implicit* in the ability to deploy non-modal descriptive vocabulary.

Sellars has claimed that the activity of describing is unintelligible except as part of a pragmatic package that includes also not just the making of inferences, but the making of *counterfactually robust* inferences: the sort of inferences involved in *explanation*, and licensed by explicitly modal statements of *laws*. Sellars summed up the claim admirably in the title of another one of his early papers: "Concepts as Involving Laws, and Inconceivable without Them." Grasp of a concept is mastery of the use of a word, Sellars says. And that use includes not only sorting inferences (however fallibly and incompletely) into materially good and materially bad ones, but also, among the ones one takes to be materially good, to distinguish (however fallibly and incompletely) between counterfactual circumstances under which they do, and counterfactual circumstances under which they do not, *remain* good. Part of taking an inference to be materially good is knowing something about which possible additional collateral premises or auxiliary hypotheses would, and which would not, infirm it. Chestnut trees produce chestnuts—unless they are immature, or blighted. Dry, well-made matches strike—unless there is no oxygen. The hungry lioness would still chase the antelope if it were Tuesday or the beetle on the distant tree crawled slightly further up the branch, but not if the lioness's heart were to stop beating. The point is not that there is any particular set of such discriminations that one must be able to make in order to count as deploying the concepts involved. It is that if one can make *no* such practical assessments of the counterfactual robustness of material inferences involving those concepts, one could not count as having mastered them.

Against the background of this pragmatist-inferentialist claim about what is involved in the ordinary descriptive use of concepts, Sellars's claim, as I am reading him, is that explicitly modal 'lawlike' statements are statements that one is committed or entitled to whenever one is committed or entitled to endorse such patterns of counterfactually robust inference, and commitment or entitlement to which in their turn commit or entitle one to the corresponding patterns of inference. Saying that about them settles what one needs to *do* to *use* such modal statements. It does *not* say how one is thereby *describing* the world as being when one does. It does not, in particular, *describe* a pattern of inference as good (though that saying does, in its own distinctive way, *express endorsement* of such a pattern). It does not do those things for the simple reason that the use of modal expressions is *not* in the first instance *descriptive*.[11] It codifies explicitly, in the form of a statement, a feature of the use of descriptive expressions that is indissolubly bound up with, but not identical to, their descriptive use. Nonetheless, in knowing how to use vocabulary descriptively, one knows how to do everything one needs to know how to do in order to use modal vocabulary. And that is enough to show that one cannot actually be in the Humean predicament presupposed by the empiricist challenge to the intelligibility of modal vocabulary. For one cannot know how

---

[11] Sellars says: "[Mr. E.] conceives of induction as establishing principles *in accordance with which* we reason, rather than as major premises *from which* we reason" (CDCM §83: 286).

to use vocabulary in matter-of-factual descriptions ("The cat is on the mat,") and not have any grip on how to use modal, counterfactual, and dispositional vocabulary ("It is necessary for live cats to breathe," "The cat could still be on the mat if the mat were a slightly different shade of blue, but not if it turned into soup," "The cat would leave the mat if she saw a mouse,"). Although *explicitly* modal *vocabulary* is an in-principle optional superstructure on practices of deploying descriptive vocabulary, what it expresses cannot be mysterious in principle to those who can engage in those base-level practices.

In taking this line, Sellars quite properly sees himself as reviving a central idea of Kant's. The ability to use empirical descriptive terms such as 'mass', 'rigid', and 'green' already presupposes grasp of the kind of properties and relations made explicit by modal vocabulary. It is this insight that leads Kant to the idea of 'pure' concepts or 'categories', including the alethic modal concepts of necessity and possibility that articulate causal laws, which must be available a priori because and in the sense that the ability to deploy them is presupposed by the ability to deploy ordinary empirical descriptive concepts. The categories, including modality, are concepts that make explicit what is implicit in the empirical, descriptive use of any concepts at all. Though the details of *which* laws, the statements of which express counterfactually robust patterns of inference, actually obtain is an empirical one, *that* empirical descriptions are related by *rules* in the form of laws, which do support counterfactually robust inferences, is *not* itself an empirical matter, but a truth about the framework of empirical description. I want to call the underlying insight "the Kant–Sellars thesis about modality." It is the claim that in being able to use non-modal, empirical-descriptive vocabulary, one already knows how to do everything one needs to know how to do in order to deploy modal vocabulary, which accordingly can be understood as making explicit structural features that are always already implicit in what one *does* in describing.

5. Conclusion

Articulating and justifying his version of the Kant–Sellars thesis about modality is Sellars's constructive response to the empiricist tradition's "nothing-but-ism" about modality: its demand that what is expressed by modal claims either be shown to be expressible in non-modal terms, or be dispensed with entirely by semantically fastidious philosophers and scientists. This complements and completes his demonstration, in the "Phenomenalism" essay, that this critical consequence of an over-ambitious empiricism is in any case incompatible with any constructive empiricist effort to reconstruct or replace the use of target vocabularies such as objective-descriptive vocabulary, primary-quality vocabulary, and theoretical vocabulary in terms of the favored empiricist base vocabularies, if that effort is subject to even the most minimal criteria of material adequacy. Together, these arguments show what Sellars eventually made of his early intuition that the soft underbelly of empiricism, in both its traditional and its twentieth-century logistical form, is its treatment of modality.

My overall aim in this essay has been to place the arguments against empiricism presented in the first half of "Empiricism and the Philosophy of Mind" in the larger context opened up by laying them alongside the further battery of arguments aimed at the same target that derive from consideration of that tradition's views about modality. And I have been concerned to show that the methodological strategies that guide all of these discussions are Sellars's *pragmatist* insistence on looking at what one must be able to *do* in order to deploy empirical descriptive vocabulary, and his *rationalist* commitment to the necessary *inferential* articulation of the concepts expressed by the use of such vocabulary. I think that even fifty years on, there is still a lot of juice to be squeezed out of these ideas.

But I want to close with another, perhaps more frivolous suggestion. Every sufficiently engaged reading becomes a rewriting, and I have been offering here, *inter alia*, the outline of a different narrative strategy that Sellars could have adopted in the late 1950s. Under some such title as *The Limits of Empiricism*, he could have re-presented the material that in fact appeared first as roughly the first half of "Empiricism and the Philosophy of Mind," and the second halves of each of "Phenomenalism" and "Counterfactuals, Dispositions, and Causal Modalities," organized around and introduced in terms of the themes I have traced here. It is interesting to speculate about how his reception might have been different—and about where we would find ourselves today—had this been the shape of Sellars's first book.

References

Lewis, Clarence Irving, *An Analysis of Knowledge and Valuation* (La Salle, IL: Open Court, 1946).

Sellars, Wilfrid. "Concepts as Involving Laws, and Inconceivable without Them," *Philosophy of Science* 15 (1948): 287–315. Reprinted in J. Sicha (ed.) *Pure Pragmatics and Possible Worlds: The Early Essays of Wilfrid Sellars* (Reseda, CA: Ridgeview Publishing Company, 1980).

—— "Inference and Meaning" *Mind* 62 (1953): 313–38. Reprinted in J. Sicha (ed.) *Pure Pragmatics and Possible Worlds: The Early Essays of Wilfrid Sellars* (Reseda, CA: Ridgeview Publishing Company, 1980). Cited as IM.

—— "Empiricism and the Philosophy of Mind," (Presented at the University of London in Special Lectures in Philosophy for 1956 under the title "The Myth of the Given: Three Lectures on Empiricism and the Philosophy of Mind"), in *Minnesota Studies in the Philosophy of Science*, vol. I, eds. Herbert Feigl and Michael Scriven (Minneapolis: University of Minnesota Press, 1956): 253–329. Reprinted in SPR with additional footnotes. Published separately as *Empiricism and the Philosophy of Mind: with an Introduction by Richard Rorty and a Study Guide by Robert Brandom*, ed. Robert Brandom (Cambridge, MA: Harvard University Press, 1997). (Cited as B.) Also reprinted in W. deVries and T. Triplett, *Knowledge, Mind, and the Given: A Reading of Sellars' "Empiricism and the Philosophy of Mind"* (Cambridge, MA: Hackett Publishing, 2000). Cited as EPM, page references to SPR, KMG, and B editions.

—— "Counterfactuals, Dispositions, and the Causal Modalities," in *Minnesota Studies in The Philosophy of Science*, vol. II, eds. Herbert Feigl, Michael Scriven, and Grover Maxwell (Minneapolis: University of Minnesota Press, 1957): 225–308. Cited as CDCM.

—— *Science, Perception and Reality* (London: Routledge & Kegan Paul, 1963). Reissued by Ridgeview Publishing Company in 1991. Cited as SPR.

—— "Phenomenalism," in *Science, Perception and Reality* (London: Routledge & Kegan Paul, 1963): 60–105. Cited as PHM.

—— "Autobiographical Reflections," in *Action, Knowledge, and Reality*, H. N. Castañeda (ed.) (Indianapolis: Bobbs-Merrill, 1975): 277–93. Cited as AR.

—— J. Sicha (ed.) *Pure Pragmatics and Possible Worlds: The Early Essays of Wilfrid Sellars* (Reseda, CA: Ridgeview Publishing Company, 1980). Cited as PPPW.

3

Perception, Imagination, and Demonstrative Reference: A Sellarsian Account

Paul Coates

1. Introduction: Sellars and the Structure of Perceptual Experience

Sellars wrote a good deal on perception, but he never produced a synoptic account of the topic. His treatment of perception, although touching on a wide variety of issues, is incomplete, and scattered across a number of papers spanning thirty years from the nineteen-fifties until the early nineteen-eighties. He makes no attempt to resolve all the problems faced by the form of Critical Realism he endorses. Even in the more extended discussions, *Empiricism and the Philosophy of Mind* (EPM), 'Phenomenalism' (PHM), *The Structure of Knowledge* (SK), and his *Carus Lectures* (FMPP), his coverage of perceptual issues is very selective.[1]

The Critical Realist theory that Sellars adopts in EPM and his other writings has sometimes been criticised on the grounds that it amounts to a form of "indirect realism", and as such is unable

---

[1] Sellars (1956), (1963), (1975) and (1981). I shall refer in the text to works from Sellars by their conventional abbreviations.

to account for the demonstrative character of many perceptual judgements.[2] This assessment, I argue, rests on an incomplete grasp of the nature of Critical Realism and the resources available to that theory. My aim in this paper is to defend aspects of the Sellarsian account of perception, and to show how the Critical Realist account of demonstrative reference encounters fewer problems than competing theories. In outlining the Sellarsian position I shall pay special attention to Sellars's discussion of the essential role of the imagination in perception, and show how this notion constitutes a key element in any account of perceptually based reference. For the most part I shall concentrate here on vision as a paradigm case of distance perception.[3]

According to the Critical Realist theory of perception that Sellars upholds, a subject S perceives some particular physical object X, in the full sense that includes conceptual activity, if and only if the following conditions hold:

1) The object X exists;
2) The subject S has an experience E, consisting of two components:
   (i) An inner sensory, or phenomenal state E, which causes:
   (ii) An episode involving concepts of at least a low-level classificatory kind—a "perceptual taking": an intentional representational episode referring to a physical object;
3) The object X causes E to come about by an appropriate causal chain C, where C can implicitly be understood (by anyone who grasps the ordinary concept of perceiving) as the

---

[2] See, for example, the criticisms in Smith (1982), ch. 2. The general position is also attacked in McDowell (1986) and (1998). I discuss these in more detail below.

[3] For reasons I discuss in my (2007), ch. 7, distance perception forms a distinctive and important class of perceptual activity. Several background assumptions concerning the basic structure of the Critical Realist theory are defended in detail in that work. The present paper seeks to extend the discussion of demonstratively based reference that I set out there in ch. 10.

kind of causal chain which 'allows perceivers to survive in a hostile world'.[4]

In standard veridical cases of perception, the subject is *directly* aware, at the conceptual level, of the physical object he or she perceives; that is, the subject forms a noninferential perceptual thought, or "taking", referring to an *external* object. Nevertheless, the subject is at the same time *immediately* aware, nonconceptually, of inner phenomenal (or sensory) states that mediate the perception of the external object.[5]

This means that the Critical Realist is committed to three central theses concerning the perception of physical objects:

(A) The Kantian thesis

Perceptual experience contains two components: first, there is a phenomenal (or sensory) nonconceptual element, and, second, a conceptual element, or perceptual thought. 'Conceptual' here is to be understood widely; it does not necessarily imply the ability to form judgements and have self-awareness, but it does involve the exercise of a classificatory ability. In EPM, Sellars refers to these two contrasting states of mind as the 'descriptive' and the 'propositional' components of experience, respectively. In later work, they are referred to as *sensa* (or *sensing states*), and the subject's *perceptual taking*.[6]

(B) The Inner State thesis

Perceptual experiences are inner states. When a subject sees an object such as a red ball in normal daylight conditions, the reddish

---

[4] The quoted phrase is from Sellars, SSOP §89; precisely how this idea is to be cashed out is one of the points I shall explain in due course.

[5] There are good reasons for referring to the (*outer*) perceived object—usually some physical object in the subject's surroundings—as 'external' to the *inner* phenomenal states of which the subject is immediately aware; see my (2007), chs. 3 and 4.

[6] See Sellars SRPC and SSOP; in EPM (1956), the descriptive content is also referred to as 'the sense-impression'.

expanse involved in the experience is an inner mediating phenomenal state, a state that is in some way closely connected with the subject's brain, and is logically distinct from (though causally connected with) the actual physical object seen.[7] The perceived object transcends the phenomenal qualities that the subject is immediately aware of at the nonconceptual level. There are, nevertheless, important conceptual connections between (private) inner experiences and (public) external objects.

(C) The Phenomenological Directness thesis

The objects of perception are external, public objects. In having an ordinary perceptual experience—such as, for example, having a visual experience in seeing a dog chase after a ball—the concepts entertained by the subject in the perceptual taking refer directly to the physical objects he or she takes to be situated in the local environment, without any inference from a prior conceptual state. Such perceptual takings are caused by the phenomenal state immediately present in consciousness, but that phenomenal state is not the focus of the perception. Thus Sellars states in (SK):

The objects of perceptual knowledge are the objects referred to in the propositional component of the perceptual experience, and these are physical objects, not private, subjective (let alone theoretical) items.

(SK, I §59: 311)

In emphasising the fact that perceptual experiences are directed, without inference, upon external physical objects, Sellars is opposing traditional sense-data theories of the kind originally put forward by Russell and Moore.[8] It is, however, important to note that he is *not* objecting to the idea that the perceptual takings are mediated by inner phenomenal states.

---

[7] Sellars spells out the basic Critical Realist ideas in various places; in addition to the works cited above, see also PR, SRPC, and IKTE. For a good account of Sellars's views on the nature of phenomenal qualities, see Rosenberg (1982).

[8] See for example Russell (1914b) and Moore (1913–14).

According to the Sellarsian account, in normal circumstances I respond to visual input by adopting what Rosenberg calls 'the mode of perception'.[9] In looking at a dog, my perceptual taking is focused on the dog I see: I directly take there to be a dog present, without making any inference from some prior belief about my own inner experiences. While my perceptual taking is, in this sense, psychologically direct, it nevertheless has presuppositions that, if prompted, I could articulate. These relate to my own capacity as a competent perceiver, and to other contextual matters (e.g. my background belief that the lighting is normal). What is perceptually taken is represented by a complex denoting phrase, such as: 'This black dog...', or 'This brick with a red and rectangular facing surface...'.[10]

The perceptual taking is accompanied by the inner phenomenal state which causes it, and which, by virtue of its guiding role, forms a part of the experience. There is no conflict with commonsense assumptions about the directness of perception here, because I do not normally conceptualise my phenomenal state as such. However, if what Sellars claims in the later parts of EPM and elsewhere is correct, then my phenomenal state can, on occasion, also become the focus of my direct thoughts. Sellars argues in EPM that introspection provides evidence about the nature of experience, and through it we become able to correctly report our impressions, that is, our phenomenal, or sensory states. We respond to perceptual experiences "in the mode of introspection".[11] I can reflect on the experience I am having, and wonder whether it is an illusory one. It follows that concepts can be intimately connected with experiences in two quite different ways. Firstly, we can employ concepts referring directly to physical objects that transcend inner experience; such concept use is then *guided by* a nonconceptual

---

[9] See Rosenberg (2000).

[10] Sellars, SRPC Part II, in KTM: 431–6; IKTE §10, in KTM: 420.

[11] See Sellars EPM, Part XVI, §62; there are also passages in later work that support this view, such as the last part of SRPC; but for a slightly different interpretation, see Rosenberg (2000).

awareness of the phenomenal states. Secondly, when we adopt an introspective mode of attention, we are (causally) prompted to exercise concepts *referring directly* to the inner phenomenal states themselves.

One set of problems facing a Critical Realist theory of perception of the kind upheld by Sellars therefore consists in explaining, more fully, how it comes about that we can conceptualise our experiences in two different ways, so that in the usual case we are able to make demonstrative reference to objects external to phenomenal consciousness. A second set of problems that arises for the Critical Realist account concerns the relation between the two components of experience.[12] Various writers have emphasised the phenomenological unity of experience—so it can be asked, how exactly do the concepts we exercise in perception harmonise with the phenomenal aspect, so that experience presents itself phenomenologically as a unity?[13] In this paper I will show how the Critical Realist can provide answers to these two problems, drawing upon Sellars's approach to these issues in his later work.

2. The Role of the Productive Imagination in Experience:

In an important late paper, 'The Role of Imagination in Kant's Theory of Experience' (IKTE), Sellars adds a further dimension to the account of perceptual consciousness defended in his earlier work, spelling out the key role played by the imagination in accounting for the unity of perceptual experience.[14] In this paper Sellars appeals, specifically, to the role of the *productive imagination*,

---

[12] A good discussion of Sellars's account of the roles of the two components of perceptual experience, and of his reasons for that account, can be found in Williams (2006).

[13] The phenomenological unity of perceptual experience is a point that Firth emphasises (1949/50). As David Smith notes, the phenomenal and conceptual components of experience cannot simply be causally linked accompaniments of each other: Smith (2002), ch. 2.

[14] Sellars IKTE. I should emphasise that the term 'imagination' is used in a quasi-technical sense that derives from Kant.

developing ideas derived from Kant. The productive imagination is an extension of the workings of the understanding. Working from the Critical Realist assumption that visual experience contains, at a fundamental level, an inner phenomenal component, and also a conceptual classificatory component of some kind, Sellars shows how the productive imagination plays two interconnected roles in the generation of the full-blown perceptual experience:

(i) Firstly, the imagination, through its exercise in the understanding, leads to the subject *conceiving* the external object seen, as the subject takes it, *objectively*, to be. The concepts exercised by the subject refer, in the standard case, to external physical objects that are potentially independent of any observer.

(ii) Secondly, the imagination "converts" the subject's visual sensing—the underlying nonconceptual phenomenal state—into something altogether much richer, through the fusion of *images* with the visual sensing of a coloured, spatial array. The result of the imagination working on visual input from the perceptual object is a *subjective, perspectival* "sense-image-model"—a notion that I shall enlarge upon below. Subjects are able to generate appropriate images in experience because of an underlying conceptual grasp of the spatial nature of physical objects in general, even when they lack a grasp of the concept of the *specific* kind of object physically present.

Thus according to Sellars's model, there are two dimensions to the exercise of concepts in the perception. My *seeing* an object, such as a red apple, is a complex affair.[15] At the *conceptual* level, my perceptual takings, in the form of demonstrative thoughts, focus on the apple itself. I conceive of this object, this apple, as an independent

---

[15] Although Sellars is ostensibly concentrating on Kant's views of the role of concepts in perception in IKTE, he is clearly endorsing the Kantian picture.

space-occupying thing. I take it to be solid, and to have an exterior surface hidden from view. At the *nonconceptual* level, I am aware of a visual phenomenal state caused by the apple. This consists, at a basic level, of a sensing state, that is, of visual sensations of an expanse of red. Through the exercise of general concepts of physical objects, this underlying sensing state is interwoven with images to form a perspectival structure, a sense-image model, which (in an informational sense) represents the apple. Sellars is conceding to phenomenologists that visual experience is not just a matter of having visual sensations corresponding to the "two-and-a-half" dimensional surfaces of things, accompanied by beliefs about the objective spatial nature of things. He wants to do justice to the phenomenological fact that we seem to experience more than surfaces—we experience objects as solid, extended into space, having depth and hidden parts, and so on.[16] The apple I see is somehow in my consciousness as a whole, three dimensional object, a volume of edible white fruit, enclosed in its red-coloured skin.

For Sellars, the observable qualities of the apple, such as its colour, enter into visual experience in three different ways. By virtue of my perceptual thoughts, I may *take* what I see to be a red apple: I *classify* it as red. But because I am not just thinking about the apple there is also immediately present in my consciousness a *red phenomenal expanse*, roughly corresponding to the facing surface of the apple. In visual experience the phenomenal redness has *actual* existence in my consciousness. In addition, I see the apple, somehow, to *contain* a volume of white. Hence, according to Sellars, 'an actual volume of white is present in the experience [in the form of an *image*] in a way which parallels the red. We experience the red *as containing the white*' (IKTE §13, in KTM: 421). Together with the imagined white of the apple, there may be, in my perceptual experience of it, further imagined features of juiciness and coolness. Sellars claims:

---

[16] Sellars, IKTE, Part II, in KTM: 421–3, passim.

But while these features are not seen, they are not *merely* believed in. These features are present in the object of perception as actualities. They are present by virtue of being imagined.

(IKTE §21, in KTM: 422)

So such features, which are not directly seen *of* the apple, are still importantly present, in the form of *image states* in experience. The imagination operates at two levels. It is a blend of imaging and conceiving.

The sense-image-model or structure of the apple comprises the totality of what is *present*, in the nonconceptual sense, in experience; it thus combines contributions from the senses and from the imagination. The model is, necessarily, *perspectival*: it represents the object seen from the point of view of the subject (in the informational sense). Such a structure is subjective, and transient. But it is only grasped, because we exercise concepts in relation to it. I am conscious of the apple in virtue of conceptualising my inner experience, the perspectival sense-image-model, *as* a cool, juicy, solid, red-surfaced apple; I thus think of the apple as an independent, *objective*, non-perspectival, enduring thing.

It must be stressed that I am not usually aware, conceptually, of the sense-images-models *as such*. But such structures both guide and, through feedback, are guided by my conceptual interpretation of the object I take myself to be seeing. The sense-image-model of the dog approximates to what some philosophers have called the non-epistemic *appearance* of the dog, understood as an inner state.[17] At the *phenomenal, nonconceptual*, level, images of the dog are combined with the visual sensations into a unified structure, a perspectival sense-image-model.

One further, very important, element needs to be added to the analysis. Sellars speaks of the concepts we exercise in perceptual experience as connected with sets or '*sequences of sense-image-models*',

---

[17] See for example the discussion in Chisholm (1957), ch. 4, and compare also Jackson on the phenomenal sense of 'looks' (1977), ch. 2.

in the plural. To grasp the concept of an objective kind, such as an apple, or dog, in the way that enables me to apply it directly in experience, entails that I understand what it is like to perceive that object from different points of view, and through time. This leads to what Sellars, following Kant, calls the *schema* of an object. The schema of an object derives from the dual concepts I exercise of that kind of object, and also of my own body, as these are spatially related. It is, in effect, a *recipe* that gives rise to a grasp of the possible experiences of observing that object. In order to grasp what a directly recognisable kind such as a dog is, I must appreciate what it is like to see the dog from different points of view. The schema of a concept of an object of kind F relates to my implicit grasp of sequences of perspectival sense-image-models of myself looking at an object of that kind F. As Sellars expresses the point, using the example of a pyramid:

> The *concept* of a red pyramid standing in various relations to a perceiver entails a *family* of concepts pertaining to sequences of *perspectival* image-models of oneself-confronting-a-pyramid.

> (IKTE §33, in KTM: 424)

3. A Modification of the Sellarsian Analysis:

To what extent should we accept Sellars's analysis? I am assuming in this paper that Sellars is entirely correct to treat the phenomenal aspect of experience as an *inner* state.[18] But I don't find Sellars's claims about the way that images are usually present in experience entirely convincing, and in one rather dense footnote he allows that he may be conceding too much to the claims of phenomenology.

Perhaps in anticipation of eating an apple I may form an image of its white juicy centre, but I don't in corresponding fashion normally form an occurrent *image* of the whole volume of flesh

---

[18] I defend this view at length in chs. 3, 4, and 5 of my (2007). See also deVries (2006) and Williams (2006).

contained within a dog's furry exterior, although I may imagine it getting up and wagging its tail. Yet I still experience the dog as a solid, three-dimensional physical thing. So what explains the phenomenological difference? I suggest that what accounts for the different kinds of images I form are the *actions* that I would be likely to carry out in respect of the two kinds of thing, together also with facts about the behaviour (or lack of it) of the kinds themselves. Unlike some contemporary British artists, I don't usually envisage cutting the dog into two halves and displaying its insides. But I may well anticipate biting into the apple, and in consequence becoming perceptually aware of its white interior. I either *expect* to become perceptually aware of different aspects of the objects I engage with, or, at the very least, I am *prepared for* typical changes in their appearance. But the kinds of changes I expect differ from case to case. Exercising the recognitional concept of an object of a kind F is connected with my imagining, in this more dispositional sense, further experiences corresponding to my seeing the different aspects of the object that I normally come in perceptual contact with. Sometimes such further experiences would result from the object's own behaviour. What I do imagine in the case of the dog are not its insides, but how it might move and take up a different position. This explains the difference noted above between the two examples.

It might also be questioned whether actual images occur as extensively in experience as Sellars seems to be suggesting. Research has shown that people vary considerably in the extent to which they form actual images in consciousness. Some people hardly construct any visual images at all when they think and perceive, whilst at the opposite end of the spectrum there exist subjects like the one described by Luria, whose conscious life seems to revolve around the production of a great many, moderately stable images.[19]

These points suggest a plausible modification of Sellars's claims about the role of the productive imagination, one that is still

[19] Luria (1968).

consistent with his central ideas about the structure of experience. Instead of construing the role of the imagination as essentially connected with the generation of occurrent images in consciousness, we should consider its dispositional manifestations. There are many objects that we recognise directly, without inference. How an object appears is not something we normally reflect upon, yet it is the basis for our recognitional responses. In directly applying a concept of a kind, such as DOG, to the thing in front of me, I exercise an *implicit* understanding of how dogs normally appear, at the phenomenal level. As a perceiver, I respond to the patterns of experience typically associated with the object before me, in recognising objective features of the dog and its relation to me, and coming to conceptualise it as a dog.

Most importantly, I can apply recognitional concepts such as DOG and APPLE directly, because I know how objects of the corresponding kinds look under different conditions. In seeing the object in front of me as a dog, I am able to anticipate, or imagine, what it would be like if the relation between me and the dog were to change. I am therefore prepared for certain kinds of likely changes in my visual experience, at the phenomenal level. So when I classify something I am experiencing as a dog, I have *implicit expectations* about how my future experience will vary, in a way that is consistent with seeing a dog.

According to the revised account I am suggesting, the imagination plays a role in this way: in noticing that what I see is a dog, I am prepared for certain kinds of typical *transformations* to the phenomenal elements of my visual experience. I have *implicit expectations* about the probable future changes in the nonconceptual phenomenal aspect of my experience. Of particular importance are the expectations I have of the probable experiential consequences of my own actions. If I bite into an apple, a white concave surface will become visible; if I walk up to the dog, it will take up a larger region of my visual field, and so on; if I walk around it, it will present a different perspectival appearance. But I am also prepared for the way that certain individual things—humans and other living animals—will move of their own accord. There may be subtle differences between what I *anticipate*, what I *expect*, and what I am *prepared for* in any situation. But these need not concern us here. What matters is that they all involve dispositions on my part relating to typical patterns of phenomenal experience associated with the relevant kind that I observe.

These anticipations, etc, that arise in perception are not formulated in an explicit form, yet they are prompted by the concepts we form, which in turn arise because of sensory input. So my concepts are both guided by the phenomenal state that is caused by visual input from the perceived object, and through feedback make me implicitly prepared for further kinds of phenomenal experiences. In this way my concepts are unified with the phenomenal aspect of my experience: in attending to and conceptualising a given aspect of my experience as an individual belonging to a certain kind, I am prepared for transformations of that particular aspect. This, incidentally, is the cash value of Strawson's metaphor, when he speaks of *other* possible experiences "being alive" in a particular experience.[20]

Thus according to the modified Sellarsian account I am proposing here, seeing an object involves three main elements. Consider, by way of an example, the situation where I see a Dalmatian dog in front of me *as* a dog (in normal conditions). The following is true of me:

(1) Firstly, at the nonconceptual level, my visual consciousness contains a sensing, an inner phenomenal state, which is caused by input from the dog I see; this involves the nonconceptual awareness of a mainly black and white shape. It is possible also that I form certain occurrent images of other aspects of the dog. These together make up my (inner) sense-image-model of the dog.

---

[20] Strawson (1970).

(2) Secondly, I have a perceptual taking, which involves a demonstrative conceptualisation:

This dog... (is a Dalmatian/friendly/black and white in colour/lying down, etc)

In virtue of the exercise of what, for me, is a basic perceptual concept of a dog, I recognise what I see *as* a dog. The *first dimension* of the exercise of this concept consists in this referential use, directed onto a public object. In the normal course of events I may, or may not, endorse the perceptual claim I am inclined to make.

(3) Finally, I have a set of *implicit* expectations about how the nonconceptual component of experience might change. I am implicitly prepared for transformations of the sense-image-model, and particularly for transformations that occur as a result of my own actions. This is the *second dimension* of concept exercise. I do not usually reflect upon the possibility of such transformations to my experiences; but in *acting* upon the world in certain ways, I show my implicit awareness of them. These expectations play a crucial role in ordinary perception, in accounting for the connection between the two components of experience.

4. Endoscopic Minimal Access Surgery:

The connection between the two dimensions of concept exercise can be illustrated by an important category of perceptual phenomena. This comprehends cases of "displaced perception".[21]

Many surgeons now operate using a technique known as Minimal Access Surgery (or, more colloquially, key-hole surgery). This involves using a small telescopic device and instruments 3–10mm in diameter that are inserted into a body cavity, such as the abdomen or knee, through small incisions. An image of the surgical procedures inside the body is relayed by a small camera

---

[21] My usage here differs slightly from that of Dretske (1995).

mounted on the eye-piece of the telescopic device to a video monitor placed adjacent to the patient, while the operation takes place.

Surgeons need specific training for this procedure, in order to learn to use the image on the screen to guide the movements they make with the instruments. They learn to use a number of different depth cues to ascertain the exact position to which they need to move the instruments. These include occlusion, relative size, texture gradients, and motion parallax.

The training enables surgeons to acquire practical knowledge of how to integrate their actions with what they see on the monitor. Making the correct movements required to manipulate the surgical instruments whilst viewing the monitor becomes largely automatic. Seeing becomes "direct", in the sense that the perceptual thoughts, as well as the actions, of the surgeon are directed on to the internal organs and the instruments, without prior inference. The images on the monitor are not, normally, the focus of the surgeon's concepts.

The patient's exterior bodily surface prevents what we would normally term a "direct" view of the inside of the body and of the ends of the surgical instruments. Yet when surgeons are absorbed in the complexities of an operation, the patient's body and the instruments are *phenomenologically present* in their visual experience. Thus a surgeon can entertain demonstrative thoughts about the patient's inner bodily organ ('that gall bladder...'), and act directly on it.[22]

The surgeon's conceptualisation of the site of the surgery is guided by the two-dimensional images displayed on the monitor in front of him. But whilst carrying out procedures on the internal organs—for example, cutting away a gall bladder—the surgeon is not normally explicitly conscious of the images on the screen. The concepts exercised refer to what is "hidden",

---

[22] In Evans's terms, the surgeon can entertain genuine 'here' thoughts about the organs in the patient's body; compare Evans (1982), ch. 6.

though phenomenologically present, and concern the instruments and internal bodily organs. Potentially, the way the surgeon conceptualises what is seen could alter. The surgeon might pause during the operation, adopt a different attentional set, and concentrate instead on how the images on the monitor appear to be blurred because the lens is fogged up.[23] But in attending to the image on the monitor *as* such, the surgeon uses a different set of concepts.

In such cases of displaced perception, the fact that there are two different dimensions of concept employment is clearly illustrated. In performing the operation the surgeon exercises concepts relating to the patient's body in a manner that allows the integration of perception with action. Yet in doing so, the surgeon is actually responsive to matters that, during most of the course of the operation, are not thought about. The images on the screen lead *causally* to the exercise of concepts relating to the objective state of the internal organs, and guide the surgeon's actions, yet there need not be any explicit *conceptual* awareness of those images.

There are two interim conclusions about experience that may be drawn from a consideration of cases of displaced perception. For the first of these, imagine a fantasy where two patients, perhaps twins with similar bodies, are connected up to two separate monitors, which are placed side by side. Two surgeons begin operating by making similar movements of the scalpel. One of them forms a demonstrative thought, 'That gall bladder...', a thought directly prompted by looking at one of the monitors. What is essential to determining the reference of the demonstrative thought is the context, and in particular the *causal* chain linking the surgeon with one of the two patients, via one of the monitors, in a manner that allows the surgeon to integrate her actions with what she sees. The referent of the demonstrative thought is not determined merely by whatever appears on the monitor, irrespective of whether the images displayed are, in some sense, more immediately "available" to the surgeon.

---

[23] Sometimes both kinds of conceptualisation will occur near simultaneously.

There is a second conclusion that can be drawn from such cases. The images displayed on the monitor can give rise to very different kinds of conceptualisation. While absorbed in the intricacies of the medical operation, the surgeon responds to the images by forming concepts that refer directly to the patient's internal organs hidden from "direct view". For the most part, the surgeon does not think of the onscreen images that, through some complex (and perhaps indirect) process, guide thoughts and actions. When the surgeon pauses to reflect on the condition of the monitor, the images prompt the exercise of concepts in quite a different way: the concepts exercised now refer directly to the very images themselves. Displaced perception thus illustrates how the very same visual input can lead, in different contexts, to the direct employment of concepts belonging to quite different categories.

5. Conceptualising Our Own Experiences Directly:

When I hallucinate, I can attend to my phenomenal states, and conceptualise them as such. Suppose I am aware of a red after-image. According to the Critical Realist theory, I can make an identifying reference to the image. I can pick it out as the kind of state that is normally caused when I see an actual external patch of red on the surface of a physical object. But this way of characterising my after-image does not exhaust its nature. For Sellars, an inner hallucinatory state is not *defined* by reference to the external, observable physical qualities that we appeal to in order to *identify* it, as deVries and Triplett have pointed out.[24] My after-image has intrinsic qualities, and through exercising concepts that belong to the framework of inner states, I can directly refer to the phenomenal nonconceptual component of experience that is immediately present in consciousness.[25] I refer to the very same

---

[24] For discussion of this issue see deVries and Triplett (2000), p. 169.

[25] See Williams (2006), sect. 6; see also deVries (2005), ch. 8.

phenomenal state that causally prompts my introspective thought, 'This red after-image ...'.

According to the Critical Realist theory, the experiences that occur in normal veridical perception, and also in cases of illusion, are ontologically on a par with hallucinatory states. I am able to make direct reference to my perceptual experiences, and consider them as states that are, potentially, independent of the objects that cause them. Thus, when I introspect, I can reflect upon the fact that in seeing the dog in front of me, I am having an experience of a certain kind—an experience *as of* seeing a dog, but which, considered in itself, is of the same kind that could occur in a hallucination.

The examples of displaced perception provide a useful analogy, one which suggests a plausible account of the nature of introspection and its relation to perception. We are able to attend to and conceptualise our experiences in different, equally valid, ways. I can shift from attending to the external objects I see, to attending to the intrinsic nature of the experiences I have in seeing them. I can consider the experiences in themselves, as potentially independent of the objects that produce them. When introspecting, I do not discover new entities; rather, I conceptualise what is immediately present in a quite different way. It is open to me to consider experiences as causally related to external objects (as the Critical Realist claims), and not as in part constituted by them.

A full account of the way we apply concepts to our inner states would also say something about the two different aspects of concept employment. When I reflect upon the images on the monitor screen directly, and employ concepts that refer to them, I also have expectations appropriate to the likely way that images on a screen will behave. In a parallel manner, when I introspect my experiences, and consider them as subjective states, and distinct from the external objects which cause them, I have implicit expectations relating to potential changes in my experiences. I am able to act upon my experiences in ways that are very different from the ways that I act upon physical objects. For example, I can directly change my visual experience of a dog by closing my eyes, or by altering my focus so that I see the dog double. Such a change in my experience is of course very different from the change I cause to the dog when, for example, I take hold of its lead and it jumps up in an excited manner, expecting to be taken for a walk. Along such lines as these it is possible to illustrate the two dimensions of the exercise of concepts when they are applied directly to our own experiences, and to show what is distinctive about the exercise of concepts when we respond to our own experiences in the mode of introspection. The imagination plays an essential role in unifying my concepts with the phenomenal states that prompt them. We therefore have an answer to the first problem highlighted at the outset of this paper, that of explaining how the same experience can be conceptualised in quite different ways.[26]

6. Perception and the Problem of Demonstrative Reference

As we noted at the outset, Sellars's Critical Realist theory of perception has been criticised on the grounds that it is unable to provide an adequate account of demonstrative reference. According to this theory, the physical object perceived is not present in experience in any phenomenal sense. It is not immediately available to the perceiver's consciousness. It is therefore difficult, the objection runs, to explain how experience could provide the basis for our perceptual judgements. The thought is that if the phenomenal qualities of experience are understood as belonging to inner states, psychologically private to the subject, then the perception of public physical objects would be at best an indirect process. We would be unable to explain the subject's ability to make perceptual judgements about external physical objects, objects that transcend immediate experience.

---

[26] I provide a more detailed defence of this general view of hallucinations in my (2007), ch. 9.

I shall argue that it is possible to defend a Critical Realist account of how demonstrative reference is possible, and show how the application of the ideas articulated above, relating to the role of the imagination, can be used to defend Critical Realism against this line of criticism. Before elaborating the Critical Realist theory, I briefly summarise some reasons for rejecting two alternative accounts of perceptual judgement.

A first account of perceptually based reference assumes that perceptual demonstratives are supported by the subject's capacity to identify what is perceived by a grasp of some description fitting its properties. The object perceived is that which fits most closely, in certain key respects, the way that the subject *conceives* it to be as a direct result of experience. As David Smith notes, in places Sellars appears to be sketching out a version of this idea.[27] The problem, as Smith points out, is that one may see an object under all kinds of illusory conditions. It may be that none of the properties one is inclined, on the basis of experience, to attribute to the perceived object in fact belongs to it. Features believed to be central to the identification of an object, such as its position, may better fit some object that is out of view.[28]

There is another general difficulty with the description view. The reference of perceptually based demonstrative claims depends essentially upon contextual matters outside of the subject's conceptual grasp. Suppose a subject sees something in the surroundings, and takes it to be a friendly dog. As a matter of fact, the subject will not normally express the spontaneously arising perceptual taking in a form equivalent to an existentially quantified sentence, along the lines of 'there is one and only one dog at P such that it is friendly, etc'. The perceptual belief occurs naturally in a form that employs indexicals: '*that* dog over there is friendly'. The employment of indexicals is not just a contingent matter. Where perception provides the subject directly with

---

[27] See Smith (2002), p. 82. Sellars makes comments sympathetic to the description view of reference in his BD (1977) and in SRPC (1978).

[28] Smith (2002), p. 82; see also Grice (1956).

the basis for a demonstrative belief, the referent of that belief cannot be wholly specified by the subject in conceptual terms alone—indexicals, such as 'this', 'here', and 'now' are always essentially involved.[29] For such reasons, attempts to account for perceptual reference by appeal to the subject's own beliefs seem to be insufficient.

A second view seeks to explain the subject's grasp of perceptual demonstratives by reference to a distinctive interpretation of the notion of *acquaintance*. According to Russell's original formulation, acquaintance is a notion that in certain respects has broad application. Russell allows that the subject can even be acquainted with such entities as abstract logical facts.[30] Yet as far as empirical knowledge is concerned, Russell takes acquaintance to be confined to private sensible entities in consciousness, or entities such as sense-data that are related in a unique manner to the consciousness of a single subject. For Russell, sense-data are understood to be private and distinct from public physical objects.

More recently, philosophers who advocate versions of the Direct Realist view of perception have sought to remove Russell's restriction on the kind of sensible entity that acquaintance puts us in contact with. They claim that, *pace* Russell, perception makes us directly acquainted with public physical objects.[31] The immediate presence of some physical object to the perceiver's mind enables the subject to make demonstrative reference to that object. Because nothing intervenes between the perceiving subject's consciousness and the external world, the subject is directly related to the physical object seen, and comes to form concepts appropriate to the category of entity immediately present, and to be able to

[29] For a defence of this claim, see especially Burge (1977) and (2007), and Evans (1982), Brewer (1999), and Eilan (2001).

[30] Russell (1914a), p. 127.

[31] I am not concerned here with the differences that can be discerned between the various different versions of Direct Realism, but with what they hold in common, in rejecting the idea that experiences are inner states. In this general category can be included Disjunctivist views; see especially Martin (2002), and also McDowell (1986), Snowdon (1990), Bermudez (2000), and Smith (2002).

identify it in a manner that supports demonstrative claims about it. Acquaintance constitutes the mechanism of reference that makes possible the targeting of singular thoughts on the physical objects in the surroundings, so that subjects know *which* individual object it is that their perceptual thoughts concern.[32]

David Smith is appealing to this Direct Realist conception of acquaintance in rejecting Sellars's conception of perceptual experiences as inner states. He claims:

For a perceptual this-thought to succeed referentially, our senses themselves must provide an object.... We need the senses themselves to acquaint us with objects.[33]

From a Sellarsian perspective, there is a serious difficulty with this neo-Russellian revival of the notion of acquaintance. According to Russell, acquaintance is a state that is a form of sensing, or experiencing, yet it also amounts to a form of knowledge.[34] This "mongrel" conception of experience forms one of the main targets of Sellars's criticisms in the early parts of EPM, when he criticises certain empirical versions of the fallacy that he categorises as "The Myth of the Given". Sellars points out that his real target is not the alleged *inner, private*, status of experience, but the confused idea that experience can be both a *nonconceptual* state, that is, having some kind of *phenomenal* or *sensory* aspect—perhaps involving the direct awareness of the sensible qualities of actual existing entities—and yet also some kind of cognitive state providing *premisses* upon which empirical knowledge is inferentially based.[35]

Sellars would object to the very idea that the subject is able to make some sort of quasi-inferential move from the level of sensory, or phenomenal, awareness, to a conceptual grasp of what is immediately present, no matter to what ontological category it belongs. He re-states this objection in his later Carus Lectures

[32] See for example the claims made by McDowell in his (1986), sect. 2.

[33] See David Smith (2002), p. 85; 'object' here means a physical object. The remarks on p. 87 are in a similar vein.

[34] See, for example Russell (1914a) p. 167, and (1914b) sect. 2.

[35] EPM §7, in SPR: 132; in KMG: 210–11; §10, in SPR: 140; in KMG: 218–19.

(FMPP), when he describes the most basic form of "The Myth of the Given" as the principle that:

If a person is directly aware of an item which has categorial status C, then the person is aware of it *as* having the categorial status C.

(FMPP, I §44: 11)[36]

In criticising "The Myth of the Given" Sellars is therefore not so much objecting to the idea of some *direct relation* between the subject and an external physical object—although he would not countenance the existence of such a direct relation—but the more fundamental idea that it could provide some kind of evidential *support* for demonstrative judgements. Whether the Direct Realist can answer this charge is an issue I shall not attempt to resolve here. McDowell, for example, has defended the view that experience provides an unmediated openness to the world, while attempting to avoid the problems that beset the traditional notion of acquaintance.[37] This is not the place for a detailed examination of the general Direct Realist standpoint, and of the question whether it can be formulated in a manner that resists Sellars's criticisms. I shall instead turn to a consideration of a third view of demonstrative judgement, an account which, I argue, makes best sense of the Sellarsian Critical Realist analysis of experience.

7. Critical Realism and Demonstrative Reference to External Objects

As we noted at the outset, for Sellars, the connection between the subject's phenomenal level awareness and perceptual judgement is causal and not inferential. This suggests an alternative to the two views so far considered. This third view attempts to show how the Critical Realist can explain the nature of our

---

[36] See also EPM §26 and §38.
[37] See McDowell (1996), chs. 1 and 2, and (1998); for criticism, see especially deVries (2006) and Williams (2006).

perceptually based beliefs, without having to appeal to the idea that the objects of perception must be immediately present in conscious experience.

Before I develop this Critical Realist model of perceptual judgement, there is one important preliminary point to note, which concerns the precise function played by immediate experience. The main motive for acceptance of the neo-Russellian acquaintance view derives from the undoubted fact that in normal perception experience plays some sort of necessary role, without which the subject would be incapable of making demonstrative reference to objects. This fact can encourage a cognitive illusion, when we begin to reflect upon the structure of the processes that occur in perception. The illusion arises because we construe the two components of experience as being more tightly connected than they really are. If it is accepted that, on the one hand, some kind of *immediate* experience is necessary for the production of perceptual beliefs, and that on the other, our perceptual beliefs are focused directly on to physical objects, then it becomes tempting to assume that those outer physical objects *directly* perceived are identical with the very items *immediately* present.

But we do not need to equate what is immediately present in experience with the actual physical object perceived. The awareness of phenomenal qualities of some kind is certainly an essential ingredient in normal perception. This is not because it supplies the mechanism of reference; we can, in principle, make sense of the notion of "super blind-sight", where in the absence of phenomenal experience a subject directly "perceives" an object, forms judgements directly about its location and kind, and can thus make direct reference to it. The subject would simply be caused to have accurate, non-inferred beliefs that allow him or her to locate the object and communicate about it. But for normal human beings, the phenomenal aspect of inner experience is psychologically necessary for prompting the conceptual states that refer directly to external physical objects. The subject is aware that immediate experience of some kind is necessary for perceptual reference, but the necessity is causal. The subject's inner experience prompts and guides the subject's perceptual taking. This taking contains individual concepts targeted directly, without inference, upon the perceived object.[38]

With this preliminary point made, we are now in a position to show how the Critical Realist analysis of perceptual experience is able to explain how demonstrative reference to publicly located physical objects is possible. The account has several parts, corresponding to the different senses of 'explanation' that are considered relevant. I consider in turn the main features of the Critical Realist model, indicating the critical role played by the imagination.

(i) Aetiology:

One kind of explanation of the perceiver's ability to make perceptually based reference to outer objects appeals to empirical theories about the nature of evolution and connected areas of scientific enquiry. Humans, and other creatures to which we can attribute some kind of classificatory capacities, have evolved so that they are able to represent items in their surroundings, with the result that they can plan activities directed towards perceived objects. By employing perceptual mechanisms that represent objects in their vicinity, they improve their likelihood of attaining goals that satisfy their needs, and hence also their chances of survival. It is perfectly consistent to claim that internal low-level phenomenal states, having an analogue form, are causally involved in the production of higher-level representational states that relate directly to distal objects.

One development of the causal-historical account would concern questions about how this basic representational ability develops into fully-fledged linguistic behaviour. An underlying representational ability is one necessary precondition for any language training

---

[38] The development of TVSS (tactile visual sensory substitution) seems to support the separation of the notions of phenomenal immediacy and the mechanism of reference; see the discussion in Bach-y-Rita (1972).

process to be effective. On the Sellarsian view, by being a part of a community, subjects with such abilities can be inculcated into linguistic activities, in which their exercise of classificatory states becomes transformed into the employment of fully fledged high-level concepts, of the kind which have their place in inferential practices and communication, and which can in addition have a referential dimension. It is such a story that Sellars begins to sketch out in the concluding sections of EPM; the importance of training is also of course implicit in the later work of Wittgenstein.[39]

(ii) The Referential Connection:

Such explanatory accounts deal with rather different issues from those that concern the mechanisms of reference of perceptual demonstratives. We may raise the formal question: what conditions must a subject S meet, in order for S to count as referring to a particular individual object X at time T, in making the perceptually based claim, '*That* object at P is a dog'? Independently of the causal history of a perceptual experience, and its subsequent expression, we may enquire about the conditions such experiences and utterances must meet, in order to count as being *of*, or referring *to*, a specific individual.

The reason why subject S's utterance of 'That dog at P ...' in the context picks some particular object X need not be because there is an actual dog at P. Demonstrative reference can succeed even in illusory circumstances. S may actually be seeing a fox, occupying a different location. Facts about how things appear, in the nonconceptual phenomenal sense, are also insufficient, for similar reasons. The issues concerning which facts determine content are notoriously deep and difficult. The Critical Realist suggestion mooted above is that, in a formal sense, what determines which individual the subject is seeing and, in consequence, is

---

[39] See also the arguments offered in Bennett (1976), chs. 3 and 4, and in Brandom (2000), chs. 4 and 5.

referring to, is the existence of an appropriate kind of causal chain linking the subject S with the object X perceived. This is the type of causal chain that is involved in perception, and which, in the sense explored further in point (iii) below, sustains "navigational" perceptual activity: the ability of a creature to move safely about its surroundings. One further feature of the causal account has to do with the role of attention, and is also discussed briefly below; but here my concern is with the general differences between the Direct Realist and Critical Realist accounts, and not with providing a detailed analysis of perceptually based demonstrative reference. Nevertheless, if a causal theory of perception is accepted, we are provided with one very plausible candidate for the mechanism that determines the content of the individual referring expressions.

This defence of Critical Realism is consistent with Evans's claims about the requirements for the successful demonstrative identification of an object. A discussion of the full ramifications of Evans's views on this issue is beyond the scope of this paper. What may be extracted from his account is that there are two very plausible conditions necessary for demonstrative identification of objects: first, that there is a continuing information link between the perceiver and the perceived object X, which allows the perceiver to keep track of the object, and to conceive of the object demonstratively identified; second, that the perceiver is able to directly locate the object in egocentric space, so as to be able to entertain genuine "here" thoughts about that object.[40] Since Critical Realism is a version of the causal account of perception, it clearly meets the first requirement; by emphasising the directness of perceptual takings and consequent actions aimed at external objects, it also meets the second.

(iii) Communication with others

From a third-person perspective, there is normally no great practical problem in ascertaining which object another person is seeing and

---

[40] See Evans (1982), ch. 6.

responding to, and to which they are referring by their use of perceptual demonstratives. I am able to successfully communicate with others about which object I am currently attending to. This is because my reference to it, by the use of a demonstrative phrase in context ('That dog...'), is supported by potential action. I can go on, if required to *act upon* the object I refer to, for example, by pointing towards it, or by singling it out through my activity in other ways. If I reach towards a dog, another person may say, 'Be careful with that dog, he is nervous...', restraining the dog with a lead, and so on. Nothing in such interchanges presupposes my having an *immediate* awareness of the dog I am seeing, acting towards and referring directly to.

Most language users have an implicit understanding of the fact that perception is essentially integrated with action. What I have elsewhere termed 'navigational activity' takes place when a subject sees some distal object, and steers a path through the surroundings in order to reach that object and make use of it.[41] It is through the essential reliance upon distance perception that humans and other creatures are able, with a fair degree of success, to act upon distal objects, so as to satisfy their needs, and to avoid harm. This core navigational conception of the function of seeing and other forms of distance perception is understood by scientists who investigate the process; this is made clear, for example, in the influential work of Milner and Goodale.[42]

It is with this idea about the dynamic function of perception in mind that Sellars writes:

... we were given our perceptual abilities, not for the purposes of onto-logical insight, but to enable us to find our way around in a hostile environment.

(SSOP §89)

---

[41] A parallel form of navigational activity arises when a subject seeks to *avoid* some other creature; see my (2007), ch. 7.

[42] Miner and Goodale (1995).

As Strawson noted, we implicitly accept that some variation in the position or orientation of an object relative to a particular observer will produce in them a corresponding change in experience; such co-variation points to a causal link between object and experience.[43] The causal connections of the appropriate kind that occur in distance perception are those that enable navigational activity to take place. There is therefore a principled basis for distinguishing between the types of causal connections that are appropriate for normal seeing, and those abnormal situations where deviant causal chains give rise to matching experiences. Scientific investigation reveals that there is in fact a complex chain of events, starting from light waves emitted from an object, and involving (in humans) stimulation of the retina and consequent transmission of nerve impulses along the optic nerve to the cortex. This causal chain underpins vision in circumstances which allow successful action upon objects. As perceivers, we do not need to know these particular facts; all we need to know, implicitly, is that there is some reliable mechanism involved in the standard case, which enables navigation to take place.

Our conventions of demonstrative reference extend the ways in which we act upon the objects we perceive. It therefore becomes plausible to view the causal chain that underpins navigational activity as contributing to the necessary conditions that, when applied in a particular case, determine *which* particular object another person is seeing, and to which that subject's use of a demonstrative expression refers.

(iv) First-person ''knowledge which'':
This implicit understanding of the general function of perception also provides the answer to the challenge raised by McDowell and others: How do visual (and other) perceptual experiences

---

[43] Strawson (1974).

equip perceivers themselves with knowledge about *which* particular objects they are seeing (or hearing, etc)?

There is no single answer to this question, but rather a series of answers, increasing in fullness and complexity. Imagine I am looking at a dog in front of me in the park, and state of it, 'That dog is a Dalmatian'.

(a) The simplest answer is that I do know which object I refer to, just by employing the demonstrative expression, 'That dog...' in response to my present experience. I think a thought, the content of which I grasp, even though the content is in part determined by external factors. If I switched to thinking about some other individual I see—say, the cat in a nearby tree—I would be aware that I was exercising a different individual concept, relating to a distinct object, one connected with a different aspect of my visual experience.

(b) Secondly, I know which object I am referring to, in the sense that I am able to initiate actions focused on the object, because I am now thinking about that particular object. So I might throw a ball in a certain direction, intending *that dog* to run and fetch it. I might walk towards it, and so on. It is not necessary that the objects I act towards be immediately present in my consciousness. My actions are straightforwardly caused by my inner states.

(c) At a more complex level, I know implicitly which object I am referring to, because, if pressed, I would be inclined to say that it is the object I am seeing, by virtue of having a certain experience: an experience now *as of* a dog in front of me. We don't usually entertain such further reflective thoughts. As Critical Realism emphasises, perceptual takings focus directly on the external objects, conceived of as independently existing, objective entities. Yet I can also reflect upon my experience of the dog, as a subjective state—of some kind—that is involved in my seeing the dog. I need *not*, of course, think of the way the dog appears to me as involving inner phenomenal states. Someone who is puzzled by the phenomenon of double vision might reflect upon the two images, or appearances, of a dog, without attributing ontological status to those appearances.

Here the role of the imagination, which I began this paper by considering, becomes important. In reflecting upon the appearance of the dog *qua* appearance of some kind, I understand it to be, at a minimum, perspectival and subjective: I am aware that I see the dog from my point of view, and that my experience is a distinct state from that belonging to my companion. The changes that I anticipate in respect of *my experience*, of the way the dog appears to me, are different from the changes I anticipate in the dog's position as it exists objectively, as we noted earlier. What I anticipate in exercising an individual concept referring to a particular object I see is a possible change to some aspect of my experience. The aspect will involve a specific spatial region in my visual field. The imagination is involved when I use concepts that relate to my subjective experience, in thinking about it as a state of some kind connected with the dog I see. So in thinking about the dog as a direct result of seeing it, I anticipate (implicitly) one part of the overall appearance of the scene to vary in ways typical of seeing a dog. In attending to the Dalmatian dog in front of me, and not, say, a green bush, I am more prepared for a rearrangement of the appearance of a black and white shaped object in my visual field, when the dog leaps up to catch a ball.

Knowing which object I demonstratively refer to by 'That dog...' also entails an implicit understanding of the fact that the object I am referring to is *the object I see*, in being aware of the subjective appearance I now experience. This may sound circular, because of the appeal to the notion of seeing. But the circularity can be removed if the navigational account of perceiving sketched above is correct: I implicitly grasp that what enables me to see some distal object is the fact that when I look at it, I have visual experiences. If the object changes, or if our relative positions change, then my experience will co-vary with such changes. This means, in effect, that I implicitly understand that my experiences are caused by the object I see. But my implicit knowledge comprehends something more, as argued above: I am aware, in some sense, that it is only by keeping visual track of the object that I am able to navigate through an environment so as to be able to home in on it, and make use of it. To see an object is for that object to cause my experiences in a manner that supports such navigational activity. This grasp of the nature of seeing is implicitly appealed to when we attribute perceptual states to others, and can be made explicit.

We are now in a position to offer a slightly fuller outline of the mechanism of reference and its connection with attention, according to the Critical Realist theory. When I see an object, attend to it and form a perceptual taking, there is a series of causally interconnected stages, which can be summarised as follows:

1 The object X causes an inner phenomenal state E in the subject, via the causal path standardly involved when S is able to navigate about the local environment;

2 The inner phenomenal state E causes a perceptual taking P, involving a complex demonstrative that may be expressed by an utterance of the form 'This F is G' (where G can include a description of the location of X in S's egocentric space).

3 The perceptual taking P *refers to* X, but importantly, also prompts *expectations* on the part of S with respect to likely transformations of a particular aspect of the overall phenomenal state E, of the kind appropriate to the way an individual of the kind F normally appears;

4 The exercise of the concepts employed in the taking P, together with guidance from the phenomenal array, enables S to act in appropriate ways towards X: to locate it, handle it, and so on.

As I warned earlier, considerations of space preclude any detailed exposition of the Critical Realist theory of perceptual content. It is clear, however, that the theory is equipped to meet the essential condition that any account of the reference to individual objects must meet. It shows that there can be a principled basis for distinguishing the particular object referred to in the perceiver's demonstrative thought from the various other objects in the visual scene. This is a condition that the Direct Realist accounts fail to meet. The existence of the appropriate kind of causally connected events, involving the above stages, is what determines that the subject is referring to a unique object in forming a perceptually based demonstrative thought. The demonstrated object is the one that initiates the sequence, and is the focus of the subsequent extended actions (these actions may involve self-correction on the subject's part).

It is because I implicitly grasp something of the nature of this complex causal connection that I know which object my perceptual beliefs refer to. I implicitly know that the object X I am referring demonstratively to by my use of 'This F...' is the object that meets the following condition:

> X is the object that is causally related to my current perceptual experience by whatever causal mechanism is essentially involved when I am able to perceptually navigate around my current surroundings so as to attain my goals, etc ...; it is the object that appears in my experience in the way that I expect F type things to appear.

It might be argued that I could, in theory, articulate the facts I grasp implicitly about the causal chain that connects me with the object I am referring to, when I make a demonstrative claim, 'That Dog ... etc'. However, it should be noted here that implicitly grasping such conditions does not mean that I could, in principle, set out in detail a definite description specifying which particular object I perceive. For one thing, my knowledge of the precise causal chain involved in perception is indirect—I am unable to specify the details of the actual physical and physiological causal chain that underlies my ability to perceptually navigate. More importantly, as we noted earlier, there is an irreducibly contextual aspect to demonstrative claims. I have to appeal to *my* experiences, and *my* surroundings. For this reason perceptual demonstratives cannot be reduced to definite descriptions.

8. Conclusion

Sellars's ideas about the productive imagination, as spelt out in his later work, provide the crucial link that explains how the phenomenal and conceptual components of experience can be unified. I am suggesting in this paper that we should understand the role of the imagination as, in part, dispositional. The imagination produces in the perceiver an implicit awareness, or set of expectations, of the likely ways in which the phenomenal, or sensory, aspect of an experience will be transformed. Such expected transformations result from the concepts exercised by the perceiver, which also have the role of referring directly to what is perceived. In the standard case, this exercise leads to demonstrative judgements aimed directly at the perceived object.

When we come to explain our ability to form demonstrative thoughts about the physical objects in our locality, we correctly think of our experiences as necessary, but are tempted to misconstrue the reason for this. The mistake is to assume that the entities to which our demonstrative thoughts refer directly must be immediately present in consciousness. The fact that experience equips us to directly identify—at the conceptual level—the outer objects we perceive is perfectly compatible with the claim that there is also a nonconceptual level, at which phenomenal *inner* states mediate such identifying claims. A careful formulation of the causal theory of perception, along the lines of the Critical Realist version upheld by Sellars, can account for the various different aspects of perceptual experience. We do not need to appeal to neo-Russellian notions of acquaintance. By acknowledging the essential causal connection between perceptual object and experience, Critical Realism is able to provide a satisfactory account of demonstrative reference.[44]

References

Works by Wilfrid Sellars:

Sellars, W. (1955) 'Physical Realism', *Philosophy and Phenomenological Research*, 15, 13–32; reprinted in Sellars (1963a). Reprinted in PP. (PR)

—— (1956) 'Empiricism and the Philosophy of Mind', in Feigl, H. and Scriven, M. (eds.), *Minnesota Studies in The Philosophy of Science, vol. I: The Foundations of Science and the Concepts of Psychology and Psychoanalysis*, 253–329 (Minneapolis: University of Minnesota Press); reprinted in Sellars (1963a). (EPM); also republished as a book with an Introduction by Rorty, R., and a Study Guide by Brandom, R. (1997) (Cambridge, MA: Harvard University Press). Also reprinted in W. A. deVries and T. Triplett, *Knowledge, Mind, and the Given: A Reading of Sellars's 'Empiricism and the Philosophy of Mind'* (Indianapolis, IN: Hackett, 2000).

—— (1963a) *Science, Perception and Reality* (London: Routledge & Kegan Paul). (SPR)

—— (1963b) 'Phenomenalism', a paper presented at the Wayne State University Symposium in the Philosophy of mind in December, 1962; in Sellars (1963a). (PHM)

—— (1975) 'The Structure of Knowledge: (1) Perception; (2) Minds; (3) Epistemic Principles', in Casteñeda, H. (ed.), *Action Knowledge and Reality*, 295–347 (Indianapolis: Bobbs-Merrill). (SK)

—— (1977a) 'Berkeley and Descartes: Reflections on the "New Way of Ideas"' in Machamer, P. and Turnbull, R. (eds.), *Studies in Perception: Interpretations in the History of Philosophy and Science*, 259–311 (Columbus: Ohio State University Press). Reprinted in KTM. (BD)

---

[44] This is a revised version of a paper read at the conference commemorating Wilfrid Sellars, *Empiricism and the Philosophy of Mind after Fifty Years*, held at the Institute of Philosophy, London University, in June 2006. I am grateful for comments received from my fellow participants during the conference, from Bruce Kuklick, and from an anonymous referee.

Sellars, W. (1977*b*) 'Some Reflections on Perceptual Consciousness' in Bruzina, R. and Wilshire, B. (eds.), *Selected Studies in Phenomenology and Existential Philosophy*, 169–85 (The Hague: Nijhoff). Reprinted in KTM. (SRPC)

——(1978) 'The Role of Imagination in Kant's Theory of Experience' in Johnstone, H. W. (ed.), *Categories: A Colloquium*, 231–45 (Pennsylvania: Pennsylvania State University). Reprinted in KTM. (IKTE)

——(1981) 'Foundations for a Metaphysics of Pure Process' (The Carus Lectures), *The Monist*, 64, 3–90. (FMPP)

——(1982) 'Sensa or Sensings: Reflections on the Ontology of Perception', *Philosophical Studies*, 41, 83–111. (SSOP)

——(2002) *Kant's Transcendental Metaphysics: Sellars's Cassirer Lectures Notes and other Essays* (Atascadero, CA: Ridgeview Publishing). (KTM)

Other works cited

Bach-y-Rita, P. (1972) *Brain Mechanisms in Sensory Substitution* (New York and London: Academic Press).

Bennett, J. (1976) *Linguistic Behaviour* (Cambridge: Cambridge University Press).

Bermudez, J. (2000) 'Naturalized Sense-Data', *Philosophy and Phenomenological Research*, 61, 353–74.

Blackburn, S. (1984) *Spreading the Word* (Oxford: Clarendon Press).

Brandom, R. (2000) *Articulating Reasons* (Cambridge, MA: Harvard University Press).

Brewer, B. (1999) *Perception and Reason* (Oxford: Clarendon Press).

Burge, T. (1977) 'Belief *De Re*', *Journal of Philosophy*, 74, 338–62.

——(2006) 'Postscript to "Belief *De Re*" ' in his (2007), 65–81.

——(2007) *Foundations of Mind* (Oxford: Clarendon Press).

Chisholm, R. (1957) *Perceiving: A Philosophical Study* (Ithaca: Cornell University Press).

Coates, P. (2007) *The Metaphysics of Perception: Wilfrid Sellars, Perceptual Consciousness and Critical Realism* (Oxford: Routledge).

deVries, W. (2005) *Wilfrid Sellars* (Chesham: Acumen).

——(2006) 'McDowell, Sellars, and Sense Impressions', *European Journal of Philosophy*, 14:2, 182–201.

—— and Triplett, T. (2000) *Knowledge, Mind, and the Given: Reading Wilfrid Sellars's Empiricism and the Philosophy of Mind* (Indianapolis: Hackett).

Dretske, F. I. (1995) *Naturalizing the Mind* (Cambridge, MA: MIT Press).

Eilan, N. (2001) 'Consciousness, Acquaintance and Demonstrative Thought', *Philosophy and Phenomenological Research*, 63, 433–40.

Evans, G. (1982) *The Varieties of Reference* (Oxford: Clarendon Press).

Firth, R. (1949, 1950) 'Sense-data and the Percept Theory', *Mind*, 58 and 59, 35–56, 434–65, reprinted in Swartz, R. J. (ed.) (1965).

Foster, L. and Swanson, J. W. (eds.) (1970) *Experience and Theory* (Amherst: University of Massachusetts Press).

Grice, P. (1961) 'The Causal Theory of Perception', *Proceedings of the Aristotelian Society*, suppl. vol. 35, 121–52.

Jackson, F. (1977) *Perception* (Cambridge: Cambridge University Press).

Kripke, S. (1980) *Naming and Necessity* (Oxford: Basil Blackwell).

Luria, A. R. (1968) *The Mind of a Mnemonist*, trans. by Lynn Solotaroff (New York: Basic Books).

McDowell, J. H. (1986) 'Singular Thought and the Extent of Inner Space', in Pettit, P. and McDowell, J. H. (eds.) (1986).

—— (1998) 'Having the World in View: Sellars, Kant, and Intentionality' (The Woodbridge Lectures), *The Journal of Philosophy*, 95, 431–91.

Martin, M. (2002) 'The Transparency of Experience', *Mind and Language*, 17, 376–425.

Milner, A. D. and Goodale, M. A. (1995) *The Visual Brain in Action* (Oxford: Oxford University Press).

Pettit, P. and McDowell, J. H. (eds.) (1986) *Subject, Thought, and Context* (Oxford: Clarendon Press).

Rosenberg, J. (1982) 'The Place of Color in the Scheme of Things: A Roadmap to Sellars's Carus Lectures', *The Monist*, 65, 315–35.

—— (2000) 'Perception vs. Inner Sense: A Problem about Direct Awareness', *Philosophical Studies*, 101, 143–60.

Russell, B. (1914*a*) 'The Nature of Acquaintance', *The Monist*, reprinted in his (1956).

—— (1914*b*) 'The Relation of Sense-data to Physics', *Scientia*, 4, reprinted in his (1917).

—— (1956) *Logic and Knowledge*, ed. Marsh, R. C. (London: Allen and Unwin).

—— (1917) *Mysticism and Logic* (London: Unwin Books).

Swartz, R. J., (ed.), (1965) *Perceiving, Sensing, and Knowing* (New York: Doubleday, Anchor).

Smith, A. D. (2002) *The Problem of Perception* (Cambridge, MA: Harvard University Press).

Snowdon, P. (1990) 'The Objects of Perceptual Experience', *Proceedings of the Aristotelian Society*, suppl. vol., 64, 121–50.

Strawson, P. F. (1970) 'Imagination and Perception', in Foster, L. and Swanson, J. W. (eds.) (1970).

—— (1974*a*) 'Causation in Perception', in his *Freedom and Resentment and Other Essays* (1974*b*).

—— (1974*b*) *Freedom and Resentment and Other Essays* (London: Methuen).

Williams, M. (2006) 'Science and Sensibility: McDowell and Sellars on Perceptual Experience', *European Journal of Philosophy*, 14:2, 302–25.

4

Some Sellarsian Myths

Paul Snowdon

The usual fate of philosophers is that their reputation and fame decline posthumously (often quite rapidly). Of course this tends not to happen to those who make such an impression in their own lifetime that they are taken, even then, to be amongst the giants of the subject. To a few, though, it happens that, after their deaths, their reputation and fame increases. This is true, for example, of Frege, but also, arguably, of Wilfrid Sellars. There is no doubt, I think, that the quality of Sellars's thought merits this continuing and growing attention. That is not however to say that we should believe all of what Sellars claims, nor all of what is claimed about him and his influence. In this paper, I want to focus, not on the central question raised by *Empiricism and the Philosophy of Mind*, (hereafter EPM), which is, of course, whether Sellars convincingly shows that the 'given' is a myth, but, rather, on some aspects of Sellars's approach to perception, and experience more generally.[1]

---

[1] This paper has developed out of one presented to a conference in June 2006 organized by the Institute of Philosophy in London on Empiricism and the Philosophy of Mind after Fifty Years. The paper for the conference had the title 'Sellars on Perception', but having broadened its subject matter a little I have modified the title. That talk also started with what I called a *negative* reminiscence, which I am relegating in this version to a footnote. I went up to Oxford in 1965 to study PPE at University College. At the end of my first year, I think, in the summer term, Sellars was giving the prestigious Locke Lectures. This is not something that a first year undergraduate would normally attend or be expected to attend. However, after a few weeks of the term, my then tutor, P. F. Strawson, told me that I must go to hear them. The reason given was not that they were of such remarkable quality

1. Sellars's Objectives and Some Questions

If we ask what Sellars's general purpose in EPM is, I suggest that we can boil it down to three main elements. The first is, of course, to demonstrate that the 'given' is a myth. The word 'demonstrate' might be too strong, but Sellars surely thought that he provides enough to persuade us that 'giveness' is a myth. Although I shall not attempt to evaluate the issue of this myth, I cannot forbear to make a few remarks at this point about that supposed myth. Although Sellars introduces the term 'giveness' in the very first sentence and also alludes to the idea of a general framework of giveness, presumably a repeated structure definitive of giveness in all its possible forms, he refrains from giving a definition of that general structure. It may be that Sellars supposed that any reader worth his salt would simply know what was meant. If he assumed that he was sadly mistaken. We are therefore in the position of readers of many philosophical works where we have to locate the identity of targets on the basis of the hints at characterization that are given but also on the basis of the ways that the writer attacks the idea.[2] The given has to be whatever Sellars's critical claims count against. It is absolutely clear that the idea of 'giveness' is a conception of the acquisition of knowledge. For the 'given' to be received is for knowledge to be generated (or present). So, the idea

and clarity that I might benefit intellectually, but that the audience had dropped to such a small number that, in order to stop the embarrassment, it had to be boosted in some way, and 'Univ' undergraduates were the obvious seat fillers. I therefore had the privilege of attending some of Sellars's Locke lectures of that year, at the tender age of 19. But we now come to the point at which my reminiscences merit the description 'negative'. I can recall the room, one of the smaller rooms in Examination Schools, and I can recall, in a vague way, the motley crew seated there and wondering who they were, but I cannot for the life of me recall Sellars himself—nothing of what he said nor of how he said it have remained in my memory—apart from the fact, or so it seems to me, that a number of times he used the words 'in strictu sensu', which initially puzzled me, but which I eventually translated as 'strictly speaking'. It is because of the terrible hole at the heart of these memories—the absence of Sellars himself—that I call this a *negative* reminiscence.

[2] An obvious example where this route to interpretation must be employed is in understanding what Hume means by 'necessary connexion'. John Mackie provides an exemplary version of this route.

of 'giveness' is an epistemological idea. But what epistemological idea is it? The most helpful elucidation that Sellars himself offers in EPM comes at the beginning of §32. There he describes one form the myth takes as involving two elements. The first is that there are certain facts that can be known noninferentially by a subject in a way which does not presuppose any other knowledge. The second element is that this knowledge is the 'ultimate court of appeal' for all factual claims about the world. Now, one might wonder why Sellars calls this 'one' form of the myth. My conjecture is that he thinks that there can be a version of the myth relating to a priori knowledge, which the present characterization with its emphasis on matters of worldly fact will not fit. But in the light of this and in the light of the evident point that Sellars's own objections to the given consist in an attempt to show that all knowledge does presuppose a structure of knowledge, the core idea of giveness would seem to be the claim that it is possible to gain knowledge (in some way or another) which does not presuppose or involve in any way at all other knowledge. Perhaps what should be said is that this is the conception of giveness in the argument of EPM.

What, then, does Sellars bring against the possibility of giveness thus characterized? I think that the answer to this question is that Sellars has two main lines of thought. The first line of thought rests on the claim that knowledge is, as one might say, knowledge that P (for some P), and having that knowledge requires the possession of the concepts internal to the proposition or thought P. Allied to this is the further idea that to possess concepts requires knowledge of various sorts. Sellars seems to espouse a conception of concept possession which might be called both holistic, requiring a whole body of background, and cognitive, where the background must be knowledge. A clear example of this sort of claim are the remarks that Sellars makes about possession of the concept 'red' in §19, a section which Sellars starts by announcing, completely correctly, that he is now 'out of step' with logical atomism. The possible weakness in this line of thought is that Sellars needs to show that all concepts require background knowledge for their possession, and the doubt has to be that Sellars does not present any general argument covering all *possible* concepts. Interestingly, Sellars's approach here brings out a contrast between his rejection of the given and one way of describing what he was proposing that might look plausible. It would not seem mad to link Sellars's rejection of the given to the idea that some would express by saying all our views are parts of an overall theory. We cannot, as it is said, step outside our *theory*. According to this way of speaking there are no *non-theoretical* givens; there is simply the evolution of a theory, propelled by some force which somehow impinges on the theory from time to time, causing changes. People who espouse this are, or might be regarded as, conceptual holists, and so in agreement with Sellars. There is also a clear sense in which 'giveness' is alien to this conception. The difference, though, is that for Sellars the background must constitute knowledge of some sort (as well, perhaps, as other things). This links to Sellars's understanding, as I am proposing, of the given in terms of knowledge acquisition not presupposing knowledge. This means, I think, that one could endorse the slogan about concepts requiring a background theory, conceptual holism of that sort, without opposing the given as Sellars understands it. One could suppose that once the theory was in place, none of it as known to be true, but hypothesized as true, the subject can in suitable circumstances acquire knowledge not dependent on other knowledge. This leaves us with the question, which I shall make no attempt to answer, whether the definition of giveness that Sellars was, on my reading, presupposing in EPM, accurately homes in on the conception that he really wanted to reject.

Sellars does have, on my reading, a second objection to giveness. This rests on Sellars's conception of knowledge. Sellars seems to have held that for an acceptance of a claim to count as knowledge not only must the acceptance, as Sellars puts it, 'have authority', which means, roughly, be an instance of a reliable belief formation process, but 'this authority must in some sense be recognized by the person' forming the belief.[3] In that section Sellars reveals that he understands by such recognition knowledge. In effect, then, Sellars's point is that the given is impossible because acquisition of knowledge presupposes knowledge in order for the acquisition to count as *knowledge* acquisition. There are two weaknesses, or possible weaknesses to this line of thought. The first is that we need to be convinced that the conception of knowledge on which it depends is correct. The second is that we need convincing, as one might say, that the conception is actually coherent. Does it not generate some sort of unacceptable regress? Sellars has some notorious reactions to this worry in sections 36 and 37.

If my reading of the main elements in Sellars's criticism of the given is correct, we can say that he does not himself seem to think that the crucial incoherence in the given is that episodes of giveness would involve an immediate conceptual registering of some non-conceptual fact, that is, would involve some sort of transition from a non-conceptual input to a conceptual uptake. The problem is, rather, that the conceptual side presupposes knowledge, and that knowledge as an achievement presupposes knowledge.[4]

That is all the engagement I wish to have here with the myth of the given. What other aims does Sellars have in EPM? Sellars's second aim, and this is not easy to express in a precise way, is to vindicate and explain the role in our thought of reference to what he calls 'inner episodes' or 'impressions' (or what we might perhaps call experiences). The third aim, which is clearly related to the second, and again at this point will remain rather imprecise, is to give an account of the nature of (some of) our perceptual judgments and concepts, in particular our talk of appearances.

---

[3] EPM §35, in SPR: 167–8; in KMG: 247; in B: 74.
[4] I mean this comment to apply to the reading of Sellars which John McDowell has brilliantly presented in his *Mind and World*, see especially ch. 1. It is not a criticism of McDowell's argument, merely a noticing that it does not seem to be Sellars's argument.

Why, it might be asked, is Sellars doing this second thing? There are, I believe, two reasons. The first is that at the time he was thinking through the argument of EPM it was quite usual to be sceptical about the existence of such things. Sellars sees himself as combating this philosophical movement, personified, for him, by Ryle. We might say that he is trying to attack what he perceives as the behaviourism of his times.[5] There is, though, a second aspect. Sellars wants to defend the idea that inner episodes are real and also the subject matter of our thought and talk, but he wishes to do so without the myth of the given reappearing. He needs an explanation of the way we think about the inner which is not a version of the given. How in outline does Sellars try to achieve this? The answer grew out of Sellars's deep reflections on the nature of science. In effect, Sellars suggests that we should think of our reference to inner episodes as akin to the way that science postulates unobserved entities. We talk about such things but they are not given, they are, rather, postulated. This leads to an interesting complexity in Sellars's thought. Throughout EPM Sellars tries to be scrupulous about the distinction between analysing our extant thought and talk and providing an explanation of some of the things we register in that thought. This is, indeed, a significant distinction within the theory of perception. Are philosophers who introduce sense-data analysing or explaining? However, Sellars believes that the analysis of our ordinary thought involves recognizing that parts of it are themselves explanatory of other parts. So the analysis involves the recognition of explanations, the contents of which can themselves receive further explanations corresponding to moves beyond analysis. Sellars is attempting to present this complex analysis in the final part when giving the two Myths of Jones.

My efforts to engage with these Sellarsian projects can be presented as an attempt to answer three general questions. One

---

[5] The role of Ryle as the representative of this denial of the inner is one aspect of what one might call the 'Britishness' of EPM, by which I mean the extent to which the philosophers discussed are British. Thus Ayer receives considerable attention, as do the traditional empiricists. Ryle is the most discussed modern philosopher in EPM.

crucial question is whether Sellars does provide an adequate analysis of the role in our thought of thought about experience. I want in the final part of this paper to try to make some progress with that question. A second question, though, that I wish to answer relates to the third objective that I have claimed Sellars has. Is Sellars's account of our perceptual concepts convincing? But I am also moved to ask a third question. This question is inspired by Richard Rorty's introduction to Robert Brandom's edition of EPM. Rorty presents in that introduction his conception of the importance for American philosophy of Sellars's work. He ranks Sellars with Quine and Wittgenstein.[6] The role, or at least one of the roles, he assigns to Sellars is to have got rid of the sense-datum theory. This is what Rorty says in a footnote; 'Austin's criticisms of Ayer in his posthumous *Sense and Sensibilia* played the role in Britain which Sellars's article played in America. Though they greatly admired Austin, American philosophers had already pretty much given up on sense-data by the time *Sense and Sensibilia* appeared.'[7] Of course, Rorty's remark is open to different interpretations. I assume, though, that he is not offering it simply as sociological remark. It is not that Sellars wrote and then the sense-datum theory was abandoned. It is rather that Sellars gave reasons which were accepted for abandoning it. The third question, therefore, that I wish to ask is whether Sellars does in fact give a refutation (or something close to a refutation) of the sense-datum theory as Rorty implies. In order to begin on that question I want to start right at the very opening of EPM where Sellars turns his attention to the classical version of the sense-datum theory.[8]

---

[6] Richard Rorty, "Introduction," in *Empiricism and the Philosophy of Mind: with an Introduction by Richard Rorty and a Study Guide by Robert Brandom*, R. Brandom (ed.) (Cambridge, MA: Harvard University Press, 1997): 1–2.

[7] Rorty, "Introduction": 2.

[8] I would like to cancel at this point what might be read as my motivation for asking this question. I am in no way tempted to turn clocks back by resuscitating the sense-datum theory. I am interested simply in determining how far Sellars's arguments discredited the view.

2. The 'Classical Concept of a Sense-Datum'

Sellars makes it clear in the first paragraph of EPM that his aim is to attack the 'philosophical idea of giveness'. The impression is conveyed that Sellars is not alone in being an opponent of the given, but we are given no very definite indication as to who the other opponents are. Moreover, he does not say there what that idea of 'giveness' is, but he immediately draws the important distinction between what he calls 'the framework of giveness' and the specific candidates which might be, or have been, supposed to be given. He then turns his critical attention to what he took to be a prime specific candidate, endorsed as such in a major philosophical tradition. Sellars calls the concept of this candidate for giveness the 'classical concept of a sense datum'. Part of his point in calling this conception the 'classical' conception is to contrast it with a non-classical approach to the introduction of sense-data which suggests that it amounts simply to a new language for saying what could already be said using appearance talk. This idea, associated with Ayer, is the second specific version of the given that Sellars turns his critical attention on.[9] What I want to scrutinize, though, is his discussion of the so-called classical version.

As I read him, Sellars develops two main points in this early discussion which might be taken to count against the classical conception, the first which he believes is not decisive, but the second of which is supposedly decisive. The third main element in Sellars's discussion is a suggested explanation as to why the mongrel concept has seemed attractive. I want to consider what our attitude should be to each of these three ingredients in Sellars's discussion.

What does Sellars actually mean by the 'classical concept of a sense datum'? The answer is that it stands for the theory that having an experience is to be analysed as consisting in standing in a relation, that can be called 'sensing', to a sense-datum, which is,

---

[9] Sellars analyses this 'heterodox' version of the sense-datum theory in Part II of EPM.

of course, a certain type of entity or particular, and further that the occurrence of such a sensing can be equated to (is the selfsame thing as) the noninferential knowing that something or other is the case. It may be too strong to talk of an equation, but the doctrine under scrutiny certainly includes the claim that the acquisition of knowledge about it is *part of* what the sensing of a sense-datum is. I shall, however, continue to talk of an equation. When Sellars strikingly describes this concept as a 'mongrel' he is alluding to this equation, which is the core of this theory.

Sellars straight away locates a prima facie problem for this view. He points out that where we are dealing with knowledge, or knowing, we are dealing with something that involves the subject being related to a fact, that is to something's being the case, whereas the sense-datum account of experience involves a subject standing in a relation to a particular entity, a particular sense-datum. The first problem, therefore, is based on the thought that the equation at the core of the mongrel concept cannot be right because it equates something which must be a relation to a fact with something that is a relation to a particular entity, which itself is clearly *not* a fact.

Sellars points out, though, quite correctly, that these observations do not show that the equation is incorrect. The reason is that it remains open for a supporter of the mongrel concept to say that the relation between the subject and the sense-datum, both of which are particular objects, is itself to be analysed in terms of knowledge. Thus, for S to sense sense-datum D is for S to know some fact concerning D. The different overall forms of 'sensing a sense-datum' and 'knowing a fact' do not block that equation.

Sellars could have drawn our attention to the fact that we employ such words as 'recognize' or 'identify' which relate particulars, but which seem properly analysable in terms of cognition and knowing a fact. Thus, we say 'S recognized that man' or 'S recognized that tune', remarks which relate S to objects. It is, however, obvious that it is built into the relation in question obtaining that the subject acquires or has knowledge concerning the object. Such locutions have the same form as 'sense' but clearly involve (or can be equated with) the knowing of facts.

What, according to Sellars, does block the equation, is that there is a fundamental difference between simply having an experience, which is what the theory is analysing as sensing a sense-datum, and getting to know some fact, which is that the latter type of occurrence can only occur after a period in which concepts are acquired, whereas having an experience is something that can occur without any period spent acquiring concepts. If one holds that having an experience consists in sensing a sense-datum, then sensing must have properties which distinguish it from coming to know something. I shall call this the *Acquisition Argument*.

I want to make some comments on this Acquisition Argument.

(1) It seems to me that there are two slightly different ways the Acquisition Argument is presented. On one presentation Sellars gives it as an *ad hominem* point. His claim is that people in what he calls the empiricist tradition themselves hold that sensing sense-data is what experience consists in and that the ability to have experiences is unacquired, but they also hold that concepts need to be acquired in order to have knowledge. He links this last idea to what he calls their 'nominalistic proclivities' (EPM §6, in SPR: 132; in KMG: 210; in B: 21). The claim then is that the classic empiricist sense-datum theorists are inconsistent.

Now, this would bring out an inconsistency in a certain traditional combination of views, and so would be an interesting comment on a complex position, if we agree that such a position existed and was popular. But on its own it would be of little philosophical significance. Maybe, for example, the so called nominalistic proclivities of the traditional empiricist are simply mistaken. If so Sellars would have assembled no evidence against the mongrel concept at all.

On the *ad hominem* reading there are also two other remarks that I wish to make. It is at least a question how accurate it is to describe the empiricist tradition as nominalistic, if by that

Sellars means treating cognition and thought as term involving, centred, that is on terms or names. Empiricism is a long tradition but in its seventeenth- and eighteenth-century forms the main emphasis was surely on the priority of thought to language. They developed a theory of the nature of language which regarded it as an expressive device for pre-existing thought. This was not nominalistic. Prompted by this observation, there is some temptation to remark that there is an ambiguity in the term 'nominalism'. If it means understanding classification and sorts without reliance on universals, then empiricists were nominalists. If it means understanding classification as 'name involving', then there is no particular closeness between empiricism and nominalism. Second, Sellars himself makes the very insightful remark that the problems with classification and thought that afflicted these early empiricists concerned what he calls determinable categories (that is to say, abstract categories) rather than determinate categories, and he adds that they 'take for granted that the human mind has an innate ability to be aware of certain determinate sorts—indeed that we are aware of them simply by virtue of having sensations and images' (EPM §28, in SPR: 160; in KMG : 239; in B: 62). Sellars's remark brings out that such empiricists might have regarded sensing a sense-datum of determinate type T as amounting to thinking that it is of that type, and hence as having the right content to be knowledge. In that case it seems to me Sellars has himself suggested an answer, of sorts, to his own *ad hominem* point. There is no denying, though, that it would not be a good answer.[10]

---

[10] It is natural to ask when reading EPM why Sellars gave it that title, where this question is focused on the inclusion of the term 'empiricism'. Just what does Sellars understand by that, and what is his attitude to it? It does not properly answer these important questions, but nonetheless it seems true, and is perhaps relevant, to point out that EPM says many deep things about the empiricist tradition, and the remark about empiricist attitudes to concepts is one of these insightful comments. As to what Sellars is trying to say about empiricism, the crucial question is whether Sellars thinks that empiricism is definitionally committed to the idea of the given. If he thinks so then amongst the morals of EPM is that empiricism is also a myth. If it is not then Sellars need not be read as saying anything in general about empiricism at all. Sellars, alas, does not define empiricism. What Sellars does though is to link his employment of the term 'empiricism' to the adjective 'traditional', and there is no

The second reading of the Acquisition Argument is stronger; Sellars himself is claiming that, as he puts it, the capacity for experience is unacquired, and that the capacity for knowledge is acquired. Hence, the mongrel equation has to be mistaken.

(2) At times Sellars states the contrast between the capacity for experience and the capacity for knowledge in an over-extreme way. He says that the former is unacquired whereas the latter is acquired. Strictly, it seems, the capacity for experience is acquired in the course of the development of the organism. Sellars's contrast is, rather, that in the life of organisms such as us, there is a time when the capacity for experience has been acquired but the capacity for knowledge has not. (Sellars's way of speaking plainly involves no serious error.)

(3) Although it seems to me that the Acquisition Argument does have the ring of truth, and so casts real doubt on the mongrel equation, there are some rather imponderable doubts that can be raised about it. The aim of someone trying to avoid its conclusion must be to suggest that the capacity for knowing is coeval with the capacity for experience. Showing that, or making it plausible, would not, of course, amount to a full defence of the equation, since the two elements might not be equatable despite being coeval, but it would block Sellars's argument against the equation.

One move that might be made is to ask Sellars himself why he is so sure that all knowing capacities are, in his sense, acquired. Now, it is, of course, no adequate ground for Sellars's conviction that it is plain that lots of concepts are acquired; to use a phrase of Sellars's, it would be 'very odd indeed' to deny this. But that evident truth does not threaten the equation. Now, Sellars himself would appeal at this point to one of his basic convictions, which he calls Psychological Nominalism, and which he summarizes as the 'denial that there is any awareness of logical space prior to, or independent

doubt that Sellars understands by that view (traditional empiricism) something committed to the given. He seems in EPM not to have indicated whether non-traditional empiricism would receive his support.

of, the acquisition of language' (EPM §31, in SPR: 162; in KMG: 241; in B: 66). It is obvious that we acquire language posterior to having experiences, and so given psychological nominalism, Sellars's point is clinched.

Now, I have neither the ingenuity nor the time here, to decide whether psychological nominalism is correct, except to make three comments. (a) The notion of acquiring a language is not totally clear, but I take it the language in question is meant to be a pre-existing public language, and so this opinion cannot be defended by arguing that access to logical space requires a vehicle for thinking and cogitation, and care would certainly need to be taken over the precise meaning of 'acquisition'. (b) It is simply not obviously true, and in no sense is it true in virtue of being an obvious consequence of the definition of 'awareness of logical space', and (c) as far as I can tell, Sellars in EPM advances nothing approaching a reason to adopt psychological nominalism. I myself would not want to put any weight on it and do not think that the Acquisition Argument can rely on it. It has the status of a Sellarsian dogma (or, perhaps, myth).

When not supported by this dogma, three lines of possible reply to the Acquisition Argument suggest themselves. One is that some concepts are innate and hence do not need acquiring. A second is that every occurrence of the experience in some way itself contains the elements necessary for conceptualization. A third is a move encountered even now in intelligent circles, that basic knowing is not conceptual, but somehow pre-conceptual, and hence points about the acquisition of concepts are irrelevant. Sellars, in EPM, does not work his way into or through, any of these suggestions, and so we can say that there are a few unguarded flanks to the Acquisition Argument.

(4) Let us grant, though, that Sellars's premises are reasonable and that the 'mongrel concept' is untenable. What would that show? What it, in effect, shows is that it is a mistake to equate having an experience with a knowing. But it shows nothing as

to how we should think of having an experience. In particular it does not show that the basic analysis of experience should not be in terms of a sensing relation to a sense-datum (that is to say—a relation to a particular of that kind). And secondly, it does not show that once we have acquired concepts we are not in a position to gain knowledge of the character of the elements in such an experience, in such a manner, as to qualify as something being given.

At least in this opening salvo, it cannot be said that Sellars has revealed any error on the sense-datum account of experience, nor in the view that ultimately facts about such items are given to us. These two ideas therefore survive the initial engagement with the 'mongrel concept'.

In fairness to Sellars, it needs pointing out that he himself accepted this estimate of what had been achieved by the Acquisition argument. At the beginning of section 10, after his insightful scrutiny of what Sellars calls Ayer's 'heterodox' approach to sense-data, according to which talk of sense-data has the status of an artificial language re-expressing what is already expressed by 'appearance' talk, Sellars remarks that 'a reasonable next step would be to examine these two ideas and determine how that which survives criticism in each is properly combined with the other' (EPM §10, in SPR: 140; in KMG: 218; in B: 33). He means by the two ideas the ideas that the mongrel conception equates. He therefore reveals his own recognition that the force of that argument is against the equation and not the two elements considered separately.

(5) Sellars concludes §7 with an explanation of the popularity of the mongrel concept, and this is the third element in his treatment with which I wish to engage with in this section. If the mongrel concept has been popular, then Sellars is right to ask why. §7 is quite long, but amongst other things Sellars says this:

Rather they would take the contrapositive of the argument, and reason that *since* the foundation of empirical knowledge *is* the non-inferential knowledge of such facts, it *does* consist of members of a class which contains non-veridical members. But before it is thus baldly put, it gets tangled up with the first line of thought. The idea springs to mind that *sensations of red triangles* have exactly the virtues which *ostensible seeings of red triangular physical surfaces* lack. To begin with, the grammatical similarity of 'sensation of a red triangle' to 'thought of a celestial city' is interpreted to mean, or, better, gives rise to the presupposition, that *sensations* belong in the same general pigeonhole as *thoughts*—in short are cognitive facts. *Then*, it is noticed that sensations are *ex hypothesi* far more intimately related to mental processes than external physical objects. It would seem easier to 'get at' a red triangle of which we are having a sensation, than to 'get at' a red and triangular physical surface. But, above all, it is the fact that it *doesn't make sense* to speak of unveridical sensations which strikes these philosophers, though for it to strike them as it does, they must overlook the fact that if it makes sense to speak of an experience as *veridical* it must correspondingly make sense to speak of it as *unveridical*.

(EPM §7, in SPR: 134; in KMG: 212; in B: 24−5)

It seems to me that Sellars makes two explanatory suggestions in this passage that are not very plausible. First, Sellars points out that 'sensation of a red triangle' is grammatically similar to 'thought of a celestial city', and that this tempts philosophers to think that having a sensation is like the latter a cognitive occurrence. As against this I have two observations. The first is that it is odd to think of thinking of a celestial city as cognitive occurrence. Thinking of something does not (in such cases) give us knowledge of it. This grammatical resemblance, even if it is having an influence, does not really get to where Sellars wants to get to. Second, there seems to me no more of an explanation for the temptation here than there would be in the suggestion that the fact that 'bottle of beer' is grammatically similar might lead people to think such a thing is an intellectual or cognitive occurrence. The second thing that Sellars seems to stress is that there is an attraction in thinking of sensing a sensation as a cognitive act because if one wants foundation for knowledge which is totally secure then the fact that a sensation cannot be described as 'unveridical' will make it seem the right kind of cognitive occurrence. But, again, the failure of 'unveridical' to apply to sensations seems to me to have no more explanatory role than the fact that the same expression cannot apply to, say, cricket bats might explain why cricket bats are regarded as cognitively basic. At this point, I suggest, Sellars falls victim to the popularity at his time of explaining philosophical errors in terms of superficial linguistic similarities.

3. Two Other Arguments

In EPM, as I read it, Sellars has two other objections to the two ideas considered separately. I mean that he has two apart from the completely general argument or arguments against giveness in general. Of course, these general arguments would count against the giveness of information about the character of sense-data, since they count against the giveness of anything. Those general arguments I want to engage with later.

The first more specific objection to the traditional sense-datum analysis of experience arises from the kinds of properties that sense-data are thought of as having. These properties are determined by the standard route into the theory. That route as Sellars puts it is as follows: '... the attempt to explain the facts of sense perception in a scientific style. How does it happen that people can have the experience which they describe by saying "It is as though I were seeing a red and triangular physical object" when either there is no physical object there at all, or, if there is, it is neither red nor triangular?' (EPM §7, in SPR: 132–3; in KMG: 211; in B: 22). As Sellars points out, the explanation, or the beginning of the explanation, is that the subject 'has what is called a "sensation" or "impression" of a red triangle' (EPM §7, in SPR: 133; in KMG: 211; in B: 22). In the standard theory this becomes the suggestion that the item presented is red (and triangular). Let us say that the orthodox sense-datum theory involves the idea that sense-data possess the familiar sensible properties—such as colour—and that is part of the explanation for the experience.

Now, Sellars' worry with this is expressed in §21. He says: 'One point can be made right away, namely that if these experiences are so understood that, say, the immediate experience of a red triangle implies the existence of something—not a physical object—which *is* red and triangular, and if the redness which the item has is the same as the redness which the physical object looks to have, then the suggestion runs up against the objection that the redness physical objects look to have is the same as the redness physical objects actually *do* have, so the items which ex hypothesi are not physical objects, and which radically, even categorically, differ from physical objects, would have the same redness as physical objects. And while this is, perhaps, not entirely out of the question, it certainly provides food for thought' (EPM §21, in SPR: 149–50; in KMG: 228–9; in B: 47).

Sellars is, of course, right to suggest that there is food for thought here. But exactly how substantial is the fare? It can be said that if Sellars is right then he would have refuted the standard version of the sense-datum theory. It would do so because according to the standard version, sense-data do possess such sensible properties as colour and shape and taste, etc. However, even if Sellars were right, that would not amount to a refutation of another version of the theory, according to which there are sense-data with other types of properties. The final general point is that if Sellars is correct, then the case for the sense-datum theory would be seriously weakened. Thus, Sellars is surely right to think that the standard case rests on the idea that the correct explanation of, for example, an appearance of red is the presence of a red thing. If the postulated thing cannot be red, then their postulation does not qualify as explanatory. A justification for their postulation would then be lacking.

The crucial question is whether Sellars makes a convincing case for the claim that a sense-datum cannot be, say, red. Sellars might use the following argument to support his case. (1) There are massive differences between sense-data and physical objects. As Sellars puts it, sense-data 'radically, even categorically, differ from physical objects' (EPM §21, in SPR: 150; in KMG: 228; in

B: 47). (2) Physical objects have colour. So, (3) Sense-data cannot have colour. This argument though is too quick. It rests on the assumption that if two objects, x and y, are 'radically, even categorically' different, then x and y cannot share properties. That assumption, however, is not true. Thus objects of different sorts can share such features as existence, duration, self-identity and object-hood. At some level radically different objects must be different, but we have so far been presented with no reason to suppose that radically different things cannot share colour despite differing in other important ways.

Sellars has, I think, a more interesting argument for his claim, which can be represented as follows. (4) Colour predicates have their primary application to physical objects. (5) Understanding such predicates requires or involves lots of supplementary infor-mation about colour. For example, Sellars claims 'that the latter concept involves the ability to tell what colours objects have by looking at them—which, in turn, involves knowing in what circumstances to place an object if one wishes to ascertain its colour by looking at it' (EPM §18, in SPR: 146; in KMG: 225; in B: 43). (6) Such information cannot apply to sense-data. We cannot, for example, know what are good viewing conditions for sense-data. We cannot know that because the very idea makes no sense. So, (7) ascriptions of colour to sense-data do not make sense.

This is not a wildly implausible argument, but it is unlikely, I think, to carry conviction with Sellars's opponents. I do not myself want to challenge premisses (5) and (6), but, whatever its precise role in the argument, premiss (4) is not obviously true. How has Sellars ruled out that we acquire an understanding of colour predicates in relation to colour instantiators the nature of which is not known and then extend that understanding to physical objects? This is by no means an unknown view. But more important, the argument does not quite clinch its conclusion. The problem is that it does not rule out that there is a similar way to understand colour ascriptions to non-physical objects. What would it have to be? How is it demonstrated that it is not fulfilled? The problem for this argument, I want to suggest, is that it is in a general way what might be called semantic. It relies on conditions of intelligibility as discerned in one case not being fulfilled in another. But it does not really determine what the conditions might be in the non-physical case to ground intelligibility nor does it show they are unfulfilled.

If a case is to be made for Sellars's conclusion here, I think it would have to be based on defending a claim of this form: necessarily, if x is red then x is C, where sense-data are not C. There are chances to construct such an argument, but Sellars does not really have his hands on the ingredients for it.

It cannot therefore be said that Sellars has refuted the orthodox sense-datum theory with the present line of thought.

I want now to look at another remark by Sellars which I find interesting and insightful. It is not clear what weight Sellars himself attached to his own observation, but I shall consider it as a candidate objection to, or problem-raising remark directed at, the sense-datum idea. Sellars says;

Now there is such an air of paradox to the idea that 'immediate experiences' are *mere* theoretical entities—entities, that is, which are postulated, along with certain fundamental principles concerning them, to explain uniformities pertaining to sense perception, as molecules, along with the principles of molecular motion, are postulated to explain experimentally determined regularities pertaining to gases—that I am going to lay it aside until a more propitious context of thought may make it seem relevant. Certainly, those who have thought that qualitative and existential look-ings are to be explained in terms of 'immediate experiences' thought of the latter as *the* most untheoretical of entities, indeed, as the observables *par excellence*.

(EPM §22, in SPR: 150; in KMG: 229–30; in B: 49)

One thing, I think, that Sellars is doing in this passage and section 22, from which this quotation comes, and also in section 23, is to stress the crucial distinction within his own positive view between the analysis he is offering of our perceptual language and concepts, and the explanation he will provide of the nature of sensuous experience. It might seem as if Sellars is making this point when he says; 'the very nature of "looks talk" is such as to raise questions to which it gives no answers' (EPM §22, in SPR: 152; in KMG: 231; in B: 51). In fact, as I read it, in that particular sentence the emphasis is on 'looks talk'. Sellars means that that element in our ordinary thought introduces without properly characterizing certain types of episodes. He does hold that ordinary thought embodies a further conception of them, as the second myth of Jones aims to explain. But Sellars himself thinks that the theory attained under the influence of that genius Jones itself presents a phenomenon that the philosopher can add to even now. Sellars is, therefore, himself committed to there being no paradox in a position which ultimately treats 'immediate experience', characterized in a substantial way, as a theoretical postulate.

However, Sellars's remark can be taken as bringing out what might seem to be a genuine paradox in *traditional sense-datum theory*. The appearance of such a paradox is generated by two thoughts which seem to be held together in at least one strand of traditional sense-datum theory. On the one hand, sense-datum theorists regard their postulation of sense-data as something which requires a substantial justification. There are well-known arguments with conventional names which regularly figure in the arguments they presented.[11] This might be characterized, quite reasonably, as regarding sense-data as theoretical postulates. On the other hand, they also regarded truths about sense-data as ones immediately known and as the basis for our knowledge of the world. These truths, and the items they concern, would rank as the 'obervables *par excellence*'. These two claims hardly seem consistent.

It would, indeed, seem a very strange overall theory if it was held that the immediately given, and basic, units of knowledge had such a content as 'This sense-datum is red', and that the

---

[11] I am thinking, of course, of such arguments as the argument from illusion and the argument from hallucination.

acknowledgment of the very existence of sense-data depends on what we might call weighty 'theoretical arguments'. There is though, I want to suggest, a way out of this apparent paradox. It may not be a way out that the traditional sense-datum theorists themselves had seen, or reckoned with, but it seems to provide them with a non-paradoxical conception. The way out is to hold that the content of the basic data does not itself involve the concept of a sense-datum. Once that is excluded from the basic content there is nothing paradoxical in regarding sense-data as items that require arguments to believe in. However, their role is to be the things which in fact are the things which the basic knowledge concerns. One way to spell this out is to regard the basic knowledge as of the form 'This thing is F', where nothing is explicitly conveyed as to the nature of the demonstrated item which is immediately given as F. The role of the pro-sense-datum arguments is to establish the nature of the demonstrated items. As far as I can see, this combination is not paradoxical. If Sellars did intend to bring this paradox to our attention, we should respond by gesturing to the above way out.

4. Interim Conclusions

I have so far considered three lines of thought in Sellars's engagement with the sense-datum tradition. The first is the Acquisition argument, directed at the so-called 'mongrel' concept of sense-data. My verdict on that argument is that, although there are possible lines of reply that Sellars does not investigate, it presents a serious problem for the conception of 'sensing' in a sense-datum theory that equates sensing with gaining immediate knowledge of something. However, it amounts to an objection to an equation, and once that equation is abandoned, both a sense-datum model of basic experience and the notion of facts about sense-data being 'given' remain undefeated. The second argument rested on the claim that 'sensible qualities' of the normal type, for example, colour, cannot be ascribed to sense-data. Sellars's claim certainly has some plausibility, but it cannot be said that he makes anything close to a compelling case for it. Finally, if Sellars did mean that 'paradox' point to be an objection (and it is not clear that he did) then it does not seem to work.

If fair, these assessments count against acceptance of Rorty's claim that Sellars discredited the sense-datum tradition.

There is another important aspect of Sellars's approach that needs to be brought in when considering Rorty's description of Sellars, but that will have to wait for the final section.

5. Sellars on Perceptual Concepts and Inner Episodes

We have, of course, and Sellars himself is highly conscious of it, a rich vocabulary to express facts about, and different aspects of, our perceptual experiences. We distinguish between the different senses; we describe the objects perceived in different ways, with different implications of the different ways of speaking—thus, we see Romeo, an argument between Romeo and Juliet, Romeo and Juliet arguing; we see that Romeo argued with Juliet; we also describe such episodes in terms of how things appeared to the subject—thus, we might say, Romeo and Juliet looked to be arguing, or it looked as if Romeo and Juliet were arguing. We have the categories of illusion, hallucination, and accurate or veridical perception. Within this rich structure of language and thought Sellars initially focuses throughout §§10 to 23, on appearance talk, in application to vision, which is to say 'looks' talk.

Why, it might be asked, does Sellars focus on this first? The answer is that his attention is taken by the proposal that looks-judgments count as expressions of what is given in visual perception. It catches his attention at this point because it is a commitment of Ayer's approach to sense-datum talk which Sellars has been examining, but also because it is a natural direction for an empiricist style believer in the given to go if he or she has serious doubts about the legitimacy of an expression of the facts that are supposedly given, which explicitly commits itself to sense-data. Some sort of doubts about that commitment had been raised by Sellars in the Acquisition argument. Sellars also thinks that it is the form the myth of the given will take within a view that denies there are 'inner episodes'. Sellars talks at this point of the 'crude verificationisms and operationalisms characteristic of the more dogmatic forms of recent empiricism' (EPM §10, in SPR: 140; in KMG: 219; in B: 33). Whether or not he thinks these names apply to something like Rylean behaviourism, he clearly has that approach in mind when stressing the idea of denying 'inner episodes'. Sellars, therefore, focuses on looks judgments as candidates for a certain epistemological role.

The core of Sellars's proposal is that our talk of looks is an offshoot of the central idea that perceptual experiences are, as it were, linked to claims or assertions. We make the claim in a normal successful case explicit when we report what happened as 'S saw that P'. However, in so reporting the perceptual occurrence the reporter is endorsing the truth of P. Sellars says: 'To characterize S's experience as a *seeing* is, in a suitably broad sense ... to apply the semantical concept of truth to that experience' (EPM §16 *bis,* in SPR: 145; in KMG: 223; in B: 40). The role of looks talk is to characterize the experience in terms of the linked proposition without, however, endorsing the truth of the proposition. Thus if I say that 'The tree looked green to S' I am saying that S had an experience which was similar to one which S would have had S been seeing that the tree was green, but by talking of looks I withhold my own endorsement of the truth of the claim. I do, in a sense, partially endorse it, in that I so describe the experience that I commit myself to the existence of a tree. I can describe the experience in an even less committal way by saying 'It looked to S as if there was a green tree'.

There is clearly something very plausible about Sellars's approach to 'looks'-judgments. We do link propositions to perceptual experiences in circumstances where it amounts to a seeing that P. If it is seen that P then it is true that P. Describing a perceptual episode that way commits the describer to acceptance of P. Further, when we describe other cases as ones in which it looks as if P, we do not commit ourselves to its being true that P. As describers, also, we can, as it were, modulate our language to indicate how far away from being true, or seen as being true, is P. We do, however, commit ourselves to something like its being for the subjects nonetheless as if they were seeing that P. As Sellars says: '... when I say "X Looks green to me now" I am *reporting* the fact that my experience is, so to speak, *as an experience*, indistinguishable from a veridical one of seeing that x is green' (EPM §16 *bis*, in SPR: 145; in KMG: 224; in B: 41).

On anyone's view, surely, these characterizations are insightful. But I want to argue that there are important elements in the final picture of our perceptual concepts that Sellars is proposing with which we should not agree. There are two linked thoughts about 'looks'-judgments that Sellars seems to endorse that are probably not correct. He suggests that we talk of 'looks' only when there are considerations which 'have operated to raise ... the question to endorse or not to endorse' (EPM §16 *bis*, in SPR: 145; in KMG: 224; in B: 41). But if S did see that P, and we allowed that he saw that P, hence there was no question about the truth of P, but we also asked how he managed to see that P, the obvious answer that would occur to us is that there and then it looked to S as if P. That is a fundamental explanatory dependency within our naïve thought about perception. If that is so, talk of 'looks' is not restricted to cases where Sellars's question has been raised for the describer. Second, where a question has been raised it need not be a question as to the truth of P. The doubt that occasions talk of looks may be, not over P itself, but over whether S could see that P. If we think that S has what we now call a veridical hallucination, we do not doubt that P, but rather that S saw that P. These are, however, merely minor details in Sellars's treatment, which he could easily have corrected.

Sellars seems, however, firmly committed to the much more contentious proposal that as well as linking a variety of experiences to the same proposition, we also have the thought that the experiences are the same in another way, a way that Sellars captures by talking (in a language that is slightly odd) of them sharing a 'descriptive content' (EPM §22, in SPR: 151; in KMG: 230–1; in B: 50). Now, Sellars seems to think that we have an understanding of what is shared, and he aims to present the understanding that we have achieved in the second myth of Jones (in §§60 to 63). When he describes the 'mythical theory' he says that he is attributing to it 'only those minimal features which enable it to throw light on the logic of our ordinary language about immediate experience' (EPM §60, in SPR: 191; in KMG: 271; in B: 109). This clearly reveals, I suggest, that Sellars thinks the (second) conception devised by Jones corresponds to ordinary thought (and language). We need to ask, at this point, what the myths of Jones are meant to represent. They do not represent any conjecture by Sellars as to the actual history of human thought and concept formation. (That negative feature explains why Sellars calls it a myth.) They surely are, rather, dramatic ways of presenting what one could call conceptual proposals. The point of the second myth is that it encapsulates an analysis of our extant thought, thought shared by ordinary adult humans, about what Sellars calls impressions.

Sellars thinks that our talk and thought about appearance itself can be given an account along the lines outlined in the first myth of Jones, which is his proposal as to the logic of our talk about thoughts. I shall not examine that in detail here. Sellars claims that having the category of thoughts with contents, one introducible category is that of seeing that P. He then claims that he has already explained how the terminology of looks can be grounded by extension within that framework. We in fact only have Sellars's word that our talk of seeing can be introduced on that basis. That would need properly explaining and testing. However, let us assume that Sellars has an account of our general talk of seeing-that, and of appearance.

What, one is tempted to ask, remains to be done? Sellars's claim is that an account of 'such things as impressions, sensations, and feelings' is needed (EPM §60, in SPR: 190; in KMG: 270; in B: 108). He describes such entities as those that philosophers call 'immediate experiences'. Clearly we do talk of sensations and feelings. What talk has Sellars in mind though when he cites talk of impressions? I think it is clear that Sellars holds that we ascribe to ourselves and each other, along with, say, such sensations as pain, and feelings such as embarrassment, things we call 'impressions of red'. The problem is to give an account of that part of our talk and thought. Sellars envisages such talk as representing our conception of what the common descriptive content is for the various linked perceptual experiences. We are definitely going beyond merely thinking in terms of ' "entity of the kind which is common to the situations in which there looks to be a red... object" ' (EPM §61, in SPR: 192; in KMG: 272; in B: 111).

By this point it seems to me that Sellars has misconceived our ordinary thought. First, when ordinary people talk and think about perceptual experience, they do not make much use of talk of impressions of red. It is a rather recherché mode of speech. But, second, in so far as they do, what reason is there to understand such talk as representing a positive conception of what Sellars is clearly thinking of as an internal element common to a range of experiences? I cannot really see any ground for thinking that our talk of impressions of red means any more than a matter of it looking as if there is something red. Why should it be supposed that it gives a genuine positive description of a common element?

There are large issues here which really cannot be settled quickly. However, I myself have no sense that in acquiring ordinary thought I have latched onto a conception of the intrinsic nature of a common element present whenever, say, it looks to me as if there is something red. I would have thought that I had given no thought to that and had no commitment one way or the other. Another way to make this plausible is to develop an understanding of the traditional task of the philosophy of perception. One way of conceiving the arguments that traditional philosophers put forward is as arguments designed to persuade ordinary thinkers that they should recognize that there is a common element of a type akin to sensations present whenever it looks to someone as if there is something red. This is plausibly represented as a discovery supported by argument. It invites the ordinary person to think of perception as involving something akin to sensations. This plausible conception hardly makes sense on Sellars's picture. Ordinary thought already incorporates the idea of inner impressions as central components in perception. I suggest, therefore, that the second myth of Jones in its full generality is a double myth. It is a myth in the sense that Sellars acknowledges—a dramatic story. But it is also a myth in the sense that the conceptual structure it is purporting to be a dramatic presentation of does not itself exist. There has been no introduction of impressions!

This does not mean that our thought about the inner elements that are acknowledged in ordinary ways of thinking—such things as pains, itches, and feelings—do not need a proper conceptual account. But, somewhat oddly in the second myth of Jones, Sellars makes no attempt to make our thought about such entities coherent. Thus he makes no attempt to explain our categorization of inner occurrences as pains or itches. Sellars concerns himself with such descriptive (and according to me, mythical) categories as that of 'red impression', and the elements he employs there, being formulated in terms of postulated inner replicas of red things, cannot illuminate talk of pain.[12] There are no external things for our thought of them to replicate. So, paradoxically, it seems to me, the genuine aspect of our thought that the second myth could help with remains untreated. At this point, though, an even more sceptical thought needs voicing. Is there not something totally unrealistic in a model (even allowing for its mythical status) which imagines humans with a developed conception of the external world, with the categories of things which they have observed

---

[12] In a longer treatment I would try to probe whether Sellars (alias Jones) gives us enough to really count as having a descriptive characterization of so-called impressions. It is not at all obvious that he does.

(whatever ultimately Sellars allows that to mean), but still in need of somehow attending to, and taking conceptual cognizance of, their pains and itches? Anyone with children realizes that their earliest model of the world, including of course themselves as part of it, includes such manifestly noticeable inner happenings as pains and itches. It is hard not to feel this problem when Sellars remarks that 'the language of impressions was no more tailored to fit antecedent noticings of these entities than the language of molecules was tailored to fit antecedent noticings of molecules' (EPM §62, in SPR: 195; in KMG: 276, in B: 116). This comparison of thought about internal impressions to thought about molecules is surely an indication that something is seriously wrong in Sellars's model. Is Sellars really suggesting that the same innovation was needed for thought about pains as was needed for thought about molecules? In effect, as we might say, we have no real idea as to what fixes the limits of the conceptual structures that Jones is needed to take humanity beyond.

Why did Sellars go wrong, as I have claimed, in his conception of our ordinary thought about perception and experience? My suspicion, and despite its mildly comic air it is not meant as comic, is that Sellars could address to his parents, more specifically his father, the complaint expressed in the famous poem about the mistakes of parents, by Philip Larkin. I suspect that Sellars was never given a chance to acquire the ordinary conception uncontaminated by philosophical accretions. Sellars probably absorbed a heavy notion of sense impressions with his mother's milk. It is the curse of being brought up by a philosopher.

Finally, Sellars himself after outlining Jones's second myth then introduces a new level of theorizing, which he describes as that of a 'speculative philosophical critique of ... common-sense ...' (EPM §61, in SPR: 194; in KMG: 275; in B: 115). And Sellars says that in the direction he envisages the critique going the theorist will 'come upon the particulars which sense-datum theorists profess to find ...' (EPM §61, in SPR: 194; in KMG: 274; in B: 114). This presents us with another reason not to endorse Rorty's vision of

Sellars's achievement. We can leave the details opaque, as Sellars himself does in EPM, but he has put down a marker that his own philosophical conception of experience has strong resemblances to that of the traditional sense-datum theorist. In fact, by the end, Sellars's main complaint against traditional sense-data theorists is not primarily in what they postulated but that they supposed such entities could be uncovered by what he calls analysis of the common-sense framework.

6. Conclusion

This is far from being a proper assessment of Sellars's views in EPM about perception. I have urged a picture in which they amount to a mixture of insight and illusion. Most crucially Sellars himself subscribes to a mythical conception of our ordinary thought about perceptual experience. But in contrast to Austin, whose animadversions on sense-data were, as one might say, designed to draw us away from doing the philosophy of perception, Sellars's reflections draw us into a profoundly dramatic philosophy of perception.

References

McDowell J. (1994) *Mind and World* (Cambridge, MA: Harvard University Press).

Rorty R. (1997) "Introduction," in *Empiricism and the Philosophy of Mind: with an Introduction by Richard Rorty and a Study Guide by Robert Brandom*, R. Brandom (ed.) (Cambridge, MA: Harvard University Press).

Sellars W. (1956) "Empiricism and the Philosophy of Mind". In Minnesota Studies in the Philosophy of Science, vol. I, H. Feigl and M. Scriven (eds.), 253–329 (Minneapolis, MN: University of Minnesota Press). (Originally presented at the University of London Special Lectures in Philosophy for 1956 as "The Myth of the Given: Three Lectures on Empiricism and the Philosophy of Mind".) Reprinted in SPR with additional footnotes. Published separately as *Empiricism and the Philosophy of Mind: with an Introduction by Richard Rorty and a Study Guide by Robert Brandom*, R. Brandom (ed.) (Cambridge, MA: Harvard University Press, 1997) [B]. Also reprinted in W. deVries and T. Triplett, "Knowledge, Mind, and the Given: A Reading of Sellars' 'Empiricism and the Philosophy of Mind'" (Indianapolis, IN: Hackett, 2000) [KMG].

Sellars W. (1963) *Science, Perception and Reality* (London: Routledge & Kegan Paul). Reissued (Atascadero, CA: Ridgeview Publishing, 1991) [SPR].

5

Brandom's Two-Ply Error

Willem A. deVries and Paul Coates

In his *Tales of the Mighty Dead*, Robert Brandom discusses at some
length Wilfrid Sellars's two-ply account of observation. Much of
Brandom's discussion is pithy and revealing, but we would like
to draw attention to two problems with his treatment of 'looks'-
statements that make it a less than faithful representation of Sellars's
analysis. Furthermore, to the extent that Brandom falls short of a
truly Sellarsian account of 'looks'-statements, he also prevents his
readers from appreciating fully Sellars's critique of Cartesianism.

We will very briefly review the general outline of Sellars's
proposed analysis of appearance claims in section I. In sections II
and III, we discuss the problems with Brandom's account, and in
section IV we draw some lessons about how to read Sellars on this
issue and how to understand his critique of Cartesianism.

1. The Logic of 'Looks'

Traditional theories of knowledge were constructed under the
misapprehension that all our knowledge, including our empirical
knowledge of the world around us, had to be founded upon
certainties. Where are such certainties to be found? Two thoughts
are intertwined in what we'll call the general Cartesian approach:
First, we know our own mental states first and best, because we
have a direct and immediate access to them unlike the indirect
and mediate access we have to anything extra-mental. Second,

appearances are what we know for certain, because even if I am mistaken that there is some red physical object before me, I cannot be mistaken that something looks or appears red to me. Claims about appearances are incorrigible.

These two thoughts were not always distinguished, much less disentangled, among the classical theorists, so it was often assumed that they coincide, because appearances *are* mental states that we can grasp immediately and directly. In classical empiricist thought it became virtually axiomatic that we can and do grasp appearances independently of and prior to our grasp of anything external to the mind, and that whatever grasp we have of external reality is based on and derived from our independent knowledge of appearances. Sellars's treatment of appearance claims is aimed at destroying this nexus of assumptions.

It does this by, first, destroying the notion that appearances are special kinds of objects of knowledge, and, second, giving us a way to understand such claims that frees us from the picture that their certainty is to be accounted for as a result of their immediacy or internality. How does it accomplish these tasks? Sellars ultimately offers us what Brandom terms a "two-ply" account of observational knowledge. That is, in order for an utterance of a sentence to express observation knowledge, Sellars tells us, it must be (1) a reliable symptom of the state of affairs it reports, and (2) known to be such by the reporter. In Brandom's idiolect, the production of the sentence must be the result of a *reliable differential responsive disposition* to the environmental stimuli, and "[i]t must be a committing oneself to a content that can both serve as and stand in need of *reasons*, that is, that can play the role both of premise and of conclusion in *inferences*" (Brandom, 2-Ply: 351).

The notion of observational knowledge, then, involves two distinguishable aspects or "moments," as Hegel might call them. The propositional content of one's experience is, as Sellars puts it, "wrung" from one by one's encounter with the world (EPM §16 *bis* in SPR: 144; in KMG: 223; in B: 40), but, as reflective, epistemically sensitive (or, as Brandom would say, sapient) creatures, we can—ultimately, must—adopt a normative stance toward that content, endorsing it or withholding endorsement to some degree. Sellars employs this understanding of observational knowledge in his analysis of appearance locutions. He argues that we should understand "appears," "looks," and related terms as a kind of operator that registers our unwillingness to endorse the propositional content of the relevant experience. Because such terms function as a kind of sentential operator, there is no good reason to think that appearances are a special kind of object—appearance talk functions as a modifier of the epistemic status of our normal physical object talk, not as talk about a different, perhaps even nonphysical, realm of being. The certainty of appearance claims is accounted for, not by the immediacy of our relation to or the internality of such objects, but simply in virtue of the fact that, by withholding endorsement of the propositional content of the relevant experience, there is less at stake in them, less at risk: in most cases, sincere utterance of such a sentence is adequate evidence of its truth.

By offering us a different understanding of appearances and appearance statements, Sellars hopes to liberate us from a picture, from a nexus of assumptions, that makes our access to physical objects not only problematic, but probably unjustifiable. We have not yet gone into the details of Sellars's treatment of "looks" talk, because it is in the details of his interpretation of Sellars's analysis of appearance statements that Brandom goes awry, and we will bring out the detailed structure of Sellars's analysis in our discussion of Brandom's errors.

It will, however, be useful for our argument to note at this stage that, according to Sellars, there is a further dimension to experience, one that gets short shrift on Brandom's account. In addition to the propositional content of experience, there is a further sensory (or phenomenal) nonconceptual component. As Sellars argues, 'seeing something is green is not *merely* the occurrence of [a] propositional claim' (EPM §16 *bis*, in SPR: 144;

in KMG: 223; in B: 40). There is 'something more' that philosophers have in mind when speaking of the sensory aspect of
experience as a 'sense impression' or an 'immediate experience'.
Sellars interprets the sensory component of experience as an inner
state of the subject, and in these parts of EPM refers to it as the
'descriptive content' of experience (EPM §22, in SPR: 151; in
KMG: 231; in B: 50). What is important for Sellars is the fact that
the inner sensory state is not, in ordinary perception, the focus
of our attention. In the standard case, the sensory component of
experience gives rise, without inference, to observational claims
about the physical objects in our surroundings. Sensory states are
not objects of perceptual knowledge. The exact logical status of
these sensory states, and the presuppositions incurred through our
being able to refer to them, are problems that Sellars is concerned
with throughout EPM.[1]

2. Being Red vs. Seeing Red

We discuss first a central problem with Brandom's reading of Sellars
that shows up in section III of Brandom's chapter. There Brandom
claims that Sellars finds his two-ply analysis of looks statements
to be supported by its ability "to explain features of appearance
talk that are mysterious on the contrasting cartesian approach"
(Brandom, 2-Ply: 357–8). Brandom then lists three sentences:

(i) The apple over there is red.
(ii) The apple over there looks red.
(iii) It looks as though there were a red apple over there.

He claims that "[u]tterances of these sentences can express the same
responsive dispositions to report the presence of a red apple, but

---

[1] As Sellars makes explicit, EPM §16, in SPR: 145; in KMG: 223; in B: 40. The matter
is only finally resolved in Part XVI, when Sellars explains how we are able to make direct
reports of inner sensory states. But the ability to make such reports presupposes the fact that
we have a prior ability to employ the conceptual framework for physical objects.

they endorse (take responsibility for the inferential consequences of) different parts of that claim" (Brandom, 2-Ply: 358). So, in Brandom's view, (i)–(iii) are identical in content, but differ in the endorsement of that content.

Sellars himself presents a list that might seem similar in §22 of EPM:

(*a*) Seeing that x, over there, is red
(*b*) Its looking to one that x, over there, is red
(c) Its looking to one as though there were a red object over there (EPM, §22, in SPR: 151; in KMG: 230; in B: 49–50).

It is for our purposes unimportant that Sellars's list is a list of gerundial clauses, not sentences, which he describes as themselves descriptive of three different situations that nonetheless have something important in common. There is another, philosophically important difference between Brandom's and Sellars's list. In Brandom's list, the first sentence is a straightforward physical object claim; in Sellars's list, the first situation described is not the state of some mere physical object, but an experiential, indeed an observational state of a person.

As Brandom points out, one of the goals Sellars has in mind in Parts III and IV of EPM is to argue that being red is conceptually prior to looking red, that is, that it is possible to have a conception of something's being red without having the conception of something's looking red, but not vice versa. Notice that Brandom's list makes it hard to see how Sellars could hope to accomplish this, for in his list being-red and looking-red both show up as elements of a series of sentences, which sentences contrast with each other along one dimension that is not adequate to support a claim of conceptual priority for one element overagainst the others. In order to make the claim that being-red is conceptually prior to looking-red, Sellars needs not only to distinguish different forms of "looks" claims, he must have in mind a different and stronger contrast between "looks" claims and "is" claims.

And indeed, that is just what we find in Sellars. In the orthodox Sellarsian view, a sentence such as

(1) There is a red object over there

often functions as a base-level observation report, the kind of thing that our linguistic training gives us reliable differential responsive dispositions to produce when confronted with something red in normal conditions (and that we will produce under abnormal conditions even when nothing red is there). An utterance of such a sentence makes no claim about anyone's experience.

In contrast, the claim

(2) I see there is a red object over there

is on a higher level: it makes a claim about my experience. It is on a "higher" level at very least, because it is a complex sentence that contains (1) as a proper part. But it is also significantly more complex conceptually, since it contains the concept of seeing something, a concept of a kind of experience. In Sellars's view, the statements

(3) The object over there looks red to me

and

(4) It looks to me as if there is a red object over there

are also claims at this higher level to the effect that I am having a certain kind of experience. That they are at this higher level, like claims about seeing, may be masked by their surface grammar, but that should not fool us.

On Brandom's account, it appears as if Sellars is merely concerned with a difference between *levels of endorsement*, not a difference between claims about physical objects and claims about experiences. But from different levels of endorsement, there is no argument that will establish the conceptual priority of being-red over looking-red. Considerations of endorsement are present in any claims we make about observational experience, so it would not make good sense to claim that different levels of endorsement could establish such a conceptual priority. The differences in level of endorsement necessarily coordinate contrastively with each other.

(1) does not show up in Sellars's list, because he thinks it, as a physical object statement, is distinctly different from the three expressions he lists. In Sellars's list, the case to which lookings are contrasted is not a base-level physical object claim, but a higher-level claim about an observation, in this case a seeing, which itself includes a propositional claim about a physical object. A sentence such as

(3) The object over there looks red to me

is not at the same level as the base-level observation report. It is, in Sellars's view, an essentially more complex claim, on the same level as

(2) I see there is a red object over there.

It is essentially more complex than the base-level observation report because it contains an implicit reference to and attribution of an *experience* to someone.

Now the suggestion I wish to make is, in its simplest terms, that the statement 'X looks green to Jones' differs from 'Jones sees that x is green' in that whereas the latter both ascribes a propositional claim to Jones's experience *and endorses it*, the former ascribes the claim but does not endorse it.... Notice that I will only say 'I see that x is green' (as opposed to 'X is green') when the question 'to endorse or not to endorse' has come up. 'I see that x is green' belongs, so to speak, on the same level as 'X looks green' and 'X merely *looks* green'.

(EPM §16 *bis*, in SPR: 145; in KMG: 223–4; in B: 40–1)

For Sellars, *looking* and *seeing* are on the same level, not *looking* and *being*, and this is part of his answer to the old problem of Appearance and Reality. Being red is conceptually prior to looking red for the same kind of reason that it is prior to seeing red: looking and seeing are conceptually complex states that presuppose someone's having an experience that makes a claim about reality, about what *is*. Brandom's list and his discussion of it loses this important Sellarsian insight.

3. Looks and Reports

Brandom's other misconstrual of Sellars is related to his failure to distinguish base-level observation reports about physical objects from more complex statements about our experience. Brandom incorrectly denies that "looks"-statements are reports in any sense.

Let's take a moment to get clear on Sellars's notion of a report. *Report* is, in his view, an epistemologically functional kind. That something is a report is not determined simply by its syntax, nor, in fact, by its semantics alone. Reports are those sentences we produce as actualizations of our linguistic reliable differential responsive dispositions, those declarative sentences descriptive of ourselves or our environment that are "wrung" from us by the world, and provide the de facto beginning points of our inferential activity. They are noninferential descriptive or declarative responses to the world that, once one has learned one's language properly, tend to be true in standard conditions. It is, of course, important to a report that it be truth-evaluable, for it is its tendency to be true when evoked in standard conditions that gives reports their epistemic efficacy, their ability to support other claims.

Sellars uses the neutral vocabulary of reports in the early parts of EPM, rather than talking about observation beliefs, because he has not yet revealed his analysis of mentalistic language, which is the topic of the later parts of EPM, and he does not want to appear to beg questions for or against Cartesians by employing such mentalistic language.

Brandom's interpretation of "looks"-statements is relatively succinct:

The idea is that where collateral beliefs indicate that systematic error is likely, the subject learns not to make the report 'x is ϕ', to which his previously inculcated responsive dispositions incline him, but to make a new kind of claim: '*x looks* (or seems) ϕ'. The cartesian temptation is to take this as a new kind of report. This report then is naturally thought of as reporting a minimal, noninferentially ascertainable, foundationally basic item, an appearing, about which each subject is incorrigible. Sellars's claim is that it is a mistake to treat these as reports at all—since they *evince* a disposition to call something ϕ but do not do so. They do not even *report* the presence of the disposition—that is, they are not ways of *saying* that one has that disposition.

(Brandom, 2-Ply: 356)

Elsewhere, Brandom reaffirms the thesis that looks-statements are not reports:

Since asserting 'X looks ϕ' is not undertaking a propositionally contentful commitment—but only expressing an overrideable disposition to do so—there is no issue as to whether or not that commitment (which one?) is correct.... [T]he incorrigibility of claims about how thing merely *look* simply reflects their emptiness: the fact that they are not really claims at all.

(Brandom, 2-Ply: 357)

The astute reader will have noticed a problem looming for Brandom. In the quotation from p. 356, he asserts that looks-statements are a "new kind of claim," different from observation reports about the properties of physical objects. In the quotation from p. 357, Brandom asserts that looks-statements "are not really claims at all." He cannot have it both ways.

The dialectical situation is slightly complicated by the fact that, whereas Brandom speaks of the subject's *use of expressions* of the form "looks-N," Sellars speaks of the *experiences* and the common *propositional content* they involve, including experiences that it is appropriate to characterize by reference to "looking-N." Nevertheless, it seems fairly obvious to us that Brandom goes too far in asserting that 'X looks ϕ' does not undertake a propositionally contentful commitment, that it does not even make a claim. His assertion near enough contradicts Sellars's own claim that:

The propositional content of these three experiences is, of course, but a part of that to which we are logically committed by characterizing them as situations of these three kinds.... [as a seeing that x over there, is red, its looking to one as though x over there were red,.... etc]

(EPM §22, in SPR: 151; in KMG: 230–1; in B: 50)

Good reasons can be provided for taking the relevant "looks" claims to be reports. For one thing, 'X looks ϕ' is truth-evaluable. There may not be many cases where people give it an apparently *reporting use* and it is false, but it is clearly a statement that is capable of both truth and falsity. Suppose a student of perceptual psychology misdescribes the conditions for one of the classical perceptual illusions, "Under conditions $C_1 ... C_n$, x looks ϕ". What the student says is false; it is equivalent to a conditional "If $C_1 ... C_n$, then x looks ϕ" which is false because when the antecedent is true, the consequent is false. Such occurrence inside a conditional is not a *reporting use* of the sentence, but it surely shows that such sentences do make claims or propositionally contentful commitments.[2] We also utilize appearance statements in our reasonings, such as: 'it looks scarlet, therefore it looks red', or in more sophisticated reasonings: "That alley looks dangerous (or too narrow), you'd better not go that way." If looks-statements made no claims at all, such sequences would be unintelligible, or, at least, we couldn't see them as *reasonings*. Nor could they be germanely responded to by saying, e.g., "No, I've been this way many times before, there's no problem." Denying that appearance statements are claims makes hash out of their role in our mental life.

But if it is clear that looks-statements are claims, then it seems to follow that they are claims about something. And what is it that a looks-statement makes a claim about? As Brandom points out on p. 356, looks-statements are clearly not reports of or claims about dispositions that we have. But since Brandom does not seem to notice that looks-claims are at a different level than is-claims, it may be that Brandom makes the mistake of denying that such statements

---

[2] As Sellars notes, there is a difference between an experience where a physical object looks red, and where it looks green and streaky (EPM §21, in SPR: 149; in KMG: 228; in B: 47).

are claims because he is worried that if they are claims, then the Cartesians may be right: They might be understood as claims about special kinds of objects, appearances, which are subjective, mind-dependent entities to which we have special access and on knowledge of which all our other knowledge depends.

But if this is Brandom's worry here, then it is a pity he did not pay closer attention to Sellars's text. For Sellars is clear about the fact that looks-statements are not only claims capable of truth and falsehood, but claims that can and often do have a *reporting role*. What are the claims about and what do they report?

> [W]hen I say 'X looks green to me now' I am *reporting* the fact that my experience is, so to speak, intrinsically, *as an experience*, indistinguishable from a veridical one of seeing that x is green.

> (EPM §16 *bis*, in SPR: 145; in KMG: 224; in B: 41)

Seeing-claims and looks-claims can both be used to report the nature of an experience, and they do so by stating what the propositional content of that experience is and *also* indicating the endorsement status accorded to it. The Cartesian often falls into the trap of thinking that, since in true appearance statements there need be no physical object that is being reported on, there must be some other kind of object, an appearance, that is being reported on. By putting appearance statements on the same level as seeing-statements, Sellars makes it clear that the object of the report in both cases is an experience—a funny enough object in its own right, some might complain, but something far easier to begin to get a firm conceptual grasp of than reified appearances in themselves, and which Sellars makes substantial progress towards conceptualizing in the later parts of EPM.

And a mere moment's reflection should be enough to convince one that looks-statements are often given a reporting use by competent language users. That is, they can be declarative claims about the world, noninferentially produced in us as an actualization of a reliable differential responsive disposition that tends to produce truths in well-trained language users. The reliable differential responsive disposition in such a case is essentially more complex than in the case of an observation report such as "the ball is red" because it is a response that mobilizes not just concepts of *ball* and *red*, but the concept of *experience*. It is that added complexity, once again, that accounts for the conceptual priority of being over appearing.

This is why we claim that, for Sellars, the right way to resist the Cartesian approach to experiences is to make two moves. First, we should note that the framework of experiences lacks conceptual autonomy. That is, statements or beliefs concerning our experiences presuppose that we command the physical object language, and cannot be used independently of the physical object language. This explains why perceptual reports such as "There is a red ball over there" do not show up on Sellars's list of experiential reports. Since experiential reports characterize experiences in terms of their contents, it is then easy to see that different experiential reports are distinguished by the level of endorsement of that content.

Secondly, in order to be fully resistant to Cartesian impulses, we need to properly understand the structure of perceptual experiences and the way that the propositional components they contain are directed on to the physical world. This understanding also shows us the kernel of insight in the Cartesian view. Situating it properly in a naturalistic theory, however, deprives it of its power to mislead us. The experiences that constitute our observations have a descriptive content in addition to the propositional claims they contain. They contain inner sensory states. As Sellars argues in Part XVI of EPM, we can learn to make reports of such inner sensory states when we take up a reflective attitude towards our own experiences. But this is not the normal perceptual attitude. In ordinary observation, our own sensory states are not the objects of our perceptual thoughts. Rather, they cause the noninferential perceptual takings that are directed onto the physical objects in our surroundings. So in the order of knowing, we don't begin with knowledge of our inner states (as Sellars points out in various places, e.g., SRI, in PP p. 357). In addition, whether we characterize such inner states indirectly, by reference to the physical situation in which they arise (EPM, §22, in SPR: 152; in KMG: 231; in B: 51), or directly, through characterizations of their intrinsic nature, such characterizations presuppose concepts that apply to physical objects (EPM §61 (4), in SPR: 193; in KMG: 273; in B: 113). Separating the sensory component of experience from its intentional/epistemic component prevents the "mongrel ... crossbreeding" of these two elements that besets Cartesianism. Properly understood, the sensory aspect of experience, as Sellars notes, is robbed of its 'traditional epistemological force' (EPM, §21, in SPR: 149; in KMG 228; in B: 47). The points that Sellars is arguing for in his analysis of "looks" statements should be viewed in this context.

Brandom, in stressing the "two-ply" nature of observational reports as he does, presents a misleading picture of Sellars's views on observation as a whole. He implies that the two capacities, the possession of RDRDs, and the capacity to make the appropriate kinds of commitments, exhaust the relevant dimensions of perceptual awareness (p. 365). But for Sellars there is an important further dimension—the sensory component that distinguishes an experience of the world from a mere thought about the world. To a large extent, this sensory aspect of experience is also orthogonal to the first two, in much the same sense that they are to each other, as Brandom notes in this passage. The sensory component is, nevertheless, an essential dimension of observation. When we characterize our observation reports, whether we endorse them by using 'see', or withhold commitment using 'looks', we are alluding to the fact that our reports are prompted by an experience that contains both a propositional content, and also a descriptive content.

4. Conclusion

Because Brandom does not see that appearance statements belong on the same level with seeing-statements, and not on the same level as elementary, non-complex attributions of properties to objects, his interpretation can make Sellars's view seem incoherent. Do appearance statements make claims or not? When we say how things look, aren't we reporting *something*? These are problems that arise only from Brandom's faulty interpretation of Sellars's sophisticated analysis of appearance statements.

Sellars's treatment of perception, of the appearance/reality distinction, and of the nature of experience is complex, sophisticated, and (unfortunately) not always clearly elucidated in his writings. That such a significant and astute philosopher as Brandom (operating in Sellars's home territory, no less), can get Sellars wrong on such a basic and important matter is a warning to us all to read Sellars with extreme care.

References

Brandom, Robert. "The Centrality of Sellars's Two-Ply Account of Observation to the Arguments of 'Empiricism and the Philosophy of Mind' " in *Tales of the Mighty Dead: Historical Essays in the Metaphysics of Intentionality* (Cambridge, MA: Harvard University Press, 2002): 348–67.

deVries, Willem, and Triplett, Timm. *Knowledge, Mind, and the Given: Reading Wilfrid Sellars's "Empiricism and the Philosophy of Mind"* (Indianapolis/Cambridge, MA: Hackett Publishing, 2000). Cited as KMG.

Sellars, Wilfrid. "Empiricism and the Philosophy of Mind" (Presented at the University of London in Special Lectures in Philosophy for 1956 under the title "The Myth of the Given: Three Lectures on Empiricism and the Philosophy of Mind"), in *Minnesota Studies in the Philosophy of Science*, vol. I, eds. Herbert Feigl and Michael Scriven (Minneapolis: University of Minnesota Press, 1956): 253–329. Reprinted in SPR with additional footnotes. Published separately as *Empiricism and the Philosophy of Mind: with an Introduction by Richard Rorty and a Study Guide by Robert Brandom*, ed. Robert Brandom (Cambridge, MA: Harvard University Press, 1997). (Cited as B) Also reprinted in W. deVries and T. Triplett, *Knowledge, Mind, and the Given: A Reading of Sellars' "Empiricism and the Philosophy of Mind"* (Cambridge, MA: Hackett Publishing, 2000). Cited as EPM, page references to SPR, KMG, and B editions.

—— *Science, Perception and Reality* (London: Routledge & Kegan Paul, 1963). Re-issued by Ridgeview Publishing Company in 1991. Cited as SPR.

—— "Scientific Realism or Irenic Instrumentalism: A Critique of Nagel and Feyerabend on Theoretical Explanation" in *Boston Studies in the Philosophy of Science*, vol. 11, eds. Robert Cohen and Max Wartofsky (New York: Humanities Press, 1965): 171–204. Reprinted in PP. Cited as SRI.

—— *Philosophical Perspectives* (Springfield, IL: Charles C. Thomas, 1967). Cited as PP.

6

The Tortoise and the Serpent: Sellars on the Structure of Empirical Knowledge

Michael Williams

1. Two Pictures of Knowing

At the conclusion of the pivotal section VIII of EPM ("Does Empirical Knowledge Have a Foundation?"), Sellars writes:

> *Above all*, the picture [i.e. of knowledge as resting on a foundation] is misleading because of its static character. One seems forced to choose between the picture of an elephant which rests on a tortoise (What supports the tortoise?) and the picture of a great Hegelian serpent of knowledge with its tail in its mouth (Where does it begin?). Neither will do. For empirical knowledge, like its sophisticated extension, science, is rational, not because it has a *foundation* but because it is a self-correcting enterprise which can put *any* claim in jeopardy, though not *all* at once.
>
> (EPM §38, in SPR: 170; in KMG: 250;
> in B: 78–9, emphasis in original)[1]

The elephant-and-tortoise picture is the generic conception informing foundationalist theories of knowledge (or justification),

[1] Wilfrid Sellars, "Empiricism and the Philosophy of Mind". In *Minnesota Studies in the Philosophy of Science*, vol. 1, eds. Herbert Feigl and Michael Scriven (Minneapolis: University of Minnesota Press, 1956). Reprinted in Sellars, *Science, Perception and Reality* (London and New York, Routledge & Kegan Paul/Humanities Press 1963). A more readily available version is Sellars, *Empiricism and the Philosophy of Mind: with an Introduction by Richard Rorty*

as the tail-in-mouth-serpent picture is that informing coherence theories. At least, this is a natural first reading. So Sellars seems to be saying that although the choice between foundationalism and coherentism seems forced, it is one that we can and should avoid.

How is this to be accomplished? This question is not easily answered, in large part because Sellars's attitude towards the coherence theory is not readily discerned. In EPM, Sellars is concerned almost exclusively with debunking the empiricist version of tortoise theory, with the result that he has little explicit to say about either what he takes the coherence theory to be, much less why he repudiates it. More puzzling still, aspects of Sellars's own epistemological outlook can easily suggest that he endorses a kind of coherentism.[2]

To get a handle on Sellars's strategy, we have to look beyond the sketchy treatment of the question in EPM. When we do this, we find that Sellars's strategy is not at all what some influential interpreters of EPM have taken it to be. Sellars's answer is more complex than seems generally to be appreciated. Indeed, as we shall see, it is something of an exaggeration to say that Sellars offers a full answer to the question of how to avoid the fateful choice. It would be better to say that Sellars provides materials for an answer, though he does not himself put them together as systematically as we might wish. But Sellars's answer is also more problematic than the simpler accounts of it allow. As I shall argue, Sellars's account of the structure of epistemic justification is tailored to fit his *radical fallibilism*. By Sellars's radical fallibilism I mean his conviction that even the most deeply entrenched commonsense convictions are

---

and a Study Guide by Robert Brandom (Cambridge, MA: Harvard University Press, 1997). Brandom's edition follows the 1956 version and lacks some footnotes added in 1963. It is also reprinted in the commentary *Knowledge, Mind, and the Given: Reading Wilfrid Sellars's "Empiricism and the Philosophy of Mind"* (Indianapolis, IN: Hackett Publishing, 2000). References to Sellars's essay given in the text by "EPM," section numbers, and page numbers to these editions, marked "SPR," "KMG," and "B."

[2] Laurence Bonjour incorporates Sellars's account of observational knowledge into his version of the coherence theory. Bonjour, *The Structure of Empirical Knowledge* (Cambridge, MA: Harvard University Press, 1985), ch. 6.

open to revision, a view that puts Sellars at odds with some of his warmest admirers, but which is of a piece with his rejection of the Myth of the Given in its most general form.

2. Foundations, Coherence, and the Myth of the Given

Why does it seem that we are forced to choose between the tortoise and the serpent? And what are we being invited to choose between? I suggested that, on a natural reading, the choice is between foundationalism and the coherence theory. This is not the only way to understand Sellars, but it is a good place to start.

The need to choose between foundationalism and the coherence theory arises from a familiar line of thought. Knowing, the argument goes, implies being justified (having beliefs with authority or warrant). But where does this warrant come from? In virtue of what sorts of warranting property can a (true) belief count as knowledge? Some beliefs are warranted inferentially: i.e., through being supported (deductively or inductively) by other beliefs. But surely these beliefs must themselves be warranted. Are they also warranted inferentially? If we answer "Yes", we are in danger of opening a vicious infinite regress. But how is it to be blocked? If the regress of reasons comes to an end with beliefs for which no reasons can be given, we seem to be saying that the regress is blocked by assumptions, which cannot be a source of warrant. Alternatively, we might find that in following the train of reasons, we recur to commitments that have already come up, in which case our supposed relations of support will go round in a circle. These options seem exhaustive: either we have to find reasons for reasons for reasons, and so on without end; or we just call a halt to reason-giving; or we come back to some reason already given. But in no case do we find genuine warrant. This trilemma—Agrippa's Trilemma—is one of the oldest and deepest skeptical problems. If we wish to avoid skepticism and agree that the regress of reasons is vicious, then we must put a better face on one or other of the remaining options. Perhaps we can call a halt to the regress without simply making an assumption: this is the foundationalist strategy. Or perhaps the complex relations of mutual support, in virtue of which our beliefs form a system, should be distinguished from simple circularity. This is the line pursued by the coherence theory.

According to foundationalism, epistemic warrant finds its original source in "basic beliefs" or "terminating judgments," which are warranted *non-inferentially*. And if there is to be empirical knowledge, most foundationalists have held, at least some basic beliefs must have to do with observation or experience. Because basic beliefs *confer* warrant on other beliefs, without receiving it from them, they are *epistemologically prior* to all further beliefs. They are the tortoise, or perhaps the elephant. By contrast, the coherence theory denies the need for a tortoise: our beliefs are justified, not because they rest on a privileged stratum of basic beliefs, but because they *form a system* in which they give each other *mutual* support. To invoke somewhat friendlier metaphors than Sellars's tortoise and serpent, where foundationalists postulate an *architecture* of knowledge, coherentists see an *ecology*, in which beliefs occupy different niches. By playing different functional roles (depending on their inferential relations to other beliefs), our beliefs work cooperatively to keep the system together (and perhaps moving along).

Now, many philosophers have held that the foundationalist and coherentist options are exclusive and exhaustive. But both options face serious—perhaps insuperable—problems. Since basic beliefs are supposed to provide absolute terminating points for chains of justification, foundationalists must explain the authority of basic beliefs in a way that does not make that authority covertly inferential. So, for example, they cannot trace the credibility of basic beliefs to their being formed and retained in a reliable way, for that would make their credibility depend on a reliability presupposition. As Sellars himself stresses, reconciling the ultimacy of basic beliefs with their authority is no easy task. On the other hand, coherentists must explain how mere belief–belief relations—mutual inferential support—generate genuine justification. To be sure, logical and other inferential relations between beliefs can pass justification around: but how does warrant *get into the system in the first place?*

Commonsensically, the foundationalist idea that some beliefs are inferentially warranted beliefs because others are warranted non-inferentially is very plausible. Not only are there things that we just know, observation seems to be a source of such non-inferential knowing. But this commonsensical point does not settle the issue of whether there are basic beliefs, as foundationalists conceive them. Granted, I wouldn't ordinarily be said to *infer* that there is a computer screen in front of my face, as I write these words, when I can *see* that there is. Nevertheless, in taking myself to be capable of such (apparently) non-inferential knowledge, am I not treating perception as a *generic source* of epistemic authority? And in so treating it, am I not presupposing that it is a *reliable* source: i.e., that beliefs deriving from it are *likely to be true?* A coherentist will insist that I am, which is why ordinary "non-inferential" knowledge is not *basic* in the foundationalist's sense. But now a new danger arises. This reliability-commitment, or *meta-justificatory principle* concerning perception, appears to state a general empirical fact. Won't it therefore require observational support? If so, it seems to follow that, if we hold that particular observational judgments derive their authority from such a meta-justificatory principle, we are involved in a blatant form of *epistemic circularity.* We seem forced to choose between unacceptable alternatives, just as Sellars says.

How might the choice be avoided? Presumably, we would have to argue that the familiar line of thought just rehearsed is less innocent than it is often made to appear. Perhaps the skeptic, the foundationalist and the coherentist share some unacknowledged presupposition which, once brought to light, can be seen to be optional or even misguided. If that is so, we may be able to reject the Agrippan problem altogether.

It seems clear that Sellars has something of the sort in mind. However, some readers of Sellars would argue that I am not well placed to identify the presuppositions that Sellars intends to reject because the familiar line of thought I have been exploring does not capture, in a sufficiently precise way, Sellars's sense of what is at issue. It is notable that Sellars does not address the skeptical problem directly, and there is a reason for this. Sellars thinks that skeptical problems—indeed epistemological problems generally—have their roots in a deeply misguided philosophy of language and mind. So the way to get around skepticism is not to confront the skeptic on his own terrain—the terrain of epistemology—but to shift the focus of inquiry to the skeptic's own extra-epistemological presuppositions.[3] (This is why Sellars's essay is not called "Empiricism and the Theory of Knowledge.")

Thinking along these lines, John McDowell argues that the dilemma that concerns Sellars is not the usual one between foundationalism and the coherence theory but rather an apparently forced choice between the Myth of the Given and "frictionless" coherentism. In a way, I have no objection to this: I think that "foundationalism" and "the Myth of the Given" are interchangeable. But I suspect that McDowell does not see things quite this way. On McDowell's view, the Myth of the Given *rather than* epistemological foundationalism is the tortoise.

McDowell agrees with Sellars that standard skeptical problems are shallow. The deeper problem concerns how we can so much as entertain a thought about an objective world, whether or not that thought amounts to knowledge. Our thoughts can only be about an objective world, McDowell thinks, if they are subject to some kind of external constraint, which can only be exercised through perception. But if perception only provides us with

---

[3] This is a controversial move, though one that I fully endorse. Skepticism is generally presented as an "intuitive" problem: one that arises out of everyday, average ideas about knowledge and justification. Sellars thinks, rightly, that skepticism is not intuitive at all but an artifact of philosophical theory. In exposing and criticizing the skeptic's theoretical presuppositions, Sellars is pursuing that strategy that I call "theoretical diagnosis." See my *Unnatural Doubts* (Oxford: Blackwell, 1992; Princeton, NJ: Princeton University Press, 1996), ch. 1.

further beliefs, and if our thoughts and beliefs are answerable only to other thoughts and beliefs, our "thinking" degenerates into a self-contained game with no relevance to external reality. This tempts us to look for some kind of constraint on thinking from outside what McDowell, following Sellars, calls "the space of reasons." We become tempted to suppose that our thinking is answerable to bare—that is unconceptualized—sensory presences. This is the Myth of the Given. Of course, it is hard to live with the Myth: how can non-conceptual awareness provide *reasons* for beliefs? Surely, we think, only beliefs can do that, and so we drift back to coherentism. Since we can't live with either coherentism or the Myth, we oscillate between them.[4] In repudiating the choice between the tortoise and the serpent, Sellars aims to stop this oscillation.

I am not saying that any of this is wrong in itself. However, I think that McDowell takes too narrow a view of what Sellars understands the Myth of the Given to encompass.

A problem confronting us here is that Sellars never gives a general account of the Myth, which makes McDowell's account (or anyone else's) difficult to assess. However, in EPM, Sellars does give a list of instances of the Myth; and the examples on the list suggest that McDowell's account of the Myth is overly specific. Thus:

Many things have been said to be 'given': sense contents, material objects, universals, propositions, real connections, first principles, even givenness itself.

(EPM §1, in SPR: 127; in KMG: 205; in B: 14)

Sellars thinks that few philosophers, if any, have been entirely untouched by the Myth, "not even Hegel, that great foe of 'immediacy'" (ibid.). According to Sellars, many philosophers

---

[4] John McDowell, *Mind and World* (Cambridge, MA: Harvard University Press, 1994), Lecture 1. McDowell's reading of Sellars differs on a number of important points from my own. For discussion of McDowell's reading, see my "Science and Sensibility: Sellars and McDowell on Perceptual Knowledge," *European Journal of Philosophy*, 14 (August 2006): 302–25.

who take themselves to be attacking the Myth itself are really only attacking particular forms, such as "intuited first principles" or sense-data (ibid.). By Sellars's standards, McDowell is such a philosopher. For McDowell, the Myth of the Given is the mirage of non-conceptual awareness, which, while perhaps the principle target in EPM, cannot constitute the Myth in its general form. Whatever one thinks of propositions or intuited first principles, they are not non-conceptual. Nevertheless, they have been said to be given. Indeed, not only does McDowell attack a particular version of the Myth—the form that the Myth characteristically takes on in the context of *empiricist* foundationalism—rather than the Myth as such, I suspect that Sellars would count McDowell himself as subscribing to a widely accepted version of the Myth. But more of this in due course.

So what is the Myth in its general form? The answer is: epistemological foundationalism in *its* general form. The foundationalist thinks that there are things we know that are *absolutely* noninferential and therefore *intrinsically* authoritative. As intrinsically authoritative, they constitute a permanent framework within which all inquiry must take place. As providing the framework for inquiry, they are themselves argumentatively untouchable, thus unrevisable. But as we already know, Sellars thinks that *any* claim can be put in jeopardy, just not all claims at once. But in adopting radical fallibilism, Sellars is not just thinking of particular claims but of entire ways of thinking: entire conceptual schemes.

Generically, then, the tortoise and the serpent stand for the choice between foundationalism and the coherence theory, as I initially claimed. At the most general level, this is the choice between accepting that there are permanent elements of thought and lapsing into self-sealing or frictionless coherentism, which recognizes no constraint at all. Granted, in EPM, Sellars is mainly concerned with a particular species of tortoise. But his aim is to avoid tortoises altogether, and to do so without getting swallowed by the serpent. The question is whether he pulls this off, and if so how.

3. Empiricism and the Myth

As a way into why Sellars is unhappy with the empiricist's tortoise, let us look more closely at the idea of a basic belief. There are two points to bear in mind. First, the claim that basic beliefs are 'non-inferential' makes an *epistemological* and not merely a *psychological* point. A belief is not 'non-inferential' merely in virtue of being spontaneous. The foundationalist demands beliefs that possess *primitive warrant*. Second, the foundationalist does not want merely to *give a list* of basic beliefs but to *identify a type*: traditionally, by reference to what basic beliefs are about. Thus traditional foundationalism is committed to the *content theory of epistemic status*:

(CTE) Beliefs are basic (or not) in virtue of their semantic content, what they are about.

For empiricists, beliefs about the contents of experience—how one is appeared to—have often been taken to fill the bill.

With these points in mind, we can turn to Sellars's subtle account of what empiricist foundationalism involves. According to Sellars:

One of the forms taken by the Myth of the Given is the idea that there is, indeed *must be*, a structure of particular matter of fact such that (*a*) each fact can not only be non-inferentially known to be the case, but presupposes no other knowledge of particular matter of fact, or of general truths; and (*b*) such that the non-inferential knowledge of facts belonging to this structure constitutes the ultimate court of appeal for all factual claims—particular and general—about the world.

(EPM §32, in SPR: 164; in KMG: 243; in B: 68–9)[5]

In this crucial passage, Sellars identifies two empiricist commitments. The first asserts the absolute epistemic priority of

---

[5] The reference to "one of the forms taken by the Myth" does not compromise my claim that the generic Myth is foundationalism. Sellars is simply pointing out that empiricist foundationalism is a foundationalism of *particular* facts (as opposed, say, to intuited first principles).

observational (or perhaps experiential) knowledge. Call this the *Priority Thesis*:

> **(Pr)**. Non-inferential observational knowledge is the ultimate source of warrant for all other beliefs.

Traditional foundationalists think that the Priority Thesis commits them to an atomistic conception of basic knowledge: basic beliefs, as intrinsically credible, must not be beholden to *any* collateral commitments. Call this the *Encapsulation Thesis*:

> **(E)**. Epistemologically ultimate knowledge must be encapsulated, i.e., logically independent of any further knowledge.

The Encapsulation Thesis is empiricism's Achilles heel.

Why do empiricists suppose that **Pr** entails E? Well, perhaps it just seems obvious that basic observational knowledge must be encapsulated. But if it does, it shouldn't. Sellars continues:

> It is important to note that I characterized the knowledge of fact belonging to this stratum as not only non-inferential but as presupposing no knowledge of other matter of fact. It might be thought that this is a redundancy, that knowledge (not belief or conviction but knowledge) which logically presupposes knowledge of other facts *must* be inferential. This, however, as I hope to show, is an episode in the Myth.
>
> (EPM §32, in SPR: 164; in KMG: 243–4; in B: 69)

Here, Sellars traces the inference from **Pr** to E to an assumption that he means to deny, the *Independence Requirement*:

> **(I)**. A person's knowing that P cannot be non-inferential if his knowing (or having a warranted belief) that P logically presupposes his having other knowledge (or warranted belief).

Commitment to **I** is what leads foundationalists to hold that **Pr** → E. But why commit to **I**? The obvious answer is: *to avoid epistemic circularity*. The foundationalist's thought is that the claim of basic beliefs/judgments to possess *primitive* rather than *derived* warrants would be compromised if such beliefs logically presupposed other warranted beliefs.

At first glance, I may seem obvious, even trivial. But as Sellars sees, I will be false, and the inference from **Pr** to **E** blocked, if not *every* logical presupposition of someone's knowing (or warrantedly believing) something automatically concerns the conferring of warrant. How might this be? Well, perhaps certain presuppositions go with holding a given belief *at all*, with or without warrant.

That Sellars has something along these lines in mind is suggested by the penultimate paragraph of section VIII of EPM. He writes:

> If I reject the framework of traditional empiricism, it is not because I want to say that empirical knowledge has *no* foundation. For to put it this way is to suggest that it is really 'empirical knowledge so-called', and to put it in a box with rumours and hoaxes. There is clearly *some* point to the picture of human knowledge as resting on a level of propositions—observation reports—which do not rest on other propositions in the same way that other propositions rest on them. On the other hand, I do want to suggest that the metaphor of 'foundation' is misleading in that it keeps us from seeing that if there is a logical dimension in which other empirical propositions rest on observation reports, there is another logical dimension in which the latter rest on the former.
>
> (EPM §38, in SPR: 170; in KMG: 250; in B: 78)

Here Sellars exploits just the kind of distinction that his isolation of the Independence Requirement points towards. There are, he suggests, two "logical dimensions" in which propositions can depend on other propositions. So while observation reports come first in one dimension—that of epistemic priority—they carry logical presuppositions in the other. There is no epistemic circularity so long as the dimensions are distinct: in particular, so long as one of them is not directly involved in warranting.

What are the two dimensions? Since Sellars is a *semantic holist*, a natural thought is that he is arguing that the *semantic interdependence* of basic and non-basic knowledge is compatible with the priority of observation. This is Robert Brandom's view. Brandom writes:

> The only sense in which there is no foundation for empirical knowledge is the sense in which the observation reports, which in a certain sense are its foundation, themselves rest (not inferentially, but in the order of *understanding* and sometimes of justification) on other sorts of knowledge. Observation reports … do not constitute an autonomous stratum of the language—a game one could master though one had as yet not mastered the inferential use of any expressions.

> (Brandom, Study Guide: 162)

Even to be a potential observer, a subject must be capable of making (verbal) judgments (with semantic content), as opposed having mere reactive (vocal) dispositions. How different kinds of statements/beliefs are warranted is a further matter. We have our two dimensions. Or do we?

4. Semantic Holism and the Myth

Sellars says many things that seem to support the reading just suggested. In the sections of EPM leading up to the pivotal section VIII, Sellars's criticisms of traditional empiricism repeatedly involve semantic themes. Here are three examples.

First, against philosophers who think that the foundations of knowledge rest on knowledge of "appearances", Sellars argues that talk of an object's *looking* green is parasitic on talk of its *being* green; and from this point he moves quickly to at least a qualified form of semantic holism. Thus:

> [T]he ability to recognize that x looks green presupposes the concept of *being green*…. [T]his in turn involves knowing in what circumstances to view an object to ascertain its colour…. One can have the concept of green only by having a whole battery of concepts of which it is one element….

> (EPM §19, in SPR: 147–8; in KMG: 226; in B: 43)

Notice especially that to have the *concept* of something's being green one must know about the proper conditions for viewing it. On this view, there is no mastery of observational concepts without background knowledge of the world and our ways of knowing about it. The Encapsulation Thesis must be false *for semantic reasons.*

Second, a recurrent motif of EPM is that empiricists set the foundations of knowledge at the wrong level: that of "appearances" or "impressions" or "sense-data." The source of this error is a failure to distinguish between the *conceptual* episode of seeing that something appears red and the *non-conceptual* episode of having a sensation of redness. Since the capacity to have sensations is one that we share with babies and animals, empiricists come to suppose that we have a primitive, pre-linguistic ability to know redness when we see it. For example:

... Locke, Berkeley and Hume ... all take for granted that the human mind has an innate ability to be aware of certain determinate sorts—*indeed, that we are aware of them simply by virtue of having sensations and images.*

(EPM §28, in SPR: 160; in KMG: 239; in B: 62)

Sellars resists this thought by invoking "psychological nominalism," according to which there is no "awareness of logical space prior to, or independent of, the acquisition of a language" (EPM §31, in SPR: 162; in KMG: 241; in B: 66). Again, empiricist *epistemology* is found wanting for *semantic* reasons.

Third, Sellars warns us that we will not escape the Myth of the Given *merely* by moving the foundations of knowledge from the level of appearances to that of reports on how perceptible objects really are. In particular, we will not do so if we think that the meaning of a basic descriptive term is fixed or grasped *ostensively*, by exposure to examples. To make this supposition is to imagine that "the process of teaching a child to use language is that of teaching it to discriminate elements within a logical space of particulars, universals, facts, etc., of which it is already undiscriminatingly aware" (EPM §30, in SPR: 161–2; in KMG: 241; in B: 65). To suppose this is to fall in, once again, with the idea of prelinguistic quasi-conceptual awareness already found in Locke, Berkeley, and Hume. Rejecting this idea, Sellars (like Wittgenstein) insists on a sharp distinction between ostensive *learning* and linguistic *training*. But even accepting this distinction, we will still go badly wrong if we accede to

[the] temptation to assume that the word 'red' means the quality of *red* by virtue of these two facts: briefly, the fact that it has the *syntax* of a predicate, and the fact that it is a response (in certain circumstances) to red objects.

(EPM §31, in SPR: 162; in KMG: 242; in B: 66)

While such responsive habits can, indeed must, be acquired piece-meal, for this very reason they must not be confused with mastery of concepts. It follows that a behaviorist version of empiricism fares no better than its classical predecessor. I shall return to this claim. For now, the point is that, once more, Sellars's arguments against empiricist epistemology turn on semantic considerations.

A similar strategy is on display in the explicit anti-foundationalist argument of section VIII of EPM. As we would expect, Sellars finds that the central challenge for foundationalism is to make plausible the idea of a stratum of belief that is epistemologically basic, or as he says "ultimate," and nevertheless authoritative. How can knowledge be non-nonferential and yet be *knowledge*? How can it be *ultimate* and yet have *authority*? How can basic observation reports be intrinsically *credible*? The traditional response to these questions, Sellars thinks, turns on an account of the meanings of the terms employed in reporting observations. The fundamental idea is that, "whereas ordinary empirical statements can be correctly made without being true, observation reports resemble analytic statements in that being correctly made is a sufficient as well as a necessary condition of their truth"; and further, "that 'correctly making' the report 'this is green' is a matter of 'following the rules' for 'this', 'is' and 'green' " (EPM §33, in SPR: 166; in KMG: 245; in B: 72). Presumably, the rules in question are something like this:

> Rule for 'this'. Say/think 'this' while focusing attention on an object in/region of one's visual field.
>
> Rule for 'green'. Say/think 'is green' if and only if the object to which one is attending is/appears visibly green.

If these rules are followed, one cannot make a false report. Nevertheless, in making an observation report, one records a *contingent* fact.

Sellars makes three comments. Although in ordinary usage a report is made *by* someone *to* someone, an observation report, in the technical sense, is the mere registering (by an observer) of a fact. Nevertheless, the technical idea of an observation report retains the idea that making a report is an action: something one *does* (voluntarily, on purpose). So while in Sellars's view not all correctness is the correctness of actions—a matter of what one ought to *do*—the empiricist's account of the rules governing the correctness of observation-reports is definitely of the "ought-to-do" variety. It follows, and this is the third comment, that the rules for making reports are to be followed knowingly: one does not say or think "green" as a *trained response* to the *presence* of something green; rather one does so *deliberately* on the basis of one's *awareness* of being in the presence of a green thing. As Sellars says, this account of the intrinsic credibility of observation reports brings us "face to face with givenness in its most straightforward form" (EPM §34, in SPR: 167; in KMG: 246; in B: 73). The proposed semantics of basic observation reports traces their authority to

nonverbal episodes of awareness—awareness that something is the case, e.g. that *this is green*—which nonverbal episodes have an intrinsic authority…which the *verbal* performances…properly performed 'express'. One is committed to a stratum of authoritative nonverbal episodes ('awareness'), the authority of which accrues to a superstructure of *verbal actions*, provided that the expressions occurring in these actions are properly *used*. These self-authenticating episodes would constitute the tortoise on which stands the elephant on which rests the edifice of empirical knowledge. The essence of the view is the same whether these intrinsically authoritative episodes are such items as the awareness that a certain sense content is green or such items as the awareness that a certain physical object looks to oneself to be green.

(EPM §34, in SPR: 167; in KMG: 246–7; in B: 73)

Sellars adds no criticism of this appeal to the Given, which involves the very ideas he has already rejected in the arguments scouted above.

This diagnosis of how empiricism is led to its peculiar version of the Myth seems to complete the case for the view that Sellars's intention is to rescue non-inferential observational knowledge from its association with epistemic atomism by arguing that the "logical presuppositions" that come with *semantic* holism can be distinguished from a form of dependence that would impugn a claim to *epistemic* priority.

A further advantage of understanding Sellars this way is that it accounts for why he so often seems to be a kind of coherence theorist. Commitment to semantic holism is something that Sellars shares with the traditional coherence theorist. However, traditional coherentists are not just semantic holists: they are epistemic holists too, rejecting the very idea of a class of *epistemically distinguished* propositions. A standard objection to coherentism is that, by virtue of rejecting the priority of observation, it offers no way of distinguishing between genuine empirical knowledge and elaborate fictions. Sellars echoes this thought in his reference to 'rumours and hoaxes'. But having distinguished the two logical dimensions, we can see that semantic holism no more implies epistemic holism than the priority of observation implies encapsulation. We can avoid choosing between the tortoise and the serpent.

5. Epistemic Reflexivity and Epistemic Circularity

Brandom's account of Sellars's strategy cannot simply be *wrong*. Sellars *is* a semantic holist; he *does* deny that observation reports constitute an autonomous stratum of language; and he nevertheless maintains that such reports play a distinguished role in the regulation of our more theoretical commitments. Even so, questions remain. One is philosophical: is drawing the distinction between semantic inter-dependence and epistemic asymmetry *sufficient* to show us the way between the horns of the dilemma? Another is interpretative: is this distinction between semantic and epistemic—the order of understanding and the order of knowing—what Sellars had in mind in calling attention to the two dimensions of logical dependence? The answer to both questions is "No."

There is a further complication. Although Sellars wants to retain the empiricist idea that observation reports have some kind of epistemic privilege, he seems not to be just a semantic holist but *some* kind of epistemic holist too. Recall the general form of the Myth of the Given: that certain commitments, as constituting the framework of inquiry, are themselves unrevisable. In rejecting the Myth, Sellars claims that anything can be revised, if revising it promotes an increase in the explanatory coherence of our worldview. Indeed, far from erecting a firewall between his semantic holism and his epistemic holism, Sellars thinks that the two are intimately connected. This is because Sellars thinks that scientific progress typically involves *conceptual innovation*, rather than the piling up of results couched in terms of a fixed vocabulary. To be sure, in science we aim at the formulation of laws of nature ("nomologicals"), which are accepted or rejected on empirical grounds: this is why observation reports are so important. However, we should not think of empirical justification in terms of the

foundationalist myth of an unchanging "observation language."
On the contrary,

> ... instead of justifying nomologicals by an appeal to observation statements
> the predicates of which would have conceptual meaning independently
> of any commitment to laws, the problem is rather that of deciding
> *which* conceptual meaning our observation is to have, our aim being to
> manipulate the three basic components of a world-picture: (a) observed
> objects and events, (b) unobserved objects and events, and (c) nomological
> connections, so as to achieve a world-picture with a maximum of
> 'explanatory coherence'.[6]

While providing for epistemic constraint, an account of observation
reporting must allow for changes in conceptual meaning even at
the level of the most basic observational predicates. This looks like
epistemic holism defended on semantic grounds.

There is a more specific difficulty to be faced. Distinguishing
between semantic and epistemic dependence will address the
problem of epistemic circularity only if semantic and epistemic
considerations can be kept neatly separate, and Sellars's account of
observation statements suggests that they can't.

To appreciate the problem, we must take note of a further constraint that Sellars imposes on an account of observation reporting.
We know that avoiding serpent theory means avoiding epistemic
circularity. However, in the case of observation reports, the problem of epistemic circularity arises only if we are committed to what
Willem deVries calls *Epistemic Reflexivity*[7]:

> (ER) For a person to have knowledge of some particular fact,
> via the exercise of some cognitive faculty or capacity,
> C, the person must know that C is a reliable source of
> information.

---

[6] Wilfrid Sellars, "Some Reflections on Language Games," in SPR. Also in *In the Space of Reasons*, eds. Kevin Scharp and Robert Brandom (Cambridge, MA: Harvard University Press, 2007). Subsequent references to this volume given by "ISR." Quotation p. 356/54.

[7] Willem deVries, *Wilfrid Sellars* (Chesham: Acumen, 2005). See pp. 111–12.

If observation reports derive their authority from knowledge of our reliability as observers, and if this reliability knowledge is justified by particular observational evidence, we seem to be forced into the mutual-support structure of justification postulated by the coherence theory. Since Sellars is committed to epistemic reflexivity, but wants to avoid embracing the serpent, he needs to argue that this is not so.

Some interpreters think that Sellars goes wrong in insisting on epistemic reflexivity in such an unqualified way.[8] However, Sellars's commitment to ER runs deep, for it can be seen as a consequence of what McDowell calls Sellars's "master-thought":

... in characterizing an episode or state as that of *knowing*, we are not giving an empirical description of that episode or state; we are placing it in the logical space of reasons, of justifying and being able to justify what one says.

(EPM §36, in SPR: 169; in KMG: 248; in B: 76)[9]

Modern externalists avoid issues of epistemic circularity by saying that mere *de facto* truth-reliability in belief formation is a warranting property. But Sellars pre-emptively dismisses this idea. As mere "empirical description," predicating *de facto* truth-reliability of a reporting capacity is not an *epistemic* characterization at all. For Sellars, reliability considerations get into the logical space of reasons only by being *acknowledged*.

Sellars, then shares with his empiricist opponent the problem of combining the authority of observation statements with some form

---

[8] I am thinking particularly of Brandom. See Brandom, Study Guide: 157–9. In *Mind and World*, McDowell takes Sellars to task for treating impressions as opaque, thus needing to be connected with reality via reliability-knowledge. McDowell says that, on his view, impressions are "transparent," a view which I take to be intended to remove reliability-knowledge from the picture. See *Mind and World*, Afterword, Part I. In his Woodbridge Lectures, McDowell argues that Sellars himself had a view of impressions as transparent. But again, this takes reliability-knowledge out of the picture. See John McDowell, "Having the World in View," *Journal of Philosophy*, 95: 9 (September 1998): 431–91. Subsequent references given by "HWV." McDowell's new account of Sellars on impressions is given in Lecture 1.

[9] For McDowell's gloss on the master-thought, see HWV p. 433.

of epistemic priority. Sellars begins by offering a proto-externalist account of that authority. Thus:

An overt or covert token of 'This is green' in the presence of a green item...expresses observational knowledge if and only if it is a manifestation of a tendency to produce overt or covert tokens of 'This is green'—given a certain set—if and only if a green object is being looked at in standard conditions.

(EPM §35, in SPR: 167; in KMG: 247; in B: 73–4)

Linking a term's observational use with its involvement with a trained, reliable reporting disposition is vitally important for Sellars, because it undermines the empiricist's commitment to a permanent observation language geared to a fixed range of proper sensibles. If what we can observe, thus know non-inferentially, is a matter of what we can be trained to report on reliably, the observable/theoretical distinction is empirical and methodological rather than ontological. Sellars thus makes a decisive break with the content theory of epistemic status, one of foundationalism's core commitments. Still, as we have seen, a purely externalist-reliabilist account of observation statements is not open to Sellars. Sellars identifies two hurdles that his account must clear. The first concerns the authority of observation reports. According to Sellars,

...[T]he only thing that can remotely be supposed to constitute such authority is the fact that one can infer the presence of a green object from the fact that someone makes this report.

(EPM §35, in SPR: 167; in KMG: 247; in B: 74)

That is, a reporter is authoritative to the extent that his making a report can be recognized by *others* as symptomatic of the presence of whatever he is reporting on. Authority is a public matter, socially conferred. However, the "decisive" hurdle is that the authority of observation reports must be recognized *by the reporter himself.* Sellars writes:

...[T]o be the expression of knowledge, a report must not only *have* authority, this authority must *in some sense* be recognized by the person whose report it is.... [T]he point is ... that observational knowledge of any particular fact, e.g. that this is green, presupposes that one knows general facts of the form *X is a reliable symptom of Y*.

(EPM §35, in SPR: 168; in KMG: 247; in B: 74)

This is the commitment to epistemic reflexivity demanded by the master-thought. But now the problem stares us in the face. Sellars's endorsement of epistemic reflexivity appears in the context of *explaining the authority* of observation reports. So why doesn't endorsement of epistemic reflexivity lead to epistemic circularity, hence (as traditional empiricists charge) to an unacceptable coherentism? Why hasn't Sellars jumped off the tortoise only to get swallowed by the serpent? Doesn't Sellars acknowledge as much when he takes increased explanatory coherence to be the ultimate warrant for a change in our world-picture?

There are two possible replies. One is that while a person must *acknowledge* his observational reliability, he need not *consult* that knowledge to enter an authoritative observation report. That is to say, to report with authority a person need not *even unconsciously* invoke the "reliability inference":

1. I just spontaneously uttered 'This is green'.
2. Such utterances on my part are reliable symptoms of the presence of green objects.
3. So there is a green object in front of me.

In this way, our observation reports are genuinely non-inferential. The other reply invokes the distinction between learning and justification. Sellars himself calls attention to the apparent threat of a regress. Observation reports, it seems, presuppose prior reliability-knowledge, which rests on yet prior observation reports ... and so on. His reply, in short, is that although we have to *acquire* our world-view as a whole (through training and acculturation), once we have it we can treat our spontaneous observation reports as possessing the special authority that our world-view accords them.

While both points are correct as far as they go, neither disposes of the problem of epistemic circularity. In both cases, the empiricist will say, Sellars only advances a *psychological* claim. However, the issue on the table is not what thought-process we go through in making an observation report, or how our world-picture is acquired, but *the structure of epistemic justification.* If particular observation reports depend for their authority on reliability-commitments, Sellars is stuck with epistemic circularity. In consequence, he is forced to make peace with the serpent, which he does when he stresses the ultimate importance of explanatory coherence. But why does Sellars claim to offer a way of avoiding the choice between tortoise and serpent, if he is really a serpent-theorist all along? Clearly, we have not got to the bottom of this question.

6. The Two Dimensions: Sellars's Later Account

Sellars concedes that his treatment of the authority of non-inferential reporting in EPM is sketchy at best. In "More on Givenness and Explanatory Coherence,"[10] he quotes the "two dimensions" passage and comments

To the extent that this passage was one of my notorious promissory notes, I hope that the present essay provides some of the cash.

(MGEC 191)

In MGEC, Sellars focuses on the authority of spontaneous judgments of introspection, perception, and memory (IPM judgments). He is especially interested in the function and status of certain epistemic or meta-justificatory principles. This interest leads him to

---

[10] Wilfrid Sellars, "More on Givenness and Explanatory Coherence." Originally in George Pappas (ed.), *Justification and Knowledge* (Dordrecht: Reidel, 1979). Reprinted in Jonathan Dancy (ed.), *Perceptual Knowledge* (Oxford: Oxford University Press, 1988). References to this reprinting given in the text by "MGEC" and page number.

an account of the two dimensions very different from the one we have been considering so far.

Sellars is responding to a defence of foundationalism offered by Roderick Firth. Firth argues that "the statement 'It looks to me as if I am seeing something red' ... has a certain degree of warrant for me because it is a statement ... that purports to characterize (and only to characterize) my present experience."[11] Letting P_E be the property of being about my present experience, this amounts to the suggestion that P_E is a non-inferential warrant increasing property (WP). According to Sellars, Firth's claim requires that the meta-judgment

MJ$_1$: Judgments which have P_E are likely to be true,

if warranted, has by Firth's standards a non-inferential warrant. To see this, compare MJ$_1$ with

MJ$_2$: Judgments which are believed by members of the American Geographical Society are likely to be true.

MJ$_2$ is an *inductively warranted* warrant principle, thus inferentially warranted by anyone's standards. Now according to Firth, a statement can be inferentially warranted either by itself being inductively warranted or by being derived from an inferentially warranted principle. (In the latter case, it has an inferential WP, such as being believed by members of the AGS.) So MJ$_1$ cannot be like MJ$_2$. If it were, judgments about my present experience would have an inferential property and would be inferentially warranted. Thus MJ$_1$ must have a non-inferential warrant.

What could this non-inferential warrant be? Given Firth's assumption that warrants are either inductive or somehow intrinsic, the only available answers are

(1) it is self-evident or axiomatic that it is reasonable to accept MJ$_1$;

---

[11] Roderick Firth, "Coherence, Certainty and Epistemic Priority," *Journal of Philosophy*, 61: 19 (October 1964): 545–57. The passage quoted is on p. 553. This essay has also been reprinted in Dancy, op. cit.

(2) it is reasonable to accept MJ_1 because, if it is false, no empirical statements are warranted.

Sellars comments:

Both these answers would turn us aside with a stone instead of the bread which ... we intuitively feel must be there. Self-evidence is too atomistic an interpretation of the authority of epistemic principles; while the second answer—which amounts to the old slogan 'this or nothing'—is too weak.

(MGEC 186)

So what has gone wrong? Sellars has already dropped a large hint by asking

... suppose that P' is the property of belonging to a theory of persons as representers of themselves-in-the-world, which although it has good explanatory power and is capable of refinement by inductive procedures, *was not* (and, indeed, could not have been) *arrived at* by inferences guided by inductive canons however broadly construed. Would P' be an *inferential* WP or an *explanatory* but not *inferential* WP?

(MGEC 183)

Call this theory "T".

We shall come back to T in a moment. But first, according to Sellars, MJ_2 is both a criterion for assessing geographical knowledge and an (inductively confirmed) empirical statement. He asks,

But what of MJ_1? And what of such principles as

MJ_3: If a person ostensibly perceives (without ground for doubt) something to be Φ (for appropriate values of Φ) then it is likely to be true that he perceives something to be Φ.

MJ_4: If a person ostensibly remembers (without ground for doubt) having ostensibly perceived something to be Φ (for appropriate values of Φ) then it is likely to be true that he remembers ostensibly perceiving something to be Φ.

Might not these also be *both* principles which provide criteria for adjudicating certain empirical knowledge claims *and* empirical knowledge claims in their own right?

(MGEC 186–7)

Surely not: the very suggestion lands us (again!) in blatant epistemic circularity. What we need is

a way in which it could be *independently* reasonable to accept MJ_1, MJ_3 and MJ_4 in spite of the fact that a ground for accepting them is the fact that they belong to T, which we suppose to be an empirically well-confirmed theory.

(MGEC 188)

But what could that be?

An answer emerges when we reflect that T is not a *particular theory*, arrived at by inductive reasoning but rather the *framework* within which particular inquiries are carried out. If we want to know how we got into this framework, the answer is presumably to be sought in

a special application of evolutionary theory to the emergence of beings capable of conceptually representing the world of which they have come to be a part.

(MGEC 190)

With respect to *how we got into* T, both the question and answer are *causal* rather than *epistemic*. But if we want to raise the epistemic question—Why is it reasonable to accept T?—the answer is that

the necessary connection between being in the framework of epistemic evaluation and being agents ... constitutes the objective ground for the reasonableness of accepting *something like* theory T.

(MGEC 190)

More precisely,

... [S]ince agency, to be effective, involves having reliable cognitive maps of ourselves and our environment, the concept of effective agency involves that of our IPM judgments being likely to be true, that is, to be correct mappings of ourselves and our circumstances ... [I]f the above argument is sound, it is reasonable to accept

MJ$_5$: IPM judgments are likely to be true,

simply on the ground that unless they *are* likely to be true, the concept of effective agency has no application.

(MGEC 190)[12]

This secures independent warrant for IPM judgments. However, we haven't yet fully explained how these can be *both* warranting principles and inductively confirmable empirical hypotheses. Here is the "linchpin" of the argument.

We must carefully distinguish between having good reason to accept MJ$_5$ and having good reason to accept a proposed *explanation* of *why* IPM judgments are likely to be true.

... To explain why IPM judgments are likely to be true *does* involve finding inductive support for hypotheses concerning the mechanisms involved and how they evolved in response to evolutionary pressures. And *this* obviously presupposes the reasonableness of accepting IPM judgments.

... MJ$_5$ is epistemically prior to the reasonableness of particular IPM judgments, whereas the particular IPM judgments are epistemically prior to *explanations* of the likely truth of IPM judgments.

(MGEC 190–1)

This puts a very different gloss on the two dimensions. What we have is not semantic interdependence versus epistemic priority but two dimensions of epistemic priority. Epistemic principles are basic in the order of fundamental epistemic warrant. But IPM judgments are epistemically prior to explanations of why epistemic principles hold. This argument is suggestive. But what does it really

---

[12] A similar line of thought has recently been developed independently by Crispin Wright. See Wright, "Warrant for Nothing (and Foundations for Free)," *Aristotelian Society*, Suppl. vol. LXXVIII (2004), pp. 167–212. See especially Wright's discussion of "entitlements of rational deliberation" at pp. 197–200.

amount to? There are several points to be made in answer to this question.

Clearly, Sellars intends to offer a response to the charge that IPM judgments are 'non-inferential' only in a psychological sense. It is true that for Sellars being non-inferential is primarily a psychological matter. But being non-inferential in Sellars's sense turns out to have epistemic significance, since the reasonableness of accepting non-inferential judgments derives from the *non-inductive* reasonableness of accepting *T*. The independent reasonableness of accepting MJ_5 is built into any epistemic subject's self-conception as a "finite knower in a world one never made" (MGEC 189). So has Sellars defused the threat of epistemic circularity? A traditionally-minded epistemologist is likely to say that he hasn't. Sellars *thinks* that he has because he has provided independent and non-inductive reasons for accepting theory *T*. But the reply to this will be that Sellars's reasons are *non-inductive* by virtue of being *non-epistemic*. The reasons for accepting are *strategic*: as finite knowers in a world we never made, we have no choice but to sign up to some set of epistemic principles. But taking an epistemic justification to be one that has to do with the likelihood a proposition's being true, Sellars gives no such justification. Rather, he argues that we are not *culpable* in accepting *T*, since accepting some set of epistemic principles is unavoidable. In so far as we have epistemic reasons for accepting *T*, those reasons are inductive and involve judgments that derive their authority from *T* itself. Sellars does not avoid epistemic circularity.

Sellars does not give this objection the attention it deserves. But taking up hints that he does provide, there are replies that we can make on his behalf.

The need to incorporate into our world view something like T is not merely strategic or pragmatic. Having the ability to justify and criticize claims is part and parcel of being in the logical space of reasons, which is itself the condition for manifesting conceptual abilities of any sort. The account of the "two dimensions" in MGEC extends rather than replaces that given by Brandom, largely, provided that we are careful not to draw too sharp a contrast between semantic and epistemic considerations. Such a contrast has no place in Sellars's thinking. His inferentialist semantics are thoroughly epistemic, in that conceptual content is determined in large measure by inferential, thus potentially justificatory, relations. Thus, in MGEC, Sellars's strategy for avoiding epistemic circularity is to distinguish the distinct roles that reliability commitments play in the game of giving and asking for reasons. But since to be a conceptual animal just is to play the game, and since the game *must* contain something like T, our justification for accepting T is a "merely pragmatic" affair. What Sellars offers is akin to a transcendental argument.

It is also important not to forget Sellars's proviso that his argument only underwrites the reasonableness of accepting *something like T*. With the progress of inquiry, guided by T, we gain empirical evidence that T is true, while refining its content through gaining a more sophisticated understanding of the scope and limits of our basic cognitive capacities. T, which validates our IPM judgments, cannot have been *wildly* off the mark, for if our IPM judgments had been wildly unreliable we would not be around to discuss their reliability. But this does not mean that T is either comprehensive or correct in all details. So not only is accepting T on non-inductive grounds not "merely pragmatic," it is not dogmatic either. Once inquiry is off the ground, anything can be revised, *including T itself.*

The importance of this point should not be underestimated. Epistemic circularity seems threatening because it appears to be *vicious*: our epistemic principles authorize certain particular judgments, which in turn confirm our principles. Surely, any epistemic principle can be "justified" this way: the pious believer who hears the voice of God in his heart knows that what he hears must be true, because this is what the voice tells him. But on Sellars's dynamic and fallibilist conception of knowledge and justification, IPM judgments, and the epistemic principles they presuppose, do not work like that. There is no guarantee that the IPM judgments we rely on will validate in detail the epistemic principles they presuppose. In fact, we know that they do not. Starting with a relatively crude set of principles, we collect data that lead us to refine our principles. The apparent "circularity" involved in the inter-dependence of IPM judgments and epistemic principles is not vicious because theory *T* is *not guaranteed to be self-confirming.*

I suggested at the outset that avoiding the choice between the tortoise and the serpent turns on identifying some unacknowledged presupposition common to the competing pictures. Now we have found Sellars's candidate. Sellars connects his "two sources of reasonableness" view with his insistence in EPM that traditional foundationalism goes wrong *above all* in its *static* picture of epistemic justification. Both foundationalism and coherentism are "time-slice" theories, for both trace warrant to some occurrent structural property of our world-picture. By contrast, Sellars insists that warrant be viewed dynamically, hence historically: our world-picture is warranted because it is the result of the rational correction of a previous picture. As Sellars says, empirical knowledge is a self-correcting enterprise. The threat of epistemic circularity is an *illusion*, engendered by the static conception of knowledge shared by tortoise- and serpent-theorists, and of course by Agrippan skeptics too.

7. An Alternative Structure

Although we have made significant progress, questions remain. However, Sellars provides the materials for some answers. Unfortunately, he does not himself develop these answers in a systematic way.

So far, I have gone along with the idea that particular non-inferential reports are warranted by reliability presuppositions. However, in my view, observation reports are not even *typically*, much less invariably warranted in this fashion. A remark of Wittgenstein's is relevant here:

... When one says that such and such a proposition can't be proved, of course that does not mean that it can't be derived from other propositions;

any proposition can be derived from other ones. But they may be no more certain than it is itself.[13]

Lots of everyday judgments (including many IPM judgments) are *more* certain than *any* epistemic principle. Indeed, in lots of cases they seem to be at the limits of certainty. Wittgenstein again:

Suppose I now say "I'm incapable of being wrong about this: that is a book" while I point to an object. What would a mistake here be like? And have I any *clear* idea of it?[14]

The answer is no: doubts do not always make sense. But if that is so, there are countless everyday judgments (again including IPM judgments) that could not possibly have their epistemic status *improved* by being derived from a principle like MJ_5. If this is so, derivability from MJ_5 is not a WP. Or more precisely, it is not *always* such a property.

In saying this, I am not repudiating epistemic reflexivity. To see why not, we must attend to a distinction—hinted at in EPM but more fully developed in *Science and Metaphysics*—between two kinds of rules, which Sellars calls "ought-to-do" and "ought-to-be."[15] Ought-to-do rules are imperatival in form; and in charting the empiricist's route to the given, Sellars notes the empiricist treats making a report (in his technical sense) as subject to such rules: for example, 'Say/think "... is red" in the presence of visible redness.' To treat reports this way is to treat reporting as an action: i.e. as done on purpose, so that it always *makes sense* to ask "Why are you doing that," even if the answer is sometimes "Just feel like it." However, since according to Sellars an observation report is a *response*, wrung from a perceiver by an object or situation, reporting cannot be *action*. I can deliberately look in the direction of the fence. But my seeing the bird—thus acquiring a disposition to report "There's a bird"—is not a further thing that I do: it is

---

[13] Ludwig Wittgenstein, *On Certainty* (Oxford: Blackwell, 1969), §1.   [14] Ibid. §17.
[15] Wilfrid Sellars, *Science and Metaphysics* (London and New York: Routledge & Kegan Paul/Humanities Press, 1968). Reissued by Ridgeview Publishing, Atascadero, CA, 1992. See ch. III, sect. VI, pp. 75–7.

something that *happens to me*. Sellars concludes that seeing is not a mental action but a mental *act*: the actualization of a trained capacity. Nevertheless, as we know from the master-thought, even involuntary reports (and their "inner" counterparts) must be fully caught up in the logical space of reasons, which means that they must be subject to epistemic norms. This is where ought-to-be rules come in. To report knowledgeably on aspects of the passing scene, I need to *be* reliable, and the conditions in which I make a report must *be* favorable for my exercise of my recognitional ability. If I find reason to think that I am not so reliable, or that the conditions in which I registered a particular observation were not favorable, then there are things that I now ought-to-do: for example, stop treating the report in question as reliable, pending further investigation. In this way, the ought-to-be rules that govern mental acts, by functioning as *rules of criticism*, engage with ought-to-dos. In this way mental acts of perceiving (and their overt expression in observation reports) are fully embedded in the logical space of reasons, of justifying and being able to justify what one says.

The distinction between the two kinds of rules suggests a new conception of the structure of epistemic justification: the "default and challenge" model of justification, to adopt Brandom's terminology.[16] On this model, being justified in believing that-p—that is to say, being entitled to take it that p for the purposes of inference and action—does not always require our having done something *specific* to earn that entitlement. To be sure, only accredited epistemic subjects can possess default (or indeed any) entitlements. But the status of epistemic subject, like that of moral agent, is acquired through training and acculturation. And what we acquire through training includes the reliable reporting dispositions that are presupposed by observation reporting. In this respect, reliability is presupposed in the order of understanding, just as Brandom says.

[16] Robert Brandom, *Making It Explicit* (Cambridge, MA: Harvard University Press, 1994). See especially pp. 176–9.

But if this is so, why insist on reliability-knowledge, as Sellars does? Because the default entitlements acquired by observation carry *defence commitments*. There may be reason to doubt the reporter's reliability in general; or we may suspect that the conditions for making the report were not favorable, so that the reporter cannot be relied on in this instance. In the face of such challenges, entitlement lapses until the challenge is answered. However, one can neither recognize legitimate challenges nor respond to them unless one knows a good deal about how observation reports can be erroneous: that is, *unless one knows a good deal about one's reliability and its limits*. Moreover, one can sometimes justify a report to a skeptical interlocutor by citing one's reliability with respect to the matter in hand. A typical case might be where one has a special recognitional capacity. ("I'm a keen ornithologist: that's how I know.")

The idea that justification conforms to a default-and-challenge structure accords well with the emphasis that Sellars places on the point that empirical knowledge is rational because self-correcting. Default justification is not a license to think what you like, since default justification is always defeasible, even at the most basic observational level. Rules of criticism are vital to the process of self-correction. So we should not view the default-and-challenge model as a structural model that competes directly with the structural models offered by foundationalism and the coherence theory. (If we try, it will look less like an alternative than like a variant form of foundationalism.) Rather, we should see it as another way of insisting that justification be viewed dynamically rather than statically. If the default-and-challenge conception offers a different structural model, it is because it insists on incorporating a temporal element.

There is an objection to attributing the view I have just sketched to Sellars. In the 1963 reprinting of EPM, Sellars adds a footnote in which he insists that it is not enough that the situation in which a report is entered *be* normal: the subject must also *know* that it is normal (EPM §22n, in SPR: 152; in KMG: 230).[17] Is this a step too far? McDowell thinks so.[18] However, it is not easy to say how demanding a conception of knowledge Sellars is working with here. Perhaps the justification involved in the subject's knowing that the situation is normal is itself default. That is, perhaps the subject counts as knowing that the situation is normal if it *is* normal and he has no reason to suppose that it isn't. If this is all Sellars has in mind, we can happily concede his point.

The idea that ought-to-be rules are rules of criticism meshes cleanly with Wittgenstein's point that particular IPM judgments, made in particular circumstances, can be as certain as any judgment ever gets to be: *more* certain even than any explicitly formulated reliability-commitment that might be thought to underwrite them. As Wittgenstein himself notes, what we learn about our reliability mostly concerns our limitations. It concerns the ways in which judgments that are ordinarily to be accepted without demur can go wrong. Only with this kind of knowledge on board can we recognize and respond to legitimate challenges to otherwise default entitlements. Given the default-and-challenge model, we can have epistemic reflexivity without epistemic circularity. And if we can have that, we can avoid the choice between the tortoise and the serpent.

As with Sellars's "two dimensions of reasonableness" view, we should see his remarks on the two sorts of rules as extending rather than revising the views sketched in EPM and MGEC. In particular, the idea that epistemic justification conforms to a default-and-challenge structure does not conflict with (and so is not an alternative to) the position that Sellars defends in MGEC. The point that we have a non-inductive warrant for accepting something like theory *T* still holds good. So does the distinction between having that warrant and being able to explain why *T*

[17] This note is not in the Brandom edition of EPM, hence the lack of a page reference in B.

[18] HWV, p. 474.

is likely to be true. What the distinction between ought-to-be and ought-to do rules adds to this picture is a more nuanced conception of the role played in epistemic justification by certain elements of *T*. It offers a more nuanced account of the dynamics of belief-revision.

8. Radical Fallibilism

Sellars presents a subtle and complex way of escaping the apparently forced choice between the tortoise and the serpent, in which the central element is a move from a static to a dynamic conception of justification. However, Sellars is a *radical* fallibilist in a way that Wittgenstein, for example, is not. So although I introduced the idea of a default-and-challenge structure to turn aside an objection that I derived from Wittgenstein—that reliability-commitments cannot always play a directly warranting role with respect to IPM judgments—we should not leap to the conclusion that Sellars's views and those of Wittgenstein can be fully reconciled. Wittgenstein thinks that many (perhaps most) ordinary observationally-based commitments are exempt from doubt (thus also from the need for justification) because expressions of doubt would be *senseless*. Our language game makes no provision for doubt. This is as true of "Here is one hand" (when my hand is in front of my face) as it is of "2 + 2 = 4." Sellars can agree with this only up to a point.

As I read him, Wittgenstein holds that there is no sense to be made of the idea that the familiar objects we encounter in everyday life do not exist. Such things are therefore with us always. This is not Sellars's view. When Sellars claims that *anything* can be called in question, he means it. For example, Sellars thinks that there may be no such things as the colored objects that populate the commonsense world, though the point has to be made with some care. Thus:

... 'Physical objects are not really coloured' makes sense only as a clumsy expression of the idea that there are no such things as the coloured physical objects of the common sense world, where this is interpreted, not as an empirical proposition—like 'There are no nonhuman featherless bipeds'—*within* the common sense frame, but as a rejection (in *some* sense) of this very framework itself, in favour of another built around different, if not unrelated, categories.

(EPM §41, in SPR: 173; in KMG: 252; in B: 82)

Sellars hastens to add that he is not making a practical proposal. He is not suggesting that we abandon everyday ways of speaking. This means that, as long as the existing framework is *used*, it will be *incorrect* to say that no object is really colored.... But this is the limit of his agreement with Wittgenstein. From Sellars's standpoint, Wittgenstein is only making a (correct) point about how things stand viewed from *within* our commonsense framework of everyday objects in Space and Time, and that framework has no unqualified claim to be the last word on how things are. To suppose that it did would be to lapse once more into the Myth of the Given in what I have called its general form. Thus Sellars says that "*speaking as a philosopher*, I am quite prepared to say that the common sense world of physical objects in Space and Time is unreal—that is, that there are no such things." Or less paradoxically, "that in the dimension of describing and explaining the world, science is the measure of all things, of what is that it is, and of what is not that it is not" (EPM §41, in SPR: 173; in KMG: 253; in B: 82). As deVries puts it, for Sellars ordinary objects have only "practical reality."[19]

In these remarks from EPM, Sellars is gesturing towards what he later described as the clash of two "images" (comprehensive conceptions) of man-in-the-world, the manifest and the scientific.[20] The manifest image embodies our commonsense picture of the world, in which we ourselves, persons, constitute a fundamental category. By contrast, the scientific image grows out of taking science to be the measure of what there really is; and in this

---

[19] DeVries, op. cit., p. 271 ff.

[20] See "Philosophy and the Scientific Image of Man," in SPR and ISR. References given by PSIM and page numbers.

world-picture, ordinary objects and, even more significantly, we ourselves find no obvious place.

Sellars thinks that the sort of philosophy exemplified by Wittgenstein—which includes not only those trends in Anglophone philosophy that emphasize the analysis of 'commonsense' and 'ordinary usage,' but Continental phenomenology as well—as "more or less adequate accounts of the manifest image of man-in-the-world." As such, they are only the latest exemplars of the 'perennial philosophy,' or 'Platonic tradition.' In this tradition, the manifest image is "endorsed as real." Thus the manifest image is taken to provide a "large scale map of reality," to which science adds only "a needlepoint of detail" (PSIM, in SPR: 8, in ISR: 376). I have no doubt that Sellars would count McDowell, like Wittgenstein, as another partisan of the manifest image, thus as a proponent of the Myth. McDowell argues that, once we set aside the Myth of the Given in the form of the Myth of a non-conceptual constraint on thinking, we can speak of everyday perceptual experience as involving "openness to the layout of reality."[21] This is not a Sellarsian thought. It is no mere oversight that McDowell does not address the Myth of the Given in what Sellars regards as its general form.[22] It is a mark of real disagreement.

---

[21] *Mind and World*, p. 26.

[22] None of this would bother McDowell, who finds Sellars's claim that we face a clash of images unconvincing: see HWV, p. 473. Brandom generally avoids discussing the supposed clash of the images, but he is clearly not very sympathetic to this aspect of Sellars's work. There is a deep reason for this. Sellars's idea of "describing" is bound up with his idea that the aim of a fundamental descriptive vocabulary is to "picture" the objects that it is about. Although Sellars is clear that picturing is not itself a *semantic* relation, the idea that picturing is a vital aspect of descriptive vocabulary has close connections with Sellars's account of truth as "semantic assertibility," and in particular with his idea that the final truth consists in assertibility in conceptual scheme CSP (for Charles Sanders Pierce): assertibililty at the limit of inquiry. These tendencies in Sellars's thought run counter to the strongly deflationary approach to semantic notions favoured by Brandom. At least, I suspect that this is Brandom's view. Brandom (personal conversation) often contrasts "left wing" with "right wing" Sellarsians. The left wingers drop worries about truth, picturing and the clash of the images in favor of a more therapeutic approach to metaphysical anxieties. For sympathetic accounts of Sellars's project of fusing the images (and of the place of picturing in that project), see James O' Shea, *Wilfrid Sellars* (Cambridge: Polity Press, 2007), chs. 1 and 6; and Jay Rosenberg, *Fusing the Images* (Oxford: Oxford University Press, 2007), chs. 1, 3, and 5. Sellars's accounts of truth and picturing can be found in *Science and Metaphysics*, chs. IV–V.

This is not the place to explore in detail Sellars's idea that the task of philosophy in our time is to fuse the images. The idea that the images clash, or that there are two such images to fuse, is controversial, even among Sellars's admirers. I bring it up only to add a last detail to our understanding of Sellars's epistemology.

We saw earlier that Sellars sometimes sounds like a coherence theorist, singling out explanatory coherence as the ultimate arbiter of what to believe. This makes sense when we remember that Sellars's rejection of the Myth of the Given in its most general form is of a piece with his thought that the most dramatic advances in understanding (and even some that are not so dramatic) involve conceptual change. The problem that faces us is not always what propositions to accept in our current vocabulary: sometimes it is what vocabulary to deploy: i.e., what concepts to have. In such matters, increasing explanatory coherence is the ultimate touch-stone of epistemic propriety. So—though I offer this suggestion with some diffidence—perhaps we should say that the conception of justification presented by the default-and-challenge conception is best seen as first and foremost a picture of routine justification *within* a conceptual framework. When we confront the need to modify the framework, different considerations come into play.

To take this position is not to embrace frictionless coherentism. The need to consider changing our concepts arises out of and is constrained by our observational interactions with a world we never made. The deep and difficult question is whether the possibilities of conceptual change are as limitless as Sellars supposes. This is a question I have not tried to answer here.

References

BonJour, Laurence, *The Structure of Empirical Knowledge* (Cambridge, MA: Harvard University Press, 1985).

Brandom, Robert B., *Making It Explicit* (Cambridge, MA: Harvard University Press, 1994).

Brandom, Robert B., "Study Guide". In *Empiricism and the Philosophy of Mind: with an Introduction by Richard Rorty and a Study Guide by Robert Brandom*, R. Brandom (ed.) (Cambridge, MA: Harvard University Press, 1997). [B]

deVries, Willem A., *Wilfrid Sellars*, Philosophy Now Series (Chesham, Bucks: Acumen Publishing and Montreal & Kingston: McGill-Queen's University Press, 2005).

Firth, Roderick, "Coherence, Certainty and Epistemic Priority," *Journal of Philosophy*, 61: 19 (Oct. 1964): 545–57.

McDowell, John., *Mind and World*, 2nd edn. (Cambridge, MA: Harvard University Press, 1996).

—— "Having the World in View: Sellars, Kant, and Intentionality. Lecture III: Intentionality as a Relation," *The Journal of Philosophy*, 95 (Sept. 1998): 471–91.

O'Shea, James, *Wilfrid Sellars* (Cambridge: Polity Press, 2007).

Rosenberg, Jay F., *Fusing the Images* (Oxford: Oxford University Press, 2007).

Sellars, Wilfrid, "Some Reflections on Language Games," *Philosophy of Science*, 21 (1954): 204–28. Reprinted in ISR; reprinted with extensive revisions in SPR.

—— "Empiricism and the Philosophy of Mind". In *Minnesota Studies in the Philosophy of Science*, vol. I, H. Feigl and M. Scriven (eds.) (Minneapolis, MN: University of Minnesota Press, 1956): 253–329. (Originally presented at the University of London Special Lectures in Philosophy for 1956 as "The Myth of the Given: Three Lectures on Empiricism and the Philosophy of Mind".) Reprinted in SPR with additional footnotes. Published separately as *Empiricism and the Philosophy of Mind: with an Introduction by Richard Rorty and a Study Guide by Robert Brandom*, R. Brandom (ed.) (Cambridge, MA: Harvard University Press, 1997). [B] Also reprinted in W. deVries and T. Triplett, *Knowledge, Mind, and the Given: A Reading of Sellars' "Empiricism and the Philosophy of Mind"* (Indianapolis, IN: Hackett, 2000) [KMG]. Cited as EPM.

—— "Philosophy and the Scientific Image of Man". In *Frontiers of Science and Philosophy*, R. Colodny (ed.) (Pittsburgh, PA: University of Pittsburgh Press, 1962), 35–78. Reprinted in SPR, ISR.

—— *Science, Perception and Reality* (London: Routledge & Kegan Paul, 1963. Reissued by Ridgeview Publishing, Atascadero, CA, 1991.

—— *Science and Metaphysics* (London and New York: Routledge & Kegan Paul/Humanities Press, 1968). Reissued by Ridgeview Publishing, Atascadero, CA, 1992.

—— "More on Givenness and Explanatory Coherence." Originally in George Pappas (ed.), *Justification and Knowledge* (Dordrecht: Reidel, 1979). Reprinted in Jonathan Dancy (ed.), *Perceptual Knowledge* (Oxford: Oxford University Press, 1988).

—— *In the Space of Reasons*, Kevin Scharp and Robert Brandom (eds.) (Cambridge, MA: Harvard University Press, 2007).

Williams, Michael. *Unnatural Doubts* (Oxford: Blackwell, 1992; Princeton, NJ: Princeton University Press, 1996).

Wittgenstein, Ludwig. *On Certainty* (Oxford: Blackwell, 1969).

Wright, Crispin. "Warrant for Nothing (and Foundations for Free)," *Proceedings of the Aristotelian Society*, suppl. vol. LXXVIII (2004): 167–212.

7

On the Structure of Sellars's Naturalism with a Normative Turn

James R. O'Shea

In recent decades an increasing number of philosophers influenced by Wilfrid Sellars have stressed the importance of a distinction between the normatively structured 'logical space of reasons' on the one hand, and the proper domain of naturalistic causal explanations characteristic of modern natural science on the other. Three major works have been of particular significance in this respect: Richard Rorty's *Philosophy and the Mirror of Nature* (1979), John McDowell's *Mind and World* (1994), and Robert Brandom's *Making It Explicit* (1994). However, each of these authors also contends that the laudable aspects of Sellars's account of the space of reasons and his famous rejection of the 'myth of the given' must be detached from the regrettable *scientism*, which they judge to be an unfortunate aspect of Sellars's own philosophy.

At the same time, on the other hand, an equally impressive group of philosophers ranging from the eliminative materialism of Paul Churchland to the various non-eliminativist scientific naturalisms characteristic of Daniel Dennett, Ruth Millikan, William Lycan, and Jay Rosenberg, have in their different ways been inspired rather than put off by Sellars's defense of a strongly scientific realist conception of reality, and in particular by his resulting investigations into how it is possible to reconcile that conception with our own experiential self-understanding as it appears within what Sellars called the 'manifest image of man-in-the-world'.[1]

What I explore in this paper is the difficult question of the nature of the relationship between the natural and the normative as it was conceived by Sellars himself. I shall argue that Sellars's own view represented an attempt to defend both the *irreducibility* of the normative space of reasons and yet, simultaneously and in another sense, its comprehensive *reducibility* from the perspective of an ideal scientific conception of the nature of reality and of the human being. Questions concerning the nature of the relationship between the 'natural' and the normative are of course among the most hotly contested issues in contemporary philosophy. It may be that Sellars's own views on this particular issue still contain insights that have not yet been mined.

1. The Normative 'Space' of Conceptual Thinking: In One Sense *Irreducible*, In Another Sense *Reducible*

Many of the recent and most well-known discussions have quite properly emphasized Sellars's conception of *knowledge* as a normative standing in the logical space of reasons, as in the following famous passage from 'Empiricism and the Philosophy of Mind':

The essential point is that in characterizing an episode or a state as that of *knowing*, we are not giving an empirical description of that episode or state; we are placing it in the logical space of reasons, of justifying and being able to justify what one says.

(EPM §36, in SPR: 169; in KMG: 248; in B: 76)

---

[1] The former philosophers (Rorty, et al.), who emphasize the quasi-Hegelian aspects of Sellars's 'space of reasons', have sometimes been characterized as the 'left wing' Sellarsians; while those philosophers who stress the importance of Sellars's naturalism and his strong scientific realism tend to be known as the 'right wing' Sellarsians. In this paper I argue that Sellars's view represented an attempt to show how the irreducibility of the normative 'space of reasons' is consistent, in another sense, with its thoroughgoing reducibility within what Sellars calls the 'scientific image of man-in-the-world'.

In a similar spirit, earlier in the same work, Sellars had claimed that

... the idea that epistemic facts can be analyzed without remainder—even 'in principle'—into non-epistemic facts, whether phenomenal or behavioural, public or private, with no matter how lavish a sprinkling of subjunctives and hypotheticals is, I believe, a radical mistake—a mistake of a piece with the so-called 'naturalistic fallacy' in ethics.

(EPM §5, in SPR: 131; in KMG: 209; in B: 19)

Furthermore, not only our epistemic states but more basically *all* our conceptual capacities generally were held by Sellars to be in some sense *irreducible in principle* to any description or explanation of those states in terms that refer only to non-conceptual processes and causal relations, however complex.

At the same time, however, in his overall views on truth and ontology Sellars defended what he called "the thesis of the primacy of the scientific image" (PSIM, in SPR: 38; in ISR: 406). As he put it in his famous (or infamous) *scientia mensura* dictum, "in the dimension of describing and explaining the world, science is the measure of all things, of what is that it is, and of what is not that it is not" (EPM §42, in SPR: 173; in KMG: 253; in B: 83). In his ontology Sellars was both a thoroughgoing nominalist and a scientific naturalist from top to bottom. If we set aside certain important distinctions that have to be made in light of his novel view of 'sensa' and sensory consciousness,[2] Sellars's naturalism took the form of a comprehensive physicalism or materialism.[3]

---

[2] The qualifications that have to be made in relation to Sellars's views on sensory consciousness do not affect the present issue. Sellars's 'sensa' are ultimately what he calls 'physical$_1$-but-not-physical$_2$' phenomena. Roughly, they are causally efficacious spatiotemporal processes (i.e., they are physical$_1$) rather than being mere epiphenomena; however, Sellars proposes that our sensa do not obey the *mechanistic* physical laws that are adequate to describe non-living (i.e., physical$_2$) matter. For further discussion see J. O'Shea (2007), ch. 6.

[3] It is important to bear in mind, though I shall not stress the point in this paper, that Sellars is a *non-reductive* physicalist in at least the following sense: he does not hold that such comparatively 'higher-level' sciences or 'special sciences' as neurophysiology, chemistry, or biology would be put out of business *as sciences* even by an ideally successful ontological reduction-by-identification of the *objects* of those sciences with systems of the sorts of objects treated in atomic physics. Our predictions and projections in terms of the empirical concepts

As applied to the crucial case of the nature of the human being, Sellars makes it clear that in the final ontological reckoning or ideal synoptic vision of the world, persons are revealed to be complex "bundles" or "multiplicities" of micro-physical processes (cf. FMPP III §125: "The way would be open to a bundle theory of persons. A person would be a bundle of absolute processes ... "; and cf. PHM 101). On Sellars's view, then, "the scientific image of man turns out to be that of a complex physical system" (PSIM, in SPR: 25; in ISR: 393).

The difficult interpretive issue, or so I believe, concerns just how Sellars conceived his account of the *irreducibility* of the norm-governed conceptual capacities of persons within the 'logical space of reasons' to be consistent with the ideal physicalist ontology and the strong *reducibility* claims that are embodied in his thesis of the primacy and completeness of the ideal scientific image of the human being. The following passage from 'Philosophy and the Scientific Image of Man' brings out the heart of this difficult issue, with reference to the essentially holistic nature of the normative space of reasons (the final sentence in particular is what I want to focus on):

... I want to highlight from the very beginning what might be called the paradox of man's encounter with himself, the paradox consisting of the fact that man couldn't be man until he encountered himself. It is this paradox which supports the last stand of Special Creation. Its central theme is the idea that anything which can properly be called conceptual thinking can occur only within a framework of conceptual thinking in terms of which it can be criticized, supported, refuted, in short, evaluated. To be able to think is to be able to measure one's thoughts by standards of correctness, of relevance, of evidence. In this sense a

and 'stances' (to borrow Dennett's useful notion) of the higher-level sciences and of the 'manifest image of man-in-the-world' will have enormous utility insofar as the relevant empirical generalizations are approximately true, well-founded phenomena. But Sellars's strong scientific realist contention is that the nature and extent of this approximation to the truth of these 'predecessor' generalizations is ultimately adequately explained only by means of their ontological identification with their theoretical successor generalizations. For further discussion see J. O'Shea (2007), chs. 2 and 6.

diversified conceptual framework is a whole which, however sketchy, is prior to its parts, and cannot be construed as a coming together of parts which are already conceptual in character. The conclusion is difficult to avoid that the transition from pre-conceptual patterns of behaviour to conceptual thinking was a holistic one, a jump to a level of awareness which is irreducibly new, a jump which was the coming into being of man.

There is a profound truth in this conception of a radical difference in level between man and his precursors. The attempt to understand this difference turns out to be part and parcel of the attempt to encompass in one view the two images of man-in-the-world which I have set out to describe. For, as we shall see, this difference in level appears as an irreducible discontinuity in the *manifest* image, but as, in a sense requiring careful analysis, a reducible difference in the *scientific* image.

(PSIM, in SPR: 6; in ISR: 374)

Suppose we grant for present purposes that Sellars is right about the essentially normative and holistic nature of conceptual thinking as expressed in the first paragraph (these are of course controversial positions in their own right). And suppose we also set to one side the interesting remark on the holistic 'jump' that Sellars says it is 'difficult to avoid' concluding was involved in the evolutionary transition from pre-conceptual patterns of behaviour to conceptual thinking proper.[4] I want to focus instead on the distinction made in the second paragraph concerning the 'difference in level' between normative conceptual thinking and non-normative, non-conceptual patterns and processes.

Given what we have already seen, it is not difficult to understand why Sellars holds that this difference in level is conceived, on the one hand, as an "*irreducible discontinuity*" within the manifest image conception of ourselves as persons-in-the-world. But what does

---

[4] Sellars's artful dodge here—his statement that *the conclusion is difficult to avoid that X*—leaves it as an exercise for the reader to figure out whether Sellars in fact believes after all that we should, or should not, come to the conclusion that X. I suspect that Sellars's hesitation here is due to the fact that he does not take it to be incumbent upon himself as a philosopher to sort out in advance what is an ongoing matter for scientific inquiry: the question as to the ultimate evolutionary origins of natural languages.

he mean by asserting that this 'difference in level' is, "in a sense requiring careful analysis, a reducible difference in the *scientific image*"? This is the difficult and (I suggest) important distinction that I want to reflect upon: namely, the general idea that the 'difference in level' between the normative space of conceptual thinking on the one hand, and naturalistically describable non-normative, non-conceptual processes on the other, is in one sense an irreducible difference, but in another sense a reducible difference. I shall refer to this in what follows as Sellars's *irreducibility-cum-reducibility* distinction or position.

There are two general tendencies of interpretation in relation to the issues raised by Sellars's irreducibility-cum-reducibility position that I want to reject as interpretations of what Sellars himself was up to. My suggestion will ultimately be that Sellars's own view can capture what ought to be retained from each of these two tendencies.

Firstly, according to what we might call the 'separating off' interpretation, Sellars in emphasizing the irreducibility-cum-reducibility distinction is following a perennial line of thinking, one which can be traced from Plato's *Phaedo* through Kant's 'phenomenal/noumenal' distinction to Wittgenstein's later philosophy, in distinguishing sharply between normative *reasons* and scientific *causes*. On this interpretation, to put it brusquely, once we occupy the naturalistic explanatory perspective of the scientific image, the normative dimension of conceptual thinking *qua* conceptual thinking is simply no longer on our radar screen as a proper scientific explanandum.

There is certainly much in Sellars's philosophy that would fit an interpretation that 'separates off' normative reasons from scientifically lawful causes in this sense—in fact, there is all that goes into the 'irreducibility' side of Sellars's irreducibility-cum-reducibility position. However, it is clear from the passage above (i.e., PSIM 6/374) that the *reducibility* side of Sellars's position is supposed to apply to *the distinction of level itself*; that is, to the distinction between the normative-conceptual and the non-normative or pre-conceptual that constitutes the difference between 'man' and his 'precursors'. It is this distinction that Sellars sees (in a sense to be explained) as a *reducible difference of level* when viewed under the regulative ideal of the final scientific image of the human being. Sellars was clearly more ambitious in his synoptic and naturalistic explanatory aims than those who share the 'separating off' tendency of interpretation would wish to embrace. For Sellars, what is on the radar screens of *both* the manifest *and* the scientific images of 'man-in-the-world' is the nature of conceptual thinking *qua* conceptual thinking, along with the crucial distinction itself between normative reasons and naturalistic causes. This is what gives Sellars's philosophy a unifying explanatory boldness—whatever judgment one might ultimately make of its success or failure—that is lacking in those philosophers who in one way or another want us to rest content with separating off the naturalistic dimension of scientific causes from the normative dimensions of the logical space of reasons.

For broadly similar reasons I do not think that what might be called the 'eliminativist' tendency of interpretation in relation to Sellars's irreducibility-cum-reducibility position can adequately capture what he was up to. An eliminativist interpretation would quite properly focus on Sellars's strong scientific realist view that the sophisticated common sense ontology or manifest image of the perceptible world is in one sense ultimately *strictly speaking false*; that it is in principle if not yet fully in practice to be *replaced* by the explanatorily superior successor ontologies of the emerging scientific image of the world. Sellars's key distinction on this view might be taken to be characterizing the normative space of conceptual thinking as in some sense constituting an 'irreducible' but ultimately *false* conceptual framework; and this framework would be 'reducible' in the sense of being in principle *replaceable* by the ideal scientific picture of ourselves and the world.

However, this global eliminativist tendency of interpretation likewise seems to miss the mark. Sellars comments on his analogy of stereoscopic vision, which he uses to describe the philosopher's task of 'fusing' or integrating the two idealized global images or conceptions of the world into one coherent image, that "the very fact that I use the analogy of stereoscopic vision implies that as I see it the manifest image is not overwhelmed in the synthesis" (PSIM, in SPR: 9; in ISR: 377). He holds that "man is *essentially* that being which conceives of itself *in terms of the image which the perennial philosophy refines and endorses*"—that is, in terms of the manifest image (PSIM, in SPR: 8; in ISR: 376). That is the 'irreducible' or '*sui generis*' side of the story. On the other side of the distinction, however, Sellars does indeed want to hold that the ontology of persons as rational agents and conceptual thinkers within the space of reasons is in principle successfully accommodated *within* the comprehensively physicalist ontology of the ideal scientific image of the world. That is the 'reducibility' side of Sellars's position, and this is what needs to be clarified without reaching for either an eliminativist sledgehammer on the one hand, or a pluralist feather on the other.

2. Sellars's Earlier Version of the Distinction: 'Logical Irreducibility' cum 'Causal Reducibility'

Some insight can be gained on the nature of Sellars's central 'irreducibility-cum-reducibility' position by going back a decade from 'Philosophy and the Scientific Image of Man' to a predecessor distinction he had introduced in his 1953 paper, 'A Semantical Solution of the Mind–Body Problem'. Sellars begins that paper with the remark that "'the mind–body problem'...is notoriously a tangle in which all the major puzzles of philosophy can be found" (SSMB ¶1: 45). He then proceeds to use the classic problem in moral philosophy concerning the relationship between 'ought' and 'is' to introduce a fundamental distinction between different senses of *reducibility*: namely, between what he calls *logical reducibility* (or irreducibility) and *causal reducibility* (or irreducibility). (Sellars's use of the term 'logical reducibility', given his wide use of the term 'logical', might also appropriately be called 'conceptual reducibility'.) As the article develops it becomes clear that for Sellars this distinction, and all that it involves, is supposed to help us understand the relationship between the intensional conceptual frameworks pertaining to mind, meaning, morals, and the modalities on the one hand, and the extensional ontology of an ideal scientific account of human-being-in-the-world on the other. It involves ways of articulating the key 'irreducibility-cum-reducibility' distinction that were to remain central to Sellars's thinking throughout his career.

The main focus in this wide-ranging paper was on the question of whether 'mental acts' defined as exhibiting intentionality or about-ness "can be reduced to items which are not mental acts, … and if so, in exactly what sense of 'reduced' '" (SSMB ¶5: 47). Sellars's ultimate answer is that the mental or intentional is *logically irreducible* yet also *causally reducible* to complex patterns of behavior and brain processes describable within an ideal extensionalist scientific frame-work. Much of the article is devoted to exploring the nature of this particular way of making Sellars's 'irreducibility-cum-reducibility' distinction.

Let us take Sellars's analogy with the traditional is/ought problem first. (It should be noted that as Sellars's distinction will apply to the case of the is/ought problem, intentional mental states such as emo-tions, beliefs, and desires will be assumed to fall unproblematically on the naturalistic, psychological side of the divide. Subsequently Sellars will adjust the relevant distinction to tackle the mind–body problem concerning the nature of intentional psychological states themselves.)

Very briefly, then, as Sellars idealizes the classic is/ought dispute, the *ethical non-naturalists* were primarily concerned to defend the idea that 'ought' is *logically irreducible* to 'is' in that the meaning of 'ought' is indefinable or unanalyzable in descriptive terms. As his example of ethical non-naturalism in this sense Sellars uses ethical intuitionism (he mentions Ross and Prichard). By contrast, Sellars describes the ethical naturalist as concerned in the first instance to defend the idea that 'ought' is *causally reducible* to 'is'. The notion of causal reducibility itself, Sellars indicates, has to do with what one has to appeal to in "a properly constructed causal explanation". In the context of the is/ought problem, he puts it as follows:

If we use 'ethical assertion' in such a way that 'Jones ought to pay his debt' is an ethical assertion, but 'Jones feels that he ought to pay his debt' is not, then we can say that to claim that Ought is causally reducible to Is is to claim that one can give a causal explanation of the history of moral agents without making ethical assertions.

(SSMB ¶6: 48–9)

As we might put it in the material mode, to say that objective moral properties are 'causally reducible' to natural properties would be to say that one can give a fully adequate causal explanation of "the history of moral agents" without appealing to any objective moral properties themselves. And in contrast to both the 'separating off' and 'eliminativist' tendencies of interpretation, this would be to give an adequate causal explanation of the history of moral agents *qua* moral agents.

That the latter is supposed to be so is indicated by Sellars's next move, in which he suggests that both the ethical non-naturalists and the ethical naturalists tended to assume that logical irreducibility and causal irreducibility necessarily go hand and hand. The ethical intuitionists, for example, who on Sellars's story were concerned in the first instance to defend the logical irreducibility of moral assertions, felt compelled to argue that "the motive (cause) of conscientious action" must be mediated by ethical beliefs or intuitions that, so to speak, latch on to objective moral properties (SSMB ¶7: 49). As Sellars describes the intuitionist view, "Human thinking on ethical matters is, as [the intuitionists] see it, ultimately grounded in and controlled by objective values and obligations. The existence of moral concepts and beliefs in the human mind [on their view] cannot be accounted for in purely naturalistic terms" (SSMB ¶7: 49). That is, the intuitionists on Sellars's story felt compelled to deny the causal reducibility of moral assertions in order to preserve their logical irreducibility to naturalistic descriptions. Causally explaining the 'history of moral agents', on their view, requires appeal to objective values somewhere in the explanans.

By contrast, the ethical naturalists, whom Sellars suggests were primarily concerned to emphasize the *causal reducibility* of ethical assertions to naturalistic terms, thereby also felt compelled to defend the *logical* reducibility or definability of ethical assertions in terms of such naturalistic descriptions. On both sides, Sellars suggests, logical reducibility or irreducibility was assumed to require causal reducibility or irreducibility.

For his own part, Sellars is of course staking out his own position, on both the 'is/ought' problem and the mind–body problem, as one of *logical irreducibility* yet *causal reducibility* (in an appropriately non-trivial explanatory sense of causal reducibility). Although his concern is not about moral philosophy *per se* in the 'Semantical Solution' paper,[5] Sellars does indicate that he takes himself to be an ethical *non-naturalist* insofar as he defends the logical or conceptual *irreducibility* of assertions of ethical obligation. In this respect he suggests that 'non-naturalism' should be understood in a broader sense than was assumed by the early intuitionists. As he puts it, "if one should use the term 'Non-naturalism' to cover any view, whether historically espoused or not, which holds that ethical terms have a cognitive meaning which is not definable in descriptive terms, then, no doubt, it is possible to be a Non-naturalist and yet accept the causal reducibility of Ought to Is" (SSMB ¶8: 49–50). Thus Sellars is also able to agree with the *ethical naturalists* insofar as he thinks that the details of his account of ethical assertions can demonstrate that they are 'causally reducible', in a non-trivial sense, to naturalistic descriptions of particular patterns of socially acquired beliefs, motivations, and behavioral dispositions of moral agents. Not unreasonably he argued that the general structure of such a position would represent a middle way between the ethical naturalist and non-naturalist positions he was discussing.

---

[5] Sellars cites his article "Obligation and Motivation," in *Readings in Ethical Theory*, eds. Wilfrid Sellars and John Hospers (New York: Appleton-Century-Crofts, 1952): 511–17.

For reasons soon to emerge, I believe that it is important for any interpretation of Sellars's overall irreducibility-cum-reducibility position to take at least brief notice of his own views on the nature of normative 'ought's themselves, for example the moral 'ought'. Briefly summarized, Sellars put forward an account of moral 'ought' statements in terms of what he called *community intentions* or 'We shall' intentions (an idea that was later developed in different ways by Michael Bratman and others). (The 'shall' terminology is Sellars's simplifying technical idiom for intentions and—if the intended time of action is *now*—volitions.) Around this he built a view of morality that was broadly Kantian or universalizing in form, but was teleological and benevolence-based in substance. Here is one summary statement Sellars gave of his moral theory in a Letter to David Solomon:

[The] fundamental intention characterizing the moral point of view has the form, '*We* shall any of *us* do that which (in his/her circumstances) promotes (maximizes) *our* common good'. I have argued that such an intention can be construed as 'categorically valid' because sharing such an intention defines what it is to be members of a community.[6]

(Letter to David Solomon, June 28, 1976, §15)

Sellars argues that on his view particular ought-judgments such as 'Jones ought to pay his debts', are objectively true or false (on the primary sense of 'true' as 'correct semantic assertibility' that Sellars defends; see *SM* IV §§24–9: 100–2). On his account, moral assertions are *intersubjectively impartial* relative to whatever community the 'We shall' can be regarded as operative over.

I am not concerned here either to analyze or to evaluate Sellars's account of the moral 'ought'. For my present purpose his key claim, on the one hand, is that whatever it is that cognitively significant moral assertions *say*, this is something that cannot be said without remaining within the 'logical space' of community

---

[6] Sellars's correspondences are available on the 'Problems from Wilfrid Sellars' website maintained by Andrew Chrucky: http://www.ditext.com/sellars/index.html.

intentions, so to speak. Moral assertions are held by him to be conceptually or 'logically' irreducible in that sense.

Underlying this account, on the other hand, Sellars put forward a naturalistic, causal explanation of the motivational efficacy of 'shall' intentions as socially acquired linguistic and psychological dispositions to follow up one's 'I shall do A' intentions and volitions, other things being equal, with the doing of A. Such a social-behavioral account of the origin, the content, and the motivational force of individual intentions, community intentions, and on that basis, of normative 'ought' statements, would not itself, as we saw him put it earlier, involve the *assertion* of any 'ought' statements (or the appeal to any objective moral properties). Yet this causal account is supposed to be more than just a trivial, subject-changing, or 'separated off' scientific explanation of various physical motions. For ideally such a *causal reduction* of normative 'ought's would explain specifically and exhaustively those particular psychological dispositions and complex patterns of behavior in which the practice of asserting and obeying intersubjectively valid moral assertions really consists. As I see it, this is the sense in which Sellars himself defends "a position which agrees with the Non-naturalist that Ought is logically irreducible to Is, and yet agrees with the Naturalist that Ought is causally reducible to Is" (SSMB ¶9: 50).

It is important to recognize that Sellars in this sense took there to be available, in principle, a fully adequate naturalistic, ultimately extensionalist account of the nature and force of normative 'ought's themselves (and the same will hold, in this sense, for his views on intentionality and meaning as well; cf. SSIS 439). In the Preface to *Science and Metaphysics*, Sellars makes the following remark in this explanatory spirit, in anticipation of his account of normative 'ought's in the final chapter of that book:

... unless and until the 'scientific realist' can give an adequate explication of concepts pertaining to the recognition of norms and standards by rational beings his philosophy of mind must remain radically unfinished business.

(*SM* p. x)

(And as we know, for Sellars, the philosophy of mind is "a tangle in which all the major puzzles of philosophy can be found" (SSMB ¶1: 45).) Here it is clear that the adequate scientific or naturalistic explication of human beings' rational recognition of norms is to be an account of such norms *qua* the norms that they are, and not merely an account of a separate scientific subject matter. Or consider the following pregnant passage from his earlier 1949 article, 'Language, Rules and Behavior':

> The historically minded reader will observe that the concept of rule-regulated behavior developed in this paper is, in a certain sense, the translation into behavioristic terms of the Kantian concept of Practical Reason. Kant's contention that the pure consciousness of moral law can be a factor in bringing about conduct in conformity with law, becomes the above conception of rule-regulated behavior. However, for Kant's concept of Practical Reason as, so to speak, an intruder in the natural order, we substitute the view that the causal efficacy of the embodied core generalizations of rules is ultimately grounded on the Law of Effect, that is to say, the role of rewards and punishments in shaping behavior. The most serious barrier to an appreciation of Kant's insights in this matter lies in the fact that most discussions in philosophical circles of the motivation of behavior stand to the scientific account (whatever its inadequacies) as the teleological conception of the adjustment of organisms to their environment stands to the evolutionary account.
>
> (LRB ¶18, fn. 3: 299–300)

(In the final sentence Sellars is clearly referring to the *current* inadequacies of such scientific accounts.) In this respect Sellars regarded himself as outlining the basis for a robustly causal-naturalistic or scientific account of the ultimate nature and force of normative rules. And it is in this non-trivial sense, I suggest, that he understood the normative in general to be *causally reducible*, though *conceptually irreducible*, to the scientific-natural.

I am aware that these last remarks are too sweeping both in themselves and as an interpretation of Sellars on the nature of normative 'ought's. But that Sellars was up to something of the kind just described is crucial for understanding his analogous views on the 'logical irreducibility yet causal reducibility' of intentionality, meaning, and conceptual thinking in general. For it is this earlier distinction, I suggest, that also underwrites Sellars's broad claim in the passage from 'Philosophy and the Scientific Image of Man' from which we started (PSIM, in SPR: 6; in ISR: 374), concerning the *manifest image irreducibility* yet simultaneously the *scientific image reducibility* of the holistic framework of conceptual thinking (or the 'space of reasons'). In the final section I will attempt to spell out in general terms how the overall structure sketched out above in the case of normative 'ought's was held by Sellars to apply to the case of meaning and conceptual thinking, along with a brief final remark on the nature of *persons* in the synoptic vision.

3. Mind, Meaning, and Persons in Sellars's Naturalism with a Normative Turn

The basis for Sellars's general approach to the mind–body problem, in a nutshell, is a normatively characterized conceptual or functional role semantics that is supposed to apply both across natural languages and by analogy to a theoretically posited 'Mentalese'. The meaning of a linguistic term, on this view, is determined by its role within a wider pattern of 'language entry' responses to objects in perception (such as a ●this apple is red●); in formal and material inference patterns (such as 'if x is red, then x is colored'); and in 'language exit' transitions as described earlier in relation to 'shall'-intentions (such as an ●I'll take the red one *now*● followed, *ceteris paribus*, by my taking the red one). The normative aspect of this view is that the relevant roles are held to be determined by communally shared implicit norms of usage or linguistic 'ought-to-be' rules. Sameness or similarity of meaning (and of thoughts), on this view, is sameness or similarity of norm-atively constrained functional role. Sellars's so-called 'Semantical

Solution of the Mind–Body Problem', in the paper we have been looking at, was in effect an early version of a conceptual role semantics and a functionalist philosophy of mind of this general kind, cleverly disguised behind a convoluted and uninviting discussion of what he tended to characterize as a possible 'ideal scientific behaviorism'.

What the complex discussion in that early paper does shed light on, however, is what Sellars's overall position of 'logical irreducibility cum causal reducibility' is supposed to amount to in the case of his views on meaning and conceptual content. The general distinction that he appeals to in this early article, and subsequently throughout his career, is between what is *asserted* by a statement—what the statement *says*, what it describes or mentions explicitly—as opposed to further information that is pragmatically *conveyed*, or implied, or *presupposed* by the statement.[7] So consider the explicitly semantic statement made by one English speaker to another that

> 'Es regnet' (in German) means *it is raining*.
> (Or using Sellars's dot-quoting device:
> 'Es regnet's (in German) are •it is raining•s.)

On Sellars's view what this explicitly semantic statement does, roughly speaking, is to call upon one's antecedent knowledge of English in order to functionally classify the German 'Es regnet' as playing a relevantly similar rule-governed role as is played in *our* patterns of linguistic behavior, and in *our* perceptual responses, inferences, and actions, by 'it is raining's. Or as Sellars puts it in the 'Semantical Solution' paper:

… [A]lthough the use of semantical statements is a correct way to *convey information* about human behavior, semantical statements do not describe human behavior. Thus " 'Es regnet' uttered by Jones mean[s] *it is raining*" does not *mention* biographical facts about the role [of] utterances of 'es regnet' in Jones' struggles with his natural and social environment, even

---

[7] In *Making It Explicit* Robert Brandom has devoted considerable attention to developing, within his own framework, this particular aspect of Sellars's semantics.

though it is a mode of speech properly designed to convey information of this kind.

(SSMB ¶59: 79)[8]

The English speaker's background familiarity with the use of 'it is raining's enables her to take from the meaning statement the information that German speakers, for example, produce 'Es regnets's in various pattern-governed ways in relation to cancelled picnics, inferences concerning wet streets, meteorological reports, and so on.

The central idea is that, on the one hand, the latter behavioral and psychological patterns are what they are primarily as a result of the communally shared 'ought-to-be' norms or rules that have shaped them (together with whatever more basic representational structures the human animal comes equipped with; see Sellars MEV). On the other hand, however, causal explanations concerning the presupposed uniformities or patterns of linguistic behavior and inner processing themselves could in principle be given in entirely naturalistic, non-normative terms. The only real relations between mind and world, on this view, are the various resulting causal relations and patterns that have come to obtain as a result of the shared norms of linguistic behavior. As Sellars puts it in *Naturalism and Ontology*:

Thus, the fact that the uniformities (positive and negative) involved in language-entry, intralinguistic and language departure transitions of a language are governed by specific ought-to-be statements in its meta-linguistic stratum, and these in turn by ought-to-bes and ought-to-dos concerning explanatory coherence, constitutes the Janus-faced character of languagings as belonging to both the causal order and the order of reasons. This way of looking at conceptual activity transposes into more manageable terms traditional problems concerning the place of intentionality in nature.

(*NAO*, V §64: 110)

---

[8] The passage as printed in SSMB appears to leave out both the 's' in 'means' and also the word 'of' (or perhaps 'plays').

And this, in broad terms, is also the sense in which the 'framework of conceptual thinking' and the 'space of reasons' are supposed to be *causally reducible*, in a non-trivial explanatory sense, within the ideal scientific image of the world.

Clearly the crucial link in this account is a certain conception of socially maintained linguistic norms and of *rule-following* behavior generally. In the article 'Truth and Correspondence' in 1962 Sellars articulated an important meta-principle in this connection concerning the essential role of normative principles in shaping corresponding behavioral uniformities: namely, that the "Espousal of principles is reflected in uniformities of performance" (TC: 216). This in effect falls out from the account of 'ought's, 'shall'-intentions, and community intentions discussed earlier. As Sellars puts it in 'Some Reflections on Language Games' (1954):

Learning the use of normative expressions involves ... acquiring the tendency to make the transition from occupying the position 'I ought now to do A' to the doing of A. This motivating role of 'ought' in the first person present is essential to the 'meaning' of 'ought'.

(SRLG §67; in SPR: 350)[9]

Sellars's further comment upon this meta-principle makes a clear connection with the key broader issue concerning *logical irreducibility* cum *causal reducibility*:

I am not claiming that to *follow* a principle, i.e. act on principle, is identical with exhibiting a uniformity of performance that accords with the principle. I think that any such idea is radically mistaken.[10] I am merely saying that the espousal of a principle or standard, *whatever else it involves*, is characterized by a uniformity of performance. And let it be

---

[9] The version of "Some Reflections on Language Games" contained in ISR is the original version published in *Philosophy of Science*. It differs significantly from the revised version published in SPR. This quote is not present verbatim in the ISR version, though a very similar passage can be found in §51 of that version on p. 48.

[10] Cf. the 'radical mistake' that is 'of a piece with the naturalistic fallacy' in the passage from EPM quoted at the outset.

emphasized that this uniformity, though not the principle of which it is the manifestation, is describable in matter-of-factual terms.

(TC: 216)

Here again is the idea that the normative principle itself is, on the one hand, conceptually irreducible to any ideal scientific explanation of it in causal-naturalistic terms. But as before, here again he also stresses that the patterns or 'uniformities of performance' themselves are in principle describable in purely naturalistic terms, and they are thus explainable *as* the particularly shaped patterns that they are. And we have also seen that on his view the normative principles or 'ought's do not themselves generate any ontologically problematic properties for the naturalist, given his particular account of 'ought's in terms of certain kinds of shared intentions and desired ends.

The upshot of this overall picture is that our normatively rule-governed linguistic practices both presuppose and systematically maintain a corresponding underlying structure of specific sorts of natural-causal connections between language (and mind) and the world. This norm/nature presuppositional structure, I believe, can be shown to hold across the board for Sellars's views on the nature of meaning, intentionality, knowledge, and truth.[11] On his account,

---

[11] To take just one instance, consider Sellars's views on the relationship between the normative 'order of signification' (or meaning) and the non-normative 'order of picturing' (mental/linguistic representations), as illustrated by his discussion of the case of possible android-robots in 'Being and Being Known' in 1960. As he sums up that account:

In this sense we can say that isomorphism *in the real order* between the robot's electronic system and its environment is a presupposition of isomorphism *in the order of signification* between robotese and the language we speak.

(BBK ¶53, in SPR: 57; in ISR: 226)

Roughly put, that a complex 'picturing' relationship or structural isomorphism—one that is ideally describable in causal-naturalistic terms—has come to obtain between the robot's inner representations and the objects and events in its environment, will be a presupposition of our semantic interpretation of the robot's inner symbolic 'language' as *meaning* this or that. Working through Sellars's papers with this basic 'norm/nature' presuppositional structure in mind reveals it to be the spinal cord of his overall philosophical system.

(Sellars's discussion in BBK of the 'intentional' framework and the 'engineering' framework for interpreting the robot anticipates aspects of Dennett's distinction between

none of those normative phenomena themselves turn out to be *relations* between language or mind and the world. Yet the rule-governed practices in which those normative phenomena consist both presuppose and themselves generate, by their very nature, specific patterns of natural-causal relations and structures. For Sellars, it is the specific nature of the resulting *non*-normative causal relations and real mind-world isomorphisms that enable our cognitive systems—at least, at the bottom level and when we've got things right—to be *mirrors of nature* that correspond to empirical reality.

This is what I take to be the overarching strategy of what might be called Sellars's 'naturalism with a normative turn'. The strategy has essentially been one of exposing what *seem* on the surface to be certain puzzling 'factualist' or 'ontological' questions, perennially seen as requiring the appeal to various problematic primitive relations and quasi-relations to reality, to be in reality various complex questions concerning how our multifarious and projected *rule-governed practices* are related to the *natural-causal uniformities* which they both presuppose and shape. My suggestion has been that this is the general logical structure of Sellars's attempt to account for the conceptual irreducibility of normative structures within an uncompromisingly scientific-naturalist ontology. What we have seen Sellars argue from the beginning of his career is that this same strategy must also be applied to normative discourse itself.

As he puts it toward the end of the 'Semantical Solution' paper:

The situation is even clearer with respect to normative discourse. Whatever users of normative discourse may be *conveying* about themselves and their community when they use normative discourse, what they are *saying* cannot be said without using normative discourse. The task of the philosopher cannot be to show how, in principle, what is said by normative discourse could be said without normative discourse, for the simple reason that this cannot be done. His task is rather to exhibit the complex relationships which exist between normative and other modes of discourse. It will be noticed that if one combines our assertion of

the 'intentional stance' on the one hand, and the 'design stance' and 'physical stance' on the other.)

the causal reduciblity of Ought to Is, with our account of mentalistic discourse, the ethical naturalist gets everything he can reasonably hope for. Yet the fact remains that what is said by 'Jones ought to pay his debt' could not be said in even an ideal [extensionalist] PMese.

(SSMB 66: 82)

This overall picture holds out the prospect of an integration of the normative with the scientific-natural that would enable us to preserve the insights of both those who emphasize the irreducibility of the logical space of reasons and those who work under the explanatory regulative ideal of an all-comprehensive scientific naturalist ontology. And this, after all, was the main goal of Sellars's original philosophical attempt to envision a synoptic, stereoscopic fusion of the manifest and scientific images of 'man-in-the-world'—a project which has subsequently splintered into the perspectives of his 'left wing' and 'right wing' admirers respectively.

Finally, a brief comment on the important question of the resulting place of *persons* within this account of Sellars's synoptic naturalism. What there ultimately *really* is, for Sellars, is, so to speak, what the ontology of the envisioned ideal scientific image finally says that there is. So in this sense persons, like everything else in nature, are ultimately complex patterns and sequences of micro-physical events (or 'absolute processes', on Sellars's ultimate account; see FMPP lecture III). How is that final ontological vision consistent with the irreducible conceptual unity of the person as a self-conscious, deliberative agent? On the one hand, as Sellars puts it, "the irreducibility of the personal is the irreducibility of the 'ought' to the 'is'" (PSIM, in SPR: 39; in ISR: 407). Yet, as we should by now expect, he also remarks in the same context that our task is to show "that categories pertaining to man as a *person* who finds himself confronted by standards (ethical, logical, etc.)... can be reconciled with the idea that man is what science says he is" (PSIM, in SPR: 38; in ISR: 406).

On this key question as to the irreducible unity of the person, Sellars believed that it was Kant who had the key insight (assuming, of course, Sellars's proposed replacement of Kant's 'things in themselves' with the micro-ontology of the ideal scientific image). The following passage from Sellars's 'Phenomenalism' paper nicely situates the complex question of the ultimate nature of persons within the *irreducibility-cum-reducibility* structure that I have been attempting to clarify:

The heart of the matter is the fact that the irreducibility of the 'I' within the framework of first person discourse ... is compatible with the thesis that persons can (in principle) be exhaustively described in terms which involve no reference to such an irreducible subject. For the description will *mention* rather than *use* the framework to which these logical subjects belong. Kant saw that the transcendental unity of apperception is a form of experience rather than a disclosure of ultimate reality. If persons are 'really' multiplicities of logical subjects <that is, swarms of micro-particles, etc.>, then unless these multiplicities used the conceptual framework of persons there would be no persons. But the idea that persons 'really are' such multiplicities does not require that concepts pertaining to persons be *analysable into* concepts pertaining to sets of logical subjects. Persons may 'really be' bundles, but the concept of a person is not the concept of a bundle.

(PHM, in SPR: 101; in ISR: 345)

On Sellars's naturalism with a normative turn, then, the normative conceptual framework of persons, too, is 'logically irreducible' yet 'causally reducible' to the categorial ontology of the ideal scientific image. Making sense of the details of that difficult distinction must be central to any attempt to come to grips with Sellars's quest for a synoptic vision of our own ultimate place in the overall scheme of things.[12] I have also suggested that Sellars's own position may bear

---

[12] For an alternative and probing account of the role of normativity within Sellars's final synoptic vision, see the final chapter of Willem deVries's *Wilfrid Sellars* (2005). As far as I can see, the different reconstruction I offer here is not inconsistent with the fundamentals of deVries's account. Within the framework sketched here, in O'Shea (2007) I am perhaps able to push the radical (in some respects Feyerabendian) nature of Sellars's scientific realist vision further than deVries might be willing to go, while nonetheless preserving in full the conceptual irreducibility of the 'manifest' framework of thinking, sensing, and practically active *persons*. In the book I emphasize Sellars's

fruitfully on more recent and ongoing controversies concerning naturalism and the irreducibility of normative standards.

References

Brandom, Robert (1994), *Making it Explicit: Reasoning, Representing, and Discursive Commitment* (Cambridge, MA and London: Harvard University Press).

Churchland, Paul (1981), 'Eliminative Materialism and the Propositional Attitudes', *Journal of Philosophy* 78.

Dennett, Daniel (1987), *The Intentional Stance* (Cambridge, MA: Bradford Books/MIT Press (NB page 341 on Sellars)).

deVries, Willem A. (2005), *Wilfrid Sellars* (Chesham, UK: Acumen Press).

McDowell, John (1994), *Mind and World* (Cambridge, MA: Harvard University Press; reissued with a new introduction, 1996).

Millikan, Ruth (2005), 'The Son and the Daughter: On Sellars, Brandom, and Millikan', ch. 4 of her *Language: A Biological Model* (Oxford: Clarendon Press).

O'Shea, James (2007), *Wilfrid Sellars*, in the *Key Contemporary Thinkers* series (Cambridge: Blackwell/Polity Press).

Rorty, Richard (1979), *Philosophy and the Mirror of Nature* (Princeton, NJ: Princeton University Press).

Rosenberg, Jay F. (1980), *One World and Our Knowledge of It* (Dordrecht, Holland: D. Reidel Publishing Co).

Works cited from Wilfrid Sellars

BBK (1960) 'Being and Being Known', *Proceedings of the American Catholic Philosophical Association*: 28–49. Reprinted in *SPR* and in *ISR*.

EPM (1956) 'Empiricism and the Philosophy of Mind', originally in *Minnesota Studies in the Philosophy of Science*, vol. I, eds. Herbert

radical claim that in the ideal synoptic vision all of the *contents* of our perceivings, inferences, and volitions would be articulated in the language of the ideal scientific image itself. The support for these claims will be found in O'Shea (2007), chs. 2, 6, and 7.

Feigl and Michael Scriven (University of Minnesota Press), 253–329. Reprinted in Sellars *SPR*.

FMPP (1981) 'Foundations for a Metaphysics of Pure Process' (The Carus Lectures) *The Monist* 64: 3–90.

ISR (2007) *In the Space of Reasons*, eds. Kevin Scharp and Robert Brandom (Cambridge, MA: Harvard University Press).

LRB (1949) 'Language, Rules and Behavior', in *John Dewey: Philosopher of Science and Freedom*, ed. Sidney Hook (The Dial Press): 289–315. Reprinted in *PPPW*.

MEV (1981) 'Mental Events', *Philosophical Studies* 39: 325–45. Reprinted in *ISR*.

NAO (1980) *Naturalism and Ontology* (Ridgeview Publishing Co.). The John Dewey Lectures for 1973–74. Reprinted with corrections in 1997.

OM (1952) 'Obligation and Motivation', in *Readings in Ethical Theory*, eds. Wilfrid Sellars and John Hospers (New York: Appleton-Century-Crofts): 511–17.

PHM (1963) 'Phenomenalism', in *SPR*: 60–105. Reprinted in *ISR*.

PPPW (1980) *Pure Pragmatics and Possible Worlds: The Early Essays of Wilfrid Sellars*, ed. and intro. Jeffrey F. Sicha (Ridgeview Publishing Co.).

PSIM (1962) 'Philosophy and the Scientific Image of Man', in *Frontiers of Science and Philosophy*, ed. Robert Colodny (University of Pittsburgh Press): 35–78. Reprinted in *SPR* and *ISR*.

SM (1967) *Science and Metaphysics: Variations on Kantian Themes*, The John Locke Lectures for 1965–66 (Routledge & Kegan Paul). Re-issued in 1992 by Ridgeview Publishing Company.

SPR (1963) *Science, Perception and Reality* (Routledge & Kegan Paul). Re-issued by Ridgeview Publishing Company in 1991.

SRLG (1954) 'Some Reflections on Language Games', *Philosophy of Science* 21: 204–28. Reprinted in ISR. Reprinted in significantly revised form in *SPR*.

SSIS (1971) 'Science, Sense Impressions, and Sensa: A Reply to Cornman', *Review of Metaphysics* 25: 391–447.

SSMB (1953) 'A Semantical Solution of the Mind–Body Problem', *Methodos* 5: 45–82. Reprinted in *PPPW*.

TC (1962) 'Truth and Correspondence', *Journal of Philosophy* 59: 29–56. Reprinted in *SPR*.

8

Getting Beyond Idealisms

Willem A. deVries

Wilfrid Sellars is known as a scientific realist. His battles against the epistemologically motivated idealism of the empiricist tradition are familiar. Less well known are the extraordinary measures he took to avoid falling into a different kind of idealism—metaphysically motivated idealism.

1. Two Classical Routes to Idealism

A good general definition of idealism is hard to come by. Roughly, the genus comprises theories that attribute ontological priority to the mental, especially the conceptual or ideational, over the non-mental. There are many species of idealism. In the modern era, we find idealists on both sides of the empiricism–rationalism divide, with the historical trend favoring idealism. But there are different routes to idealism. For example, the idealism of Leibniz is interestingly different from that of Berkeley and Hume.

It always struck me as odd that the rationalists, who emphasize the centrality of the *mentalistic* notion of reason, were more inclined to realism, while the empiricists, for whom sensory perception and its supposed apprehension of *extramental* reality was the key notion, ended up as idealists. Assumptions made by the empiricists concerning the nature of knowledge and knowledge acquisition tend to preclude knowledge of anything other than the mental, and this was taken to impose a limit on ontology as well. In an ontologically driven idealism, it is not the epistemological principles that support the primacy of the mental; rather, there is a set of ontological principles about the nature of being which lead to the conclusion that being or the real (*what* we know) has certain characteristics that only or primarily mental things have. Epistemologically motivated idealism is common in the empiricist tradition but holds little attraction for a rationalist. The atomistic ontologies of the New Way of Ideas[1] (or the New Way of Words) make the realism/idealism dispute look simpler than it really turns out to be. Once the New Way of Ideas gives way to the more sophisticated analyses of Kant and Hegel, a new and more complex analysis of the realism/idealism distinction is required. Likewise, Sellars is often regarded as a simple, straightforward scientific realist, but that is far from the whole story.

A. *The Empiricist Route to Idealism*

The basic commitment of empiricism is that all conceptual content derives from experience. The idealism of the empiricists, however, does not follow directly from this principle alone. Among the theses that combined with the empiricist principle to yield idealism are:

- the myth of the given;
- the belief that what is given is one's current mental state;
- the belief in the atomic, hierarchical, constructivist structure of the mental or conceptual realm;

[1] The "new way of ideas" is a phrase deriving from Locke's arguments with Bishop Stillingfleet (see, for example, the long note appended to *Essay Concerning Human Understanding*, 1.1.8). It has come to stand for the general representationalist theory of mind shared by most pre-Kantians, in which 'idea' stands "for whatsoever is the object of the understanding when a man thinks," (Locke, *Essay*, 1.1.8). Ideas are assumed to be internal states of mind that have representational content, with which we are directly acquainted, and that mediate any possible knowledge we have of the external, material world. In articles such as "Realism and the New Way of Words," and "Epistemology and the New Way of Words," Sellars played off this phrase by characterizing the linguistic turn of the twentieth century as "the new way of words."

- the belief in the fundamental unity of the sensory and the conceptual; and
- the belief that conceptual content is derived from sensory content by abstraction.

How these principles combined to yield forms of idealism in both eighteenth- and twentieth-century empiricism is, in general, clear:

The empiricist takes sensory experience not only to be knowledge, but to be the very paradigm of knowledge and the source—via abstraction—of *all* concepts and meaning. If sensory experience is not only what we know first and best, but also is the only and ultimate source of all conceptual content, from which all our ideas must be derived or constructed, then our concepts and our knowledge are limited to the sensory and constructions therefrom. The sensory is mental, our concepts are mental; thus, there is no way to reach beyond the mental, so the mental must be ontologically and explanatorily prior to any other form of being. This basic reasoning can be found just as much in the twentieth-century phenomenalists as in Berkeley and Hume.

After the following discussion of the form of idealism that arose out of rationalist modes of thought, I argue that Sellars's arguments in his classic "Empiricism and the Philosophy of Mind" [EPM] have both the intent and the consequence of thoroughly repudiating this empiricist path to idealism.[2] There is contention over whether Sellars intends in EPM to reject empiricism or merely

---

[2] Wilfrid Sellars, "Empiricism and the Philosophy of Mind" (presented at the University of London in Special Lectures in Philosophy for 1956 under the title "The Myth of the Given: Three Lectures on Empiricism and the Philosophy of Mind"), in *Minnesota Studies in the Philosophy of Science*, vol. I, eds. Herbert Feigl and Michael Scriven (Minneapolis: University of Minnesota Press, 1956): 253–329. Reprinted with additional footnotes in *Science, Perception and Reality* (London: Routledge & Kegan Paul, 1963); re-issued by Ridgeview Publishing Company in 1991. [SPR] Published separately as *Empiricism and the Philosophy of Mind: with an Introduction by Richard Rorty and a Study Guide by Robert Brandom*, ed. Robert Brandom (Cambridge, MA: Harvard University Press, 1997). Also reprinted in W. deVries and T. Triplett, *Knowledge, Mind, and the Given: A Reading of Sellars' "Empiricism and the Philosophy of Mind"* (Cambridge, MA: Hackett Publishing, 2000) [KMG]. Cited as EPM, page references to SPR, KMG, and B editions.

reform it, but there can be no doubt that he intends to destroy the empiricist path to idealism.

B. *Rationalism and Idealism*

The rationalists share with empiricists most of the assumptions pointed to above, but they do not accept the notion that all conceptual content must be derived from sensory content. Their model of content is importantly different from the sense-based model that dominates among the empiricists. Rationalists can be tempted to think of conceptual content as image-like and thus like the sensory, but they are ultimately committed to defining the content of a concept in terms of its logical powers. Brandom, for example, identifies significant precedents for the inferential semantics he recommends to us in the rationalists.[3]

Thus, there is no smooth path from rationalism to idealism like that from empiricism to idealism. There seems to be nothing particular about the rationalists' conception of reason that steers them directly towards idealism, with one exception. The classical rationalists all believed in the absolute priority of God, and their conception of God heavily emphasizes His intellect and creative power. Except perhaps for Spinoza, God is conceived of in primarily mental terms. In this sense, classical rationalism does naturally favor the ontological and explanatory priority of the mental. But God is a very special, indeed, exceptional being. A primarily mentalistic conception of the Divine doesn't seem incompatible with a robustly nonmental conception of nature.

Rationalism does not try to read off its ontology from antecedent epistemological commitments. Distinguishable ontological commitments, such as Leibniz's conviction that true substance must be active rather than passive, must be brought into play to push rationalism in either a realist or an idealist direction.

---

[3] See Robert Brandom, *Making it Explicit: Reasoning, Representing, and Discursive Commitment* (Cambridge, MA: Harvard University Press, 1994): 93; *Tales of the Mighty Dead: Historical Essays in the Metaphysics of Intentionality* (Cambridge, MA: Harvard University Press, 2002), chs. 4–7.

2. Blocking the Classical Routes to Idealism

Sellars attacks the five theses that underlie the empiricist route to idealism:

- the myth of the given;
- what is given is one's current mental state;
- the atomic and hierarchical structure of the mental or conceptual realm;
- the fundamental unity of the sensory and the conceptual; and
- conceptual content is derived from sensory content by abstraction.

These theses are probably not independent of each other; they emphasize different dimensions of a common understanding of the mind's relation to the world. The explicit focus of Sellars's critical arguments in EPM is the myth of the given. Idealism barely raises its head in any explicit fashion, yet by the end of EPM any empiricist form of idealism has been ruled out.

A. *The Myth of the Given*

The myth of the given is a multi-dimensional thesis, in that it has both *methodological* and *substantive* sides. The myth of the given is the doctrine that the cognitive states of any cognitive subject include some that are both (1) epistemically *basic* (independent of the epistemic status of any other cognitive state), and (2) warrant the subject's non-basic cognitive states. Such basic cognitive states are traditionally taken to be the beginning points of all knowledge and inquiry, as well as "the ultimate court of appeals for all factual claims—particular and general—about the world" (EPM §32, in SPR: 164; in KMG: 243; in B: 69).

In pre-Kantian thought, it was commonplace to assume that what is given is our own mental state: we know our minds first and best. Methodologically, the belief that one's own mental states are what is *given* encourages a deliberate naïveté about the process of understanding our own minds. We need only direct our thoughts to consciousness itself and we will, perhaps with some practice or training, gain insight into its very nature. The idea that consciousness is somehow immediate and transparent to itself discourages us from recognizing both that *theory* is called for in order to understand consciousness and the mind, and that the appropriate *philosophical* theory is distinctively *meta*.

One of the important developments in twentieth-century philosophy, one that Sellars helped solidify, is the realization that *philosophical* questions about the intrinsic characteristics of the mental fundamentally concern the *logic* of those dimensions of our conceptual framework that describe, explain, and express our mental or conscious lives.[4] This development did not *begin* in EPM, but it comes into focus there. Methodologically, Sellars replaces the enterprise of analyzing the mind or mental states with that of analyzing our *concepts* of mind and mental states. The difference is not trivial. It is the difference between a philosophy of mind that knows itself to be *philosophy* and a philosophy of mind that still confuses itself with psychology.

Turning to the substantive side, there are at least two distinguishable beliefs associated with the myth that mental states are given. One is the thesis that if x is a mental state, then we are directly conscious of it.[5] This is a very strong claim; it is often weakened to the thesis that if x is a mental state, then we *can be* directly conscious of it. The mental is always available for our direct awareness or inspection. I'll call this the immediacy of the mental.

---

[4] There are non-philosophical, i.e., empirical questions about the characteristics and structure of consciousness. Those are not in the same sense about the logic of mental discourse and are subject to very different methodologies.

[5] Locke holds something like this when he writes, "[T]o imprint anything on the mind without the mind's perceiving it, seems to me hardly intelligible. ... To say a notion is imprinted on the mind, and yet at the same time to say, that the mind is ignorant of it, and never yet took notice of it, is to make this impression nothing" (*Essay*, 1.2.5). Perhaps this is even clearer in Locke's theory of personal identity, where he discusses "that consciousness which is inseparable from thinking, and, as it seems to me, essential to it: it being impossible for any one to perceive without perceiving that he does perceive" (*Essay*, 2.27.9).

(IM) X is mental $\Rightarrow$ x is available to direct consciousness.

Conversely, it has also been held that what is available for our direct awareness is the mental. We can call this claim the mentality of the immediate:

(MI) X is available to direct consciousness $\Rightarrow$ x is mental.

The Kantian notion of the apperception necessary to any thinking being is neither identical to nor entails either of these claims.

If something is available to consciousness, it is still an open question how it appears in consciousness, *as what* it is available to consciousness. In the baldest form of the givenness of the mental, consciousness of a mental state is necessarily of that mental state *in propria persona*, that is, as the mental state it is. We can therefore distinguish a stronger form of the immediacy of the mental

(IMS) X is mental $\Rightarrow$ x is available to direct consciousness as the mental state it is.

I leave as an exercise for the reader whether there is an interesting strong counterpart to the mentality of the immediate.

Sellars denies the immediacy of the mental in both its weak and strong forms, and he denies the mentality of the immediate. He refutes the mentality of the immediate in his argument in the first half of EPM that our knowledge of medium-sized physical objects is epistemically prior to our knowledge of either sense data or appearances, which in his argument serve as proxies for mental states more generally.[6] The denial of the immediacy of the mental in both forms is the burden of the myth of the Ryleans.[7] It is intended to help us recognize, first, that there is no direct entailment between mentality and an occurrent consciousness of mentality, and second, that another story about our consciousness of the mental that does not presume its givenness is possible, plausible, and empirically sensible.

---

[6] This is the burden of EPM, parts I–VI, in SPR: 127–61; in KMG: 205–40; in B: 13–64.

[7] EPM, parts XII–XVI, in SPR: 178–96; in KMG: 258–76; in B: 90–117.

Sellars's epistemology recognizes that immediate knowledge is indispensable. But to say that a cognition is immediate is to make a methodological point about how it enters the realm of the cognitive, not a substantive point about the object of cognition or the kind of concepts it mobilizes. In self-consciousness we would expect that some relevant cognitive states will be immediate. But Sellars rejects the notion that because self-consciousness has a special form of immediacy, normal empirical inquiry is displaced in favor of direct intuition or revelation. Our self-reports have the same evidential status as other observation reports: they are justified for us to the extent that they are reliable and known to be so.[8]

Rejecting the myth of the given cuts off one of the opening moves in the empiricist route to idealism, namely, the mentality of the immediate. In refusing to set consciousness off as a special domain of inquiry, Sellars also makes more difficult a defense of his Kantian conception of reason as necessarily self-reflective than some of its proponents might hope. He cannot appeal to a special access that consciousness has to itself metaphysically.

B. *The Assimilation of the Sensory and the Conceptual*

The second thesis rejected by Sellars is the assimilation of the sensory and the conceptual.[9] For Sellars, the conceptual and the intentional realms are identical: there is no nonconceptual intentionality. Possessing conscious sensory states does not obviously entail being self-conscious. It is reasonable to attribute conscious sensory states to organisms to which it is unreasonable to attribute any kind of self-consciousness. The Kantian conception of reason, according to which rational consciousness requires self-consciousness, seems at odds with the fact that we readily attribute consciousness to animals. If it is defensible, it must be possible

---

[8] See EPM, part VIII, in SPR: 164–70; in KMG: 243–50; in B: 68–79.
[9] This is the special focus of EPM parts V and VI: in SPR: 154–61; in KMG: 233–40; in B: 53–64. But it plays an important role in the earlier parts as well.

to explain how animals can have sensory consciousness without self-consciousness. This is not easy.[10]

Still, in Sellars's eyes it is vital to abandon the idea that the sensory and the conceptual are essentially of one kind, for once we have assimilated the sensory and the conceptual, the errors accumulate quickly. This assimilation forces us to misunderstand the fundamental logic of our talk of the sensory or the intentional. Because it does not follow from

(1) John has a sensory impression of a red triangle

that

(2) There is a red triangle [in John's line of sight],

"sensory impression of…" is clearly a nonextensional context. Sellars labels this a kind of "pseudo–intentionality." In Sellars's view, it is merely *pseudo*-intentionality because (1) entails

(3) *Something, somehow* a red triangle is present to John other than as merely *believed in* or *conceived of*.[11]

This is part of the logic of the sensory that distinguishes it from the intentional.

(4) John has a thought of a pink elephant

does not entail

(5) There is a pink elephant

but neither does it entail that

---

[10] For a discussion of Sellars on animals, see deVries, "Sellars, Animals, and Thought" on the "Problems from Wilfrid Sellars" website. URL: http://www.ditext.com/devries/ sellanim.html (Accessed July 10, 2008).

[11] Sellars argues this in several places, including "Sensa or Sensings: Reflections on the Ontology of Perception," *Philosophical Studies* (Essays in Honor of James Cornman) 41 (1982): 83–111; "The Structure of Knowledge: (I) Perception; (II) Minds; (III) Epistemic Principles," in *Action, Knowledge and Reality: Studies in Honor of Wilfrid Sellars*, H.-N. Castañeda, editor (New York: Bobbs-Merrill 1975): 305–10; "Foundations for a Metaphysics of Pure Process" [The Carus Lectures], *The Monist* 64 (1981): I, §§88–98: 20–2.

(6) *Something, somehow* a pink elephant is present to John in some way other than as merely sensed.

Intentional attributions, unlike sensory attributions, are ontologically noncommittal.

Assimilating the sensory and the conceptual also interacts with the myth of the given in perverse ways, for the fact that it makes no sense to speak of a sensation as *false* has mistakenly seduced some into thinking that sensory experience is always *true*,

though for it to strike them as it does, they must overlook the fact that if it makes sense to speak of an experience as *veridical* it must correspondingly make sense to speak of it as *unveridical*.

(EPM §7; in SPR: 134; in KMG: 212; in B: 24–5)

The assimilation of the sensory and the conceptual reinforces and in turn is reinforced by the myth of the given.

C. *Abstractionism*

As long as the sensory and the conceptual are thought to be quantitatively distinct variants of some common kind, an abstractionist theory of concept acquisition is virtually impossible to avoid. According to such a theory, complex sensory impressions are caused in us, and we can simply extract the elements of the complex, thereby refining them into concepts. This involves no transition in kind or transposition into a new medium, no significant change in the intrinsic properties of the mental state—all that is required is a kind of analytic attention to experience.

As attractively simple a theory as abstractionism is, its problems are legion. First, it encourages us to get the very being of the conceptual wrong by fostering the mistaken notion that concepts are similar to sensation. It therefore encourages us to misunderstand the logic of intentional and/or sensual states. It encourages a faulty understanding of the relation between concepts and their extensions. It presupposes an atomistic structure to our concepts that cannot ultimately be made coherent. Given the complexity of sensory experience, it is difficult to explain why we acquire the concepts we do rather than some others.

Kant's notion of an unknowable thing-in-itself may owe something to his not having distinguished clearly enough between the sensory and the conceptual and retaining abstractionism for empirical concepts. In Kant's view, the *de facto* nature of human sensibility is built into the structure of every empirical concept in such a way that it is impossible to conceive of a determinate spatio-temporal structure that is independent of our subjective forms of receptivity. We cannot, in his view, develop empirically significant concepts of 11-dimensional spaces or grainy time because our concepts are so tied to and informed by sensibility that he thought it would be impossible for us to develop empirical concepts of things as they are apart from our human forms of sensibility. The other side of this coin is that Kant also does not provide tools for an adequate treatment of theoretical concepts with only indirect ties to perception. Kant's own commitment to abstractionism for every a-posteriori concept is at least partly to blame here. Or perhaps it is more revealing to blame Kant's fundamentally ahistorical conception of concepts and concept-acquisition, for he allows only empirical refinement of concepts, not conceptual revolution or categorial evolution.

If we recognize the conceptual and the sensory as really different *kinds* of representations and do a better job than Kant in disentangling the forms of sensibility from our concepts of space and time, it is possible to develop concepts that are based in sensory experience but no longer confined to the contingent form our sensory experience possesses. We might be able not only to *think* but even *know* the thing-in-itself.[12]

D. "Non-Relational" Semantics

Abstractionism serves double duty in empiricist thought: it provides both a theory of concept acquisition and the base level for a

---

[12] This is the project I take it Sellars is prosecuting in *Science and Metaphysics*.

hierarchically structured theory of meaning. Sellars rejects it for both roles. Sellars's semantics is often characterized as "non-relational," and this is unfortunate, because it encourages the uninitiated to believe that Sellars cuts *all* links between words and things. Sellars denies that 'means', 'refers', 'true', and other semantic terms can be analyzed as *relations*. All semantic (and pragmatic) terms are metalinguistic functional classifiers, in his view. Semantic predicates indicate how an expression functions in its language, often by comparing its function to the function of some other expression we are presumed to be familiar with. Saying that

'*Rot*' (in German) means *red*

or

'Snow is white' is true

is not saying how '*rot*' or 'Snow is white' relates to the world, but conveys how they function in their respective languages. The first is an indexical predication that is true if '*rot*' functions in German the way 'red' functions in English; the second is true if 'Snow is white' is a semantically ideal linguistic performance in English.[13]

But '*rot*', 'red', and 'Snow is white' function in these languages by having numerous and complex relations to other expressions, to objects and situations in the world, and to human behavior. What Sellars really objects to is the *reification* of meaning, reference, and truth, i.e., the idea that there is some *one* meaning relation to the world shared by 'red', '*rot*', 'not', 'elephant', 'quickly', 'causes', and 'ought'. Linguistic performances are complexly related to the world; therein lies the richness and flexibility of language. Our

---

[13] Sellars presented his views on meaning in a number of places. EPM, part VII, in SPR: 161–4; in KMG: 240–3, in B: 64–8, was an early foray. His theory of meaning is elaborated more thoroughly in SM, ch. III, and perhaps most perspicuously in "Meaning as Functional Classification (A Perspective on the Relation of Syntax to Semantics)," *Synthese* 27 (1974): 417–37. He treats *truth* in SM, chs. IV and V, and in "Truth and Correspondence," *Journal of Philosophy* 59 (1962): 29–56. [Reprinted in SPR.]

metalinguistic terminology abstracts from that complexity, but we should not allow it to seduce us into seeing *only* simplicity, much less hardening that simplicity into a realm of non-natural entities and relations.

Because, for Sellars, semantics provides the model for intentionality, the crude semantics of classical empiricism is tied to an equally crude model of the mind.

Sellars's treatment of semantics directly reinforces his critique of abstractionism, for abstractionism is simply a form of relational semantics. We relate to some actual instance of F in sensation and can, by the power of abstraction, isolate the idea or concept of F. The idea of F is *of F* only and simply because it preserves that relation to actual instances of F. Furthermore, because the *of-Fness* of the idea is taken to be a matter of relation to given instances of F, its employment in judgments about such instances is taken to be both *certain* and *true*. We can see here how the myth of the given, the assimilation of the sensory and the conceptual, and the direct relationality of the semantic all reinforce each other. In the empiricist tradition, this recipe leads to a form of idealism that misunderstands the structure of knowledge and our relation to the world.

E. Beyond Empiricistic Idealism

There is, of course, much more that could be said about the myth of the given, the assimilation of the sensory and the conceptual, abstractionism, and the proper construal of the semantic. The point here is to show that Sellars has put up a major roadblock at every intersection of the traditional empiricist route to idealism. The fundamental empiricist insight that all our conceptual commitments must be grounded in experience is neither motive nor reason for idealism.

In this sense, empiricism had to be saved from itself. Running to its opposite, naïve rationalism, is, however, no significant improvement, for, as we have seen, classical rationalism subscribes to many of the problematic theses that got empiricism into trouble—the myth of the given, the sameness of sense and concept, and even (sometimes) the simplicity of semantic relations—and generates insuperable difficulties of its own. The problem space within which empiricism and rationalism operated needed to be transformed. For one thing, the New Way of Ideas is not adequately sensitive to distinctions between concepts of objects and concepts of properties, between what there is and how things are. The empiricists' leveling impulse also led them far too often to pay only lip service to the further distinctions between the descriptive, the prescriptive, and the syncategorematic, between object-level and meta-level ideas or concepts. Only after Kant realized that judgment is fundamental to thinking could philosophy begin to move away from the coarse idea that the idealism vs. realism debate is about the basic objects of the world—are they material or are they mental?—to a more refined debate about the formal characteristics of the world.

This is a transformation of idealism as well, a move from thinking of the world as constituted out of *ideas* to thinking of the world as constituted by *ideals*. Post-Kantian idealists, unlike the pre-Kantians, no longer held that the world is built out of subjective, mental things—ideas—but rather that the world is built in accordance with intelligible, normative, structural principles—ideals. Organization structured by intelligible, normative principles still accords ontological primacy to the mental, but begins to leave behind the simple dualism that plagued the pre-Kantians. It is this transformed problem space that Sellars found so congenial in Kant and his successors. For Sellars saw in early twentieth-century analytic philosophy—the New Way of Words—a repetition of many of the same errors that had plagued classical empiricism.

Before we move on, let me note that not all empiricists drew the idealistic conclusion; some, for instance, rejected the idea that only one's own mental state is given.[14] Why not assert as well the

---

[14] Classically, there are the French materialists. In the twentieth century, Neurath, the physicalist stages of Carnap, and Lord Quinton's "The Foundations of Knowledge," in

givenness of certain physical objects, properties, or states of affairs? Then one faces a choice: Is the mental given as well as the physical or, radically, is the physical the sole form of the given? If it does not lead us to empiricistic idealism, the unholy alliance of theses we've been examining pushes us into one of two simplistic and extreme positions regarding the place of mind in nature: either a reductivistic naturalism or a dualistic non-naturalism that makes it difficult to locate consciousness in nature at all, both of which have been explored in detail in the twentieth-century. The reductionist dogma that is ever attractive to philosophers—the notion that there is a limited, privileged vocabulary for the description of experience in terms of which all our meaningful terms must be definable—requires that our mentalistic and our physicalistic vocabularies either have some reduction relation between them or be entirely disjoint, independent, and basic.

The new or so-called "logical" empiricist, now impressed with the primacy of the physical, tends to be a reductivist/eliminativist who believes both that the entities posited in basic empirical science are all the basic entities in the world and that the language (or in Quine's term, the ideology) of basic science is adequate to say everything worth saying. The non-naturalist or dualist shrinks in horror at this idea and, because there are important things to say that cannot be captured in the physicalistic language of basic science, proclaims the need for other, non-natural, mental entities. Occupying the middle ground between the hard-nosed reductivist and the soft-core dualist is a difficult task.

Faced with empiricistic idealism, reductionistic physicalism or outright dualism, Sellars responds by invoking a pox on all the houses. As in Kant's time, the problem space needs to be transformed. To foreshadow the denouement of this paper, we can say that Sellars essentially accepts the ontology of the reductivist and the ideology of the non-naturalist. We can recognize truths that cannot

B. Williams and A. Montefiore (eds.) *British Analytical Philosophy* (London: Routledge & Kegan Paul, 1966): 55–86.

be expressed in the vocabulary of physicalistic science without accepting the existence of supernatural objects. Sellars's mobilization of themes typical of German idealism makes this possible.

3. New Roads to Idealism

Although Kant did not endorse the idealism of his predecessors, he uncovered a new source and motive for idealism. Kant's master thought is that experience requires both sensibility and understanding, i.e., that the objects of our experience or knowledge must be constructed by us out of the raw materials provided by sensibility and in accordance with rules constitutive of the understanding. Both of these roots of our knowledge motivate his idealism.

According to Kant, sensibility has a form that is subjective and contingent to us human beings, and thus any object constructed out of the materials provided by sense will necessarily be an object only to our human point of view, an object in time and usually in space.[15] Understanding also has a distinctive formal structure that will have to be found in the objects we experience and the world they constitute: we experience *judgeables*.[16] The form of any judgeable is itself a mind-dependent feature.

Kant retains the idea that there is a mind-independent world of things in themselves, but in his view it is not and cannot be the world we experience and know. The fundamental structure of the world of our experience is determined by the formal structures of receptivity and spontaneity, and thus the mental is ontologically and explanatorily prior vis-à-vis the phenomenal world. In particular, the a-priori truths that account for the intelligibility of the phenomenal world are mind-dependent.

---

[15] This is, of course, the argument of the "Transcendental Aesthetic" in the *Critique of Pure Reason*, A19/B33–B73.

[16] As Kant says, "we can reduce all acts of the understanding to judgments, and the *understanding* may therefore be represented as a *faculty of judgment*" (A69/B94). Anything cognizable must be something about which we can make a judgment.

The *new* source and motive for idealism uncovered by Kant consists in a deeper understanding of the nature of reason. First, Kant endorses the Enlightenment's contention that reason is autonomous "in the sense that it [is] self-governing, establishing and following its own rules, independent of political interests, cultural traditions, or subconscious desires."[17] Kant does not assume that reason reflects a *de facto* order of intelligibility that can simply be *found* in the world, as, arguably, his rationalist predecessors did. Kant's insight is that reason is *reflexively self-constituting*, that is, he saw that

(1) the intelligible order we seem to *find* in the world is one we *put* there;[18]

(2) it is a condition both on there being a *world* for us and on there being an *us* in that world;[19]

(3) intelligibility is a normative standard and thus a matter of rules and evaluability; and

(4) not only are rational beings necessarily self-conscious, but this is as well an essential condition on rationality, so that one is not rationally conscious until one is a rational self-consciousness.

This is why Kant believes that consciousness presupposes self-consciousness.[20]

---

[17] Frederick Beiser, *The Fate of Reason: German Philosophy from Kant to Fichte* (Cambridge, MA: Harvard University Press, 1987): 8. Espousing the autonomy of reason entails rejecting any attempt to reduce rationality and especially the *authority* reason possesses and exercises over our beliefs and our actions to anything merely mechanical, historical, or cultural, that is, to any *de facto* causal influence on the reasoning agent. Beiser's book is an excellent review of the importance of the problem of the authority of reason in post-Kantian thought.

[18] This is Kant's "Copernican Turn."

[19] This is the necessary correlativity of the concepts of *world* and *self*. Jay Rosenberg's *Accessing Kant: A Relaxed Introduction to the Critique of Pure Reason* (Oxford: Oxford University Press, 2005) brings out this theme in Kant very well.

[20] Neither the empiricists nor the rationalists would have denied that self-consciousness is important, but they did not see it as a *structural* element of consciousness. They saw it as a content that would naturally arise for consciousness in the course of things, not as a structural requirement on there being a course of things for consciousness at all. We abstract our concepts from the things we encounter, but don't we encounter our*selves* at every turn? This line of thought fell apart with Hume, though Hume tried valiantly to tell a nearby story involving confusions and mistakes. It was left to Kant to begin to sort out the complexities of selves and self-consciousness.

Kant's new conception of reason does not itself entail idealism. But it does entail that any rational consciousness must be a complex, holistically structured entity that imposes certain structural requirements on experience and the world. Understanding the structure of reason enables one to understand the a-priori structure of experienceable reality. That there is an a-priori knowable structure to experienceable reality is for Kant a strong argument for idealism, particularly when combined with his reflections on the nature of sensibility.

This new understanding of reason motivates an idealism of a different stripe from empiricist idealisms. The question is not what the objects of experience are composed of—impressions and ideas rather than material corpuscles or stuffs—but the structural relationships that determine their natures—the structure of the necessities in which they are enmeshed. This is the real difference between Berkeleyan subjective idealism and Kant's transcendental idealism.

Post-Kantian German idealism further purified Kant's reason-based form of idealism. Hegel rejected the line of thought he took to be common to Kant and the empiricists: the sensory is subjective and mental, the sensory is a fundamental condition on all experience and cognition of objects, so the objects we experience and know must also be fundamentally subjective and mental.[21] For Hegel, there is no inference to idealism from the nature of the sensory, for the subjectivity of the sensory is itself a perfectly objective and natural fact about organisms in nature.

Hegel also rejects the idea that judgmental form is a merely subjective form of human spontaneity, even though judgmental or conceptual form is *ideal* and mind-involving. Hegel is an unabashed idealist, an *absolute* and a *formal* idealist, who develops Kant's notion that the world of experience has a kind of logical

---

[21] Hegel did not believe that Kant successfully rebutted the charges of subjective idealism that had been leveled at him since the publication of the first edition of the *Critique*. See, for instance, Hegel's *Encyclopedia of the Philosophical Sciences*, I (the "Lesser Logic") §42, Zusatz 3.

structure. Hegel's idealism, however, is motivated entirely by his analysis of the nature of concepts and their relation to the world. It is an idealism grounded in his conviction that the structure of a subjectivity, a self, is the fundamental structure that is duplicated, in different "keys" as it were, both in concepts themselves and in the objects that actualize such concepts.[22] Hegel's idealism is the thesis that entities are self-subsistent only to the extent that they have the self-constituting structure of rational subjectivity. Minds are ontologically and explanatorily primary because they are the paradigm of the self-subsistent and self-sustaining, and therefore the world-whole must itself be something like a mind. Hegel's idealism is like Leibniz's, in that it is rooted in his analysis of being and existence, not in the process of cognition.

Kant thinks that whatever is logically structured must ultimately be ideal, either a mind or mind-dependent. His phenomenal world is logically, i.e., categorially, structured. But Kant is merely a *transcendental* idealist because he does not believe that the world as it is in itself is or must be logically or categorially structured. The world as it is in itself may well have structure, but it is not *logical* structure, which is an artifact of the judging mind. Hegel, in contrast, thinks that the world *is* logically structured. There is no kind of structure, according to Hegel, that is entirely *other* than logical structure; structure and logic are tied to each other. So the structure of things as they are in themselves is itself a form of logical structure.[23] Thus absolute idealism.

In adapting the Kantian notion of logical or categorial structure, Hegel extended and in some significant ways improved on it. Hegel introduces society, intersubjectivity, history, and development into

[22] The most thorough, best documented exposition of this idea I know of is Klaus Düsing, *Das Problem der Subjektivität in Hegels Logik. Hegel-Studien*, Beiheft 15 (Bonn: Bouvier, 1976); 3. erw. Aufl. (Bonn: Bouvier, 1995). See also Robert C. Solomon, "Hegel's Concept of Geist," in *Hegel, A Collection of Critical Essays*, A. MacIntyre, ed. (Garden City, NY: Anchor Doubleday, 1972).

[23] Hegel does not offer something as crass as this, but it is as if he argues that, since there is a logic of relations, and all relations themselves have a logical structure implicit within them, all relations are, effectively, forms of logical relations.

the categories, enriching them far beyond the thin Newtonian categories found in Kant. These are welcome extensions of Kant's conception. But Hegel preserves the autonomy of reason and the explanatory primacy of the mental by spiritualizing nature and valorizing teleological explanation above causal explanation. Nature is, in his eyes, merely the self-externalization of spirit.[24] The primacy of spirit is guaranteed for Hegel because the ultimate ground of all explanation is the self-realization of the Absolute.

4. Sellarsian Idealism

Sellars characterized himself as wanting to introduce a Kantian stage into the predominantly empiricistic analytic philosophy of the first half of the twentieth century. I argue that Sellars went beyond that. First, while Kant shows the lingering influence of the epistemologically-oriented, sense-based idealism of the empiricists, Sellars shows no such lingering influence from phenomenalism. Sellars's epistemology is realistic, not idealistic, from top to bottom. Second, his philosophy embodies important Hegelian lessons concerning the importance of the social, the intersubjective, history, and development. Sellars's ideology is therefore far richer than Kant's official categorial scheme, and that enables Sellars to make good on some of Kant's failures. Third, while in the first two respects Sellars moved towards Hegel, he does *not* end up a full-fledged Hegelian. Post-Darwinian that he is, Sellars naturalizes spirit rather than spiritualizing nature.[25]

---

[24] This means that according to Hegel, nature can and must ultimately be understood as a means that spirit requires in order to realize itself fully. Hegel re-introduces teleological explanation, which most early modern thinkers had abjured, both *within* the realm of nature and *of* the realm of nature. His arguments for reintroducing teleology *within* nature are surprisingly strong, but the arguments for explaining nature as whole teleologically are not. See my "The Dialectic of Teleology," *Philosophical Topics* 19: 2 (Fall 1991): 51–70.

[25] Sellars spends time in *Science and Metaphysics* discussing how to repair the weaknesses in Kant's treatment of sensibility that exhibit Kant's inability to escape entirely from the empiricist route to idealism, but I am going to pass over these discussions and turn directly

A. The Autonomy of Reason

In Sellars's eyes, Kant was wonderfully sensitive to the complex logic of epistemological and normative reflection. His awareness of the difference between the logic of material-object and spatio-temporal event talk and the logic of epistemological and normative reflection, however, left him with a very stiff challenge: "to come up with a concept of nature which finds a place for ... the *autonomy of reason* and the *reality* of the moral point of view" (I ¶87: KTM 362). In Sellars's view, Kant failed in this task, displacing both the autonomy of reason and the reality of the moral point of view into the unknowable in-itself, and leaving mysterious their connection to the nature in which we live and have our being.

That Sellars accepts this Kantian task, despite his own materialistic proclivities, shows us how deeply Kantian he was. But that Sellars rejects the Kantian attempt to fulfill the task by distinguishing between the phenomenal and the noumenal realms shows that, like Jacobi, he could not remain a Kantian.

Sellars makes several Hegelian moves. Like Hegel, he rejects the subjectivistic tendencies that arise from an idealistic interpretation of the sensory. Hegel rejects Kant's claim that space and time can only be forms of our intuition and does not exploit any argument from the nature of our sensory experience to support his idealism.[26]

Hegel's absolute idealism constitutes his attempt to explain and defend the autonomy of reason. What is at the heart of the idea of the autonomy of reason is not reason's *separateness* from something (or anything) else, such as material nature, but the *self-determination* of reason. The antithesis of autonomy is *heteronomy*, derivation from what is other than or external to reason. That is, Hegel does not defend the autonomy of reason by running to a substance

to how Sellars hoped to be able to preserve the sound insights of German idealism and its treatment of reason while remaining a realist and naturalist.

[26] For further explanation and defense of these claims, see deVries, *Hegel's Theory of Mental Activity* (Ithaca: Cornell University Press, 1988), especially chs. 4 and 7. This resource is now available at http://pubpages.unh.edu/~wad/HTMA/HTMAfrontpage.

dualism, but by pointing out that there is a "logical space of reasons" within which all our discourse occurs and which has a structure uniquely and irreducibly its own. In particular, the salient structures in the logical space of reasons are normative structures of *justification* and *enlightenment*; they are distinct from the causal structures of the physical and even the historical realm, though such causal structures can (indeed, must) be exploited by and for the justificatory and illuminatory purposes of reason.

The autonomy of reason is not, thus, the *isolation* of reason; it does not require that reason be cut off or disconnected from nature, but that reason is *responsible* for itself, even, perhaps especially, in the face of nature. The "logical space of reasons" must in some sense stand on its own, yet it cannot be a realm entirely cut off from physical and historical nature, even if its structures are not (and are not reducible to) the causal/historical structures of nature. Trying to understand how reason can be responsive to nature while being responsible for itself has been a major task of philosophy from Kant's first *Critique* through McDowell's *Mind and World*. In the New Way of Ideas, abstractionism and the myth of the given favored the heteronomy of reason, for they are both ways in which the intelligibility or rational status of a thought are determined strictly *from outside*. The pre-Kantians had to confront difficult questions about the status of their epistemic base, whether they construed that base as a set of self-intimating sensory states or as a faculty of intuition like the natural light. The underlying problem with both rationalism and empiricism is their atomistic foundationalism, the structure of heteronomy that makes it impossible for them to do justice to the autonomy of reason.

A more profound resolution to the problem, then, will seek to remove that structure of heteronomy, abandoning both abstractionism and the myth of the given. But care must be taken that in abandoning the structure of heteronomy, one does not cut reason off from nature and the world altogether.

B. *Autonomy and Self-Constituting Reflectivity*

Key, of course, is Kant's new conception of reason as a self-constituting reflectivity. That is, rational beings and their states possess normative statuses (standings in the logical space of reasons), the possession of which is constituted by the (mutual) recognition of the possession of that status by other rational beings.[27] In Sellars this conception of reason survives in the reflexivity requirements he attaches to language, to knowledge, and to rule-following generally.[28] Sellars claims that being a full-fledged language user, knower, or rule-follower requires the possession of a conception of oneself, indeed *knowledge* of oneself, *as* a language user or rule-follower. These requirements force a form of holism on the subject of conscious experience, because they entail that conscious experiences must occur to subjects that possess a certain structure of capacities. In order to have the cognitive architecture embodied in any real language use, the cognitive architecture that makes human knowledge possible, or the cognitive architecture of a creature that is governed not just by laws but by the *conception* of laws, that cognitive architecture must provide for the possibility of reflection in a normative, metaconceptual ideology. Furthermore, a normative, metaconceptual vocabulary is possible only in an ongoing linguistic community with intersubjective practices and standards of assessment.

There is a special form of holism, Sellars argues, that makes it intelligible how the natural, material beings that are persons could also be enmeshed in normative, social, and mental facts. It is a holism of systematically and contextually determined normative types embodied in independently and naturally characterizable tokens.

---

[27] There is a lucid exposition of how, in the German idealist tradition, the authority of reason is taken to depend on the mutual recognition of rational beings in Robert Brandom, "Some Pragmatist Themes in Hegel's Idealism," in *Tales of the Mighty Dead: Historical Essays in the Metaphysics of Intentionality* (Cambridge, MA: Harvard University Press, 2002).

[28] I discuss Sellars's several reflexivity requirements in deVries, *Wilfrid Sellars* (Chesham, Bucks: Acumen Publishing, 2005). See especially p. 277.

We can see how this works pretty clearly in Sellarsian semantics. Take a meaningful word of English, say, 'red'. What meaning does it have, and why does it have it? According to Sellars, the meaning of this term is the functional role its tokens play in three dimensions of linguistic activity:

(1) in perceptual reports—it typically plays a role in reports concerning a visually detectable characteristic of objects that have certain reflectancy values in the electro-magnetic spectrum;

(2) in statements of intention—statements of certain forms typically followed (at greater or lesser remove) by activity on the part of the speaker; and

(3) in good inferences (both formal and material).

This functional role turns out to be incredibly complex. An attempt to make it fully explicit in all its glory would be impossibly long and probably unintelligible. Furthermore, it is ineluctably *normative*: the functional role of 'red' cannot be equated to its purely *de facto* use, for it can be and is used improperly, and there are innumerable occasions when it could be used properly but isn't.

This entails, ultimately, that 'red' must be enmeshed in a system of assessment: its use is responsible not only *downwards* towards the world in perception and action, but *upwards* towards a projected ideal usage. Furthermore, the rules of this system of assessment must be viewed as *constitutive* of the linguistic entities involved. The words are not existents that are present and available independently of the system of assessment. Tokens of the word 'red' are, indeed, natural entities that can be described in terms of their physical properties, but any physical entity is a token of that word only because it is playing that functional role in the incredibly complex, rule-governed, propriety-ridden behavioral economy of English-speaking people. Similar physical entities may exist outside of that context—e.g., a pattern made in the sand by a line of ants, or an infant's very first babble that just happens to sound like 'red'—but they are not tokens of 'red' at all, for the *type* is holistically context-dependent. Thus the normative types specified by their role in this system are not *reducible* to the physical types in terms of which the tokens are independently describable. But the normative typology does pick out a robust, coherent, and self-sustaining patterning of human behavior above and beyond the physical level of description. Furthermore, we have excellent reasons to regard and respect this normative typology: if it were not robust and self-sustaining, there could be no descriptions at the physical or any other level.

The idea of a self-sustaining, holistic system of rule-governed, contextually dependent, normative *types* embodied in natural *tokens* provides Sellars with a general model for the autonomy of reason. That system *is* a logical space of reasons.[29]

Post-Kantian German idealism essentially emphasizes what I have called the upwards responsibility of reason and rational agents to the ideal system. The empiricists missed this dimension of responsibility entirely, and the rationalists thought of the ideal system as a given totality independent of sensory experience. Both were wrong. The ideal must itself be discovered or constructed in the course of human experience. It is this requirement that forces reflexivity onto the system and the agents operating within the system, for they can be responsible to and for the ideal only to the extent that they are self-aware of and in their activities. Reason is autonomous, not because it is cut off from nature, but because it is a process of self-assessment, reaching for an ideal that it must constitute for itself.

Later idealists complained that Kant did not make reason adequately autonomous, for his ideal is structurally static and incumbent on individual subjectivities only severally, apparently imposed on creatures of our kind by an outside agency, God. Kant's idealism still smacks too much of *ideas* and not enough of *ideals*,

---

[29] For an argument that there is something similar going on in Hegel, see Robert B. Brandom, "Holism and Idealism in Hegel's Phenomenology," in *Tales of the Mighty Dead* (Cambridge, MA: Harvard University Press, 2002): 178–209, especially sects. VIII and IX.

which he too often postpones infinitely and calls "regulative." Later idealists emphasized the *process* of assessment and refinement by which reason takes responsibility for itself and constitutes itself in the image of its own (evolving) ideal. It is in the *process* that reason is autonomous or self-determining, and the process is already present in the here and now; the autonomy of reason is therefore not a mere promise nor a merely regulative ideal.

C. *Ontology, Reason, and Nature*

Kant preserved the autonomy of reason by removing it from nature, the realm of natural law, and transposing it into its own realm, the ultimate ground of which is unfortunately beyond our ken. In contrast, Hegel preserved the autonomy of reason by spiritualizing nature, which he conceives of as the self-externalization of spirit, as itself determined by its teleological role in the coming to self-consciousness of the Absolute. For Hegel, the normatively constituted types that are concepts are not merely present in individual subjectivities, informing their activities in the world, but they can also be found *in re*, informing the world process itself.[30] In his view, the world itself is saturated with normativity; the Absolute, God, is immanent. Hegel's world is everywhere categorially structured—subjectivity and objectivity, the spiritual and the natural, the mental and the physical. Logic is the very heartbeat of Hegelian reality. Hegel has, for instance, no qualms about saying that nature is *imperfect* in various ways; he is very willing to assess various natural phenomena in terms of a normative standard provided by the concept of the self-realization of the Absolute, which itself is developed by *logic*.

The critical divide between Kant and Hegel turns on whether categorial or logical structure is to be attributed to things as they are in themselves. Sellars is Kantian enough that he could not go along with Hegel's attribution of logical structure to reality itself. Sellars

---

[30] See deVries, "Hegel on Representation and Thought," *Idealistic Studies* 17: 2 (May 1987): 123–32; *Hegel's Theory of Mental Activity*, chs. 11–12.

hoped to avoid this kind of idealist metaphysics by employing the distinction between object-language and metalanguage and re-interpreting metaphysical claims as "material mode" expressions of formal, that is, *metalinguistic* claims about the structure of our language.[31]

Sensitive as they were to the structure of norms and ideals that are constitutive of rationality, the German idealists took the "material mode" at face value. Kant could accommodate only some of the normative ideals constitutive of reason and traditionally expressed in material mode metaphysical claims, namely, the ideals that regulate causal discourse, such as completeness of causal determination. But other, especially practical or moral ideals did not fit into his scheme of nature, so he took them to be about another realm, an intelligible realm the objects of which lie beyond our knowledge. Hegel, in contrast, drew no such distinctions: the causal maxim and moral maxims all articulate normative and in a broad sense logical principles that inform the structure and operations of an imperfect nature.

For Sellars, there turn out to be two separable ontological enterprises. Sellars's well-known dictum, that "in the dimension of describing and explaining the world, science is the measure of all things, of what is that it is, and of what is not that it is not" (EPM §41, in SPR: 173; in KMG: 253; in B: 83), tempts one to think that philosophers should cede *all* ontology to the sciences. But that's not what he means. There is material ontology, the effort to establish the fundamental nature of empirical reality, and that should be left to science. But there is also *formal* ontology, the enterprise Sellars engages in, for instance, in *Naturalism and Ontology*. Formal ontology is a philosophical enterprise aimed at clarifying the fundamental structures of any usable empirical language. It is not an empirical, descriptive enterprise but an interpretive and normative one that is necessarily conducted in a

---

[31] This is a general strategy Sellars borrowed from Carnap. For further discussion see deVries, *Wilfrid Sellars* (Chesham, Bucks: Acumen Publishing, 2005), pp. 20–2.

kind of generalized metalanguage, i.e., a language that is not *meta* to any particular natural language.[32]

In Sellars's view, formal ontology must ultimately subserve material ontology. That is, the philosophical ontologist has done her job properly when she has developed a theory of representationality that enables us to understand how conscious, thinking, physical beings—rational but material representers—can exist in and talk and think about the empirical world in which they live. This is not a matter of *reducing* the language of thoughts, concepts, and representations to the object-language of physical events in space and time, but a matter of showing (1) how these two mutually irreducible languages are connected (itself a complex task); (2) that the language of physical events and processes is more basic and more general than the language of concepts and the linguistic; and (3) that, nonetheless, the normative language in which we think about thoughts is rationally supportable on its own terms. The space of reasons is autonomous, yet dependent on the physical realm. This—Sellars's naturalism—is a fundamental commitment on Sellars's part, one of those claims for which there is no further argument beyond elaborating the whole picture and hoping that it holds up better than any alternative in the face of critique.

Post-Darwinian, nominalistic, American naturalist that he is, Sellars holds that logic is not the structure of the world.[33] Rather, the structure of the world is causal; it is empirical science's job to discover it. He agrees with Kant in refusing to attribute categorial structure to things as they are in themselves. Sellars locates the mental and the normative *within* nature, not the other way around.[34]

---

[32] It is a common mistake among philosophers from Plato to Bergmann to mistake a generalized metalanguage for object-language talk about some special nonsensible realm or some special nonsensible aspect of reality.

[33] Sellars referred often to Wittgenstein's *Tractarian* dictum 4.0312: "My fundamental idea is that the 'logical constants' do not represent."

[34] Causation itself is just another category for both Sellars and Kant. Ultimately, Sellars's vision of the world is hyper-Tractarian, for his world is the totality of objects, not facts, a sequence of one damn thing after another. I have always been bothered by this:

D. Sellarsian Idealism

Sellars's explication of the autonomy of reason flirts with idealism in spite of his attempt to locate it *within* nature. Self-determining reason always threatens to break free of the material world and assert its own dominance, and Sellars blithely endorses several lines of argument that point in that direction.

For instance, one of the characteristic themes of German idealism is that object*hood* is correlative to conceptuality. Sellars's defense of the autonomy of reason reinstates the mind-dependency of the objects of experience, but it is instructive to see where Sellars departs from his idealistic forebears.

There are several lines of argument that point to objects being language- or framework-relative (and therefore mind-dependent). Take the Kantian idea that objects are that in the concept of which the manifold of intuition is united,[35] and the further Kantian idea that concepts are essentially predicates of possible judgments,[36] then the concepts available to one are also going to determine what counts as an object. This idealistic move might be mitigated if we had some kind of direct relation to mind-independent objects that enabled us to draw our concepts from the objects themselves. This, however, would be a form of the myth of the given. The relation of *direct reference* that makes objects themselves constituents of singular propositions, for instance, has also been thought to ground a nonidealistic conception of objects, but Sellars also rejects outright any such analysis of reference in his philosophy of language. The notion of a direct semantic relation (whether meaning or reference) is as mythological as the notion of a given. Our semantic as well as our epistemic connections to objects are holistically mediated by the complex linguistic system in which references play a role.[37]

---

if *all* categorial structure is *only* in the language/conceptual framework, can there be enough empirical structure in nature to account for the presence of a language/conceptual framework? But read on.

[35] CPR B137.   [36] CPR A69/B94.

[37] For elaboration of Sellars's philosophy of language see deVries, *Wilfrid Sellars* (Chesham, Bucks: Acumen Publishing, 2005), ch. 2.

Objects, therefore, are also framework- or language-dependent. That is clear from the fact that Sellars tells us outright that the objects of the manifest image are merely phenomenal in the Kantian sense. You may well think the chair you're sitting on—that solid, gapless structure of colored matter—is real, but Sellars disagrees. It is real *in* (or *to someone operating with*) *the manifest image*, but it is not *ultimately* real.

E. Beyond Idealism?

Sellars *is* a realist, and his particular brand of realism is *scientific* realism, but that label does not itself ward off the kind of idealism we see Sellars moving towards. What science does is revise, even replace, our manifest conceptual framework. If objects in general are framework-relative, then scientific objects are also framework-relative and mind-dependent. The realism of science is as thoroughly internal as the realism of the manifest image. And a merely internal realism is just another name for idealism, no?

Sellars thinks his scientific realism does not end up as another kind of idealism, thus distinguishing him not only from German idealism but also from Peirce, despite their common ground. His notion of *picturing* is what they lacked.[38]

Unlike reference or meaning, picturing *is* a relation, and it is a *natural* relation. Its general form is *object* pictures *object*.[39] Linguistic objects—in particular, names—considered as objects in nature, as tokens of some physical kind, picture nonlinguistic objects in virtue of bearing a complex, natural, and nonsemantic relation to the objects pictured. This is the *projection relation*. Sellars holds that any empirical language must have a level at which its true, atomic statements *picture* states of affairs.

Picturing, Sellars tells us, is not truth, "Picturing is a complex matter-of-factual relation and, as such, belongs in quite a different

---

[38] See SM V ¶75: 142.

[39] Though Sellars's notion of picturing is inspired by Wittgenstein's thought in the *Tractatus*, it departs significantly from Wittgenstein's idea that *fact* pictures *fact*.

box from the concepts of denotation and truth" (SM V ¶58: 136). But pictures can be assessed as correct or incorrect:

[T]he concept of a linguistic or conceptual picture requires that the picture be brought about by the objects pictured; and while bringing about of linguistic pictures could be 'mechanical' (thus in the case of sophisticated robots), in thinking of pictures as correct or incorrect we are thinking of the uniformities involved as directly or indirectly subject to rules of criticism.

(SM V ¶56: 135–6)

And not only pictures, but picturing *schemes* can be assessed as more or less *adequate* in a way that lets us project a Peircean ideal of adequacy. The ideal in adequate picturing is a system that enables the construction of arbitrarily accurate pictures of arbitrarily delimited regions of the world. Sellars thinks that he can use the notion of an ideally adequate picture of the world to provide an "Archimedean point outside the series of actual and possible beliefs in terms of which to define the ideal or limit to which members of this series might approximate" (SM V ¶75: 142). The relatively coarse-grained framework of the manifest image does not permit the construction of such an arbitrarily adequate map of the world. Scientific progress is the development of a framework in which such an arbitrarily accurate, sub-conceptual map of the world is possible.

The notion of an ideally adequate picture, Sellars hopes, allows him to have his cake—at least in the ideal—and eat it too. First, it enables him to defend the transcendental ideality of the manifest image:

We must distinguish carefully between saying that these objects [of the manifest image] do not really exist and saying that they do not really exist *as conceived in this framework.*

(SM V ¶95: 148)

Second, he believes he can argue that the objects of the manifest image are not *merely* transcendentally ideal.

[T]he concepts in terms of which the objects of the common-sense or 'manifest' image are identified have 'successor' concepts in the scientific image, and, correspondingly, the individual concepts of the manifest image have counterparts in the scientific image which, however different in logical structure, can legitimately be regarded as their 'successors'. In *this* sense, which is not available to Kant, save with a theological twist, the objects of the manifest image do *really* exist.

(SM V ¶102: 150)

Third, the notion of picturing, Sellars believes, enables him to reject idealism once and for all.

But *no* picture of the world contains *as such* mentalistic expressions functioning *as such*. The indispensibility and logical irreducibility of mentalistic discourse is compatible with the idea that in *this* sense *there are no mental acts*. Though full of important insights, Idealism is, therefore, radically false.

(SM V ¶78: 143)

Sellars's thought here is that not only mentalistic expressions, but normative expressions in general, all turn out to be material mode metalinguistic expressions that do not, therefore, pick out *basic* objects, objects that show up at the level of adequate picturing. Mentalistic discourse and its relatives are necessarily at a higher level and dependent on an object-language, the basic terms of which occur in pictures of states of affairs.

Sellars's vision is unsettling. *All* logical structure is mind- or language-dependent, so how could one divorce the notion of an *object* from that of categorial structure? The hyper-Tractarian world of objects that Sellars claims to be the "really real" seems unrecognizable, and not just because the scientific enterprise is not yet concluded. It is a *lawless* world of pure occurrents and processes where things "just happen". Sellars's scientific realism seems to reduce not only mentality but categorial structure generally to a mere epiphenomenal illusion, a set of patterns dancing across the face of nature, incapable of explaining either thought or being. But then what is the point of calling it a *scientific* realism? The language(s) of science will have as much logical and categorial structure as any language, and scientific fact will be as mind–dependent as any other kind of fact. Our knowledge of the world, even in the scientific millennium, will perforce be knowledge of fact. Furthermore, insofar as such knowledge is grounded in a picturing relation that holds between objects or states within us and objects in nature, that relation itself will not be or constitute knowledge, nor would that "grounding" relation be a form of justification. Perhaps categorial structure is, in the end, distinguishable from logical structure, and we can deny that the logical constants represent without denying all structure to the world.

References

Beiser, Frederick, *The Fate of Reason: German Philosophy from Kant to Fichte* (Cambridge, MA: Harvard University Press, 1987).

Brandom, Robert, *Making it Explicit: Reasoning, Representing, and Discursive Commitment* (Cambridge, MA: Harvard University Press, 1994).

—— *Tales of the Mighty Dead: Historical Essays in the Metaphysics of Intentionality* (Cambridge, MA: Harvard University Press, 2002).

deVries, Willem A., "Hegel on Representation and Thought," *Idealistic Studies* 17: 2 (May 1987): 123–32.

—— *Hegel's Theory of Mental Activity* (Ithaca: Cornell University Press, 1988) available at http://pubpages.unh.edu/~wad/HTMA/HTMA frontpage.

—— "The Dialectic of Teleology," *Philosophical Topics* 19: 2 (Fall 1991): 51–70.

—— "Sellars, Animals, and Thought" on the "Problems from Wilfrid Sellars" website. URL: http://www.ditext.com/devries/sellanim.html (Accessed January 10, 2009).

—— *Wilfrid Sellars* (Chesham, Bucks: Acumen Publishing, and Montreal: McGill-Queen's University Press: 2005)

Düsing, Klaus, *Das Problem der Subjektivität in Hegels Logik. Hegel-Studien*, Beiheft 15 (Bonn: Bouvier, 1976); 3. erw. Aufl. (Bonn: Bouvier, 1995).

Hegel, Georg Wilhelm Friedrich, *Enzyklopedie der philosophischen Wissenschaften. Werke*, eds. Eva Moldenhauer and Karl Markus Michel, vols. 8–10 (Frankfurt am Main: Suhrkamp, 1970).

Kant, Immanuel, *Critique of Pure Judgment*. Trans. and ed. P. Guyer and A. Wood (Cambridge: Cambridge University Press, 1998).

Locke, John, *An Essay Concerning Human Understanding*, ed. P. H. Nidditch (Oxford: Clarendon Press, 1975).

McDowell, John, *Mind and World* (Cambridge, MA: Harvard University Press, 1994).

Quinton, Anthony, "The foundations of knowledge." In B. Williams and A. Montefiore (eds.), *British Analytical Philosophy* (London: Routledge & Kegan Paul, 1966): 55–86.

Rosenberg, Jay F., *Accessing Kant: A Relaxed Introduction to the Critique of Pure Reason* (Oxford: Oxford University Press, 2005).

Sellars, Wilfrid S., "Epistemology and the New Way of Words," *The Journal of Philosophy* 44 (1947): 645–60. [ENWW, Reprinted in PPPW].

—— "Realism and the New Way of Words," *Philosophy and Phenomenological Research* 8 (1948): 601–34. [RNWW, Reprinted in *Readings in Philosophical Analysis*, eds. Herbert Feigl and Wilfrid Sellars (New York: Appleton-Century-Crofts, 1949); also reprinted in PPPW].

—— "Empiricism and the Philosophy of Mind," (Presented at the University of London in Special Lectures in Philosophy for 1956 under the title "The Myth of the Given: Three Lectures on Empiricism and the Philosophy of Mind"), in *Minnesota Studies in the Philosophy of Science*, vol. I, eds. Herbert Feigl and Michael Scriven (Minneapolis: University of Minnesota Press, 1956): 253–329. Reprinted with additional footnotes in *Science, Perception and Reality* (London: Routledge & Kegan Paul, 1963), re-issued by Ridgeview Publishing Company in 1991. [SPR] Published separately as *Empiricism and the Philosophy of Mind: with an Introduction by Richard Rorty and a Study Guide by Robert Brandom*, ed. Robert Brandom (Cambridge, MA: Harvard University Press, 1997). [B] Also reprinted in W. deVries and T. Triplett, *Knowledge, Mind, and the Given: A Reading of Sellars' "Empiricism and the Philosophy of Mind"* (Cambridge, MA: Hackett Publishing, 2000) [KMG]. Cited in the text as EPM, page references to SPR, KMG, and B editions.

—— "Truth and Correspondence," *Journal of Philosophy* 59 (1962): 29–56. [Reprinted in SPR].

—— *Science, Perception and Reality* (London: Routledge & Kegan Paul, 1963). Republished by Ridgeview Publishing Company, Atascadero, California, 1991. [SPR].

—— *Science and Metaphysics: Variations on Kantian Themes*, The John Locke Lectures for 1965–66 (London: Routledge & Kegan Paul, 1967). Republished by Ridgeview Publishing Company, Atascadero, California, 1992.

—— "...this I or he or it (the thing) which thinks...," *Proceedings of the American Philosophical Association* 44 (1972): 5–31. The presidential address, American Philosophical Association (Eastern Division), for December 1970. [Reprinted in KTM].

—— "Meaning as Functional Classification (A Perspective on the Relation of Syntax to Semantics)," *Synthese* 27 (1974): 417–37. [Reprinted in ISR].

—— "The Structure of Knowledge: (I) Perception; (II) Minds; (III) Epistemic Principles." In *Action, Knowledge and Reality: Studies in Honor of Wilfrid Sellars*, H.-N. Castañeda (ed.) (New York: Bobbs-Merrill 1975: 305–10).

—— *Pure Pragmatics and Possible Worlds: The Early Essays of Wilfrid Sellars*, ed. and intro. Jeffrey F. Sicha (Reseda, California: Ridgeview Publishing Company, 1980). [PPPW].

—— "Foundations for a Metaphysics of Pure Process" [The Carus Lectures]. *The Monist* 64 (1981): I, §§88–98: 20–2.

—— "Sensa or Sensings: Reflections on the Ontology of Perception," *Philosophical Studies* (Essays in Honor of James Cornman) 41 (1982): 83–111.

—— *Kant's Transcendental Metaphysics: Sellars' Cassirer Lectures and Other Essays*, ed. and intro. Jeffrey F. Sicha (Atascadero, California: Ridgeview Publishing Co., 2002). [KTM].

Solomon, Robert C., "Hegel's Concept of Grist." In *Hegel, A Collection of Critical Essays*, ed. A. MacIntyre (Garden City, NY: Anchor Doubleday, 1972).

Wittgenstein, Ludwig, *Tractatus Logico-Philosophicus* (London: Routledge & Kegan Paul Ltd, 1961).

9

Functions Between Reasons and Causes: On Picturing

Johanna Seibt

In EPM Sellars exposes severe shortcomings of the classical conception of mental representations as causally given cognitive contents. Since Sellars famously characterizes his criticisms as an attempt "to kill a myth—the Myth of the Given" (EPM §63, in SPR: 195; in KMG: 276; in B: 117) and "a general critique of the framework of givenness" (EPM §1, in SPR: 128; in KMG: 205; in B: 14) Sellars's notion of the given and givenness is often identified with the particular variety of givenness that is under attack in EPM, namely, the givenness of impressions or ideas in modern philosophy. However, elsewhere Sellars affirms that "there is a dimension of givenness (or takenness) that is not in dispute" (FMPP I §87). This dimension of givenness, which ensures that when we change our concepts "we do not change that [in nature] to which we are responding" (ibid.), forms an essential part of Sellars's own account of intentionality and representation. In EPM this dimension of givenness comes briefly into view when Sellars introduces "psychological nominalism" and explains that

once sensations ... have been purged of epistemic aboutness ... the way is clear to recognizing that basic word–world associations hold, for example, between 'red' and red *physical objects*, rather than between 'red' and a supposed class of private red particulars ... [i.e., the 'ideas' or 'sense impressions' of classical empiricism, and that these "ties" of word–world associations are] *causally* mediated by sensations.

(EPM §29, in SPR: 161; in KMG: 240; in B: 64)

Sellars's basic idea is to replace the classical notion of mental representation with two relations, a field of causal "word–world associations", which is to account for the 'aboutness aspect' of classical representations; and a network of functional relations between sentences, which is to account for the 'content aspect'. As Sellars elaborates in later writings, the new non-representational approach to linguistic 'representation' capitalizes on the double-life of linguistic items as both causal and normative, which derives from the fact that function needs material embodiment and that norm–governed behavior is reflected in causal uniformities:

Thus, the fact that the underlying uniformities (positive and negative) involved in language-entry, intra-linguistic and language departure trans-itions of a language are governed by specific ought-to-be statements in its metalinguistic stratum, and these in turn by ought-to-bes and ought-to-dos concerning explanatory coherence, constitutes the Janus-faced character of languagings as belonging to both the causal order and the order of reasons. This way of looking at conceptual activity transposes into more manageable terms traditional problems concerning the place of intentionality in nature.

(NAO V §64: 130/110)

While contents as such cannot be caused, contrary to the Cartesian and classical empiricist account of mental representation, material embodiments of functions can nevertheless stand in causal relations. Sellars's notion of 'picturing' denotes, on first approximation, the causal part of this replacement strategy—the relationship that the 'Janus-faced' character of languagings establishes between natural items and natural items embodying the functions that constitute the contents of the observation sentences of a language.

On Sellars's notion of picturing hinges "the dimension of given-ness that is not in dispute". Surprisingly, while Sellars's functional analysis of content has been widely discussed and expanded, the notion of picturing has received comparatively little constructive attention.[1] Ignoring Sellars's metaphor of the "Janus-faced character of languagings as belonging to both the causal order and the order of reasons," the 'social-pragmatist movement' focused on the normative domain in the light of reason, leaving the darker causal issues to the purview of neuroscientists or behaviorists. In the following I will suggest that Sellars's account of picturing is worth a closer look if we wish to follow the trajectories of an 'anti-representationalist' philosophy of mind that Sellars draws out in sections XV and XVI of EPM.

I will argue exegetical and systematic points. On the one hand, a better understanding of 'picturing' will enable us to resolve a number of problems in Sellars's interpretation. It can help us to clarify in which way "the dimension of givenness that is not in dispute" does not commit Sellars to a realist stance in any sense of this term that contrasts with a transcendental project. Most importantly perhaps, it can help us to understand why Sellars had good reasons to insist on sensations—though 'purged from epistemic aboutness'—playing an indispensable role in a philosophical account of perceptual knowledge, i.e., in which sense he retained empiricist intuitions. On the other hand, the notion of picturing has independent systematic interest beyond such exegetical questions. Once we appreciate that picturing is not an abstract relation but a certain type of non-linear causal processing, we can envisage more easily how the tension between the natural and the normative in a Sellarsian philosophy of mind can be addressed in ways that go beyond Sellars's reliance on the principle that rule-governed behavior is reflected in causal uniformities. As I also shall argue here, the processing that Sellars calls 'picturing' can

---

[1] Early discussions can be found in Margolis 1967 and Bonjour 1973. In June 2005 I presented a precursor of this paper at the *McDowell-Sellars Conference*, arguing for a process-based conception of picturing (see sect. 5 below). In Spring 2006 Jay Rosenberg sent me a draft of his "Sellarsian Picturing" (published 2007), offering a scholarly exegesis of the relevant parts of SM and MEV together with a reconstructive analysis of the deep systematic points at issue. In reworking my 2005 paper for the EPM-conference in London I benefited, as always, in many ways from reading Rosenberg's work on the issue.

be productively connected to recent work on natural functions, the origins of normativity in nature, and anti-representational accounts of cognition in theoretical biology and cognitive science.

To restate the main objective of this paper from a somewhat different angle, the interpretation of picturing I will offer here puts functions center stage, as the category that mediates between the domains of causes and reasons by extending over parts of both. In EPM Sellars focuses on the demarcation of the logical space of reasons from the causal order, in order to show that the classical concept of a sense datum is a "mismating of ideas" (§10) such that the causal and the logical dimension are entangled in ill begotten ways. But the systematic significance of Sellars's criticism of the classical empiricist's "crossbreeding of ideas" depends *also* on the viability of his positive account about the right kind of contact between the causal and the logical or normative, as unfolded especially in his late writings, "Mental Events" (MEV, 1981) and the Carus Lectures (FMPP, 1981). So far the standard reading of Sellars's conception of the relation between the causal and the normative has focused on the 'Janus-faced character' of norm-governed items as emphasized in his writings up until the mid-1970s.[2] But a Sellarsian account of language and mind can offer more than the mere claim that items in logical space are necessarily causally embodied, or that norm-governed behavior is causally reflected. As I shall suggest here, Sellars has left us enough hints to understand Sellarsian picturing in analogy to an emergent 'dynamic regime' in natural systems (such as the formation of hurricanes, biological cells, or the organization of ant hills). Sellarsian picturing is a type of natural, causal functioning that occurs in sensory systems as the emergent 'dynamic regime' of pattern-governed functioning, which in turn engenders more encompassing dynamic regimes of normative regulation up to the "rule-following" that constitutes the space of reasons.

---

[2] For an elaboration of the irreducibility-cum-reducibility thesis implied by the 'Janus-faced' character see O'Shea, this volume, ch. 7.

1. The Initial Characterization

The purpose of Sellars's picturing relation is, roughly speaking, to accommodate the intuition that the truth of empirical statements should not be defined in terms of coherence ("semantic assertibility") alone.[3] Sellars introduces the notion of picturing in the context of an account of "factual truths", with explicit reference to Wittgenstein's "picture theory" in the *Tractatus* (SM 118; cf. also BBK and TC). One might question Sellars's decision to associate the envisaged relationship terminologically with the *Tractatus* conception of elementary propositions as pictures of facts, since in the end, as Sellars admits, the dissimilarities outweigh the similarities and the Tractarian conception serves mainly as contrast.

I shall draw a sharp distinction between what I shall *initially* characterize as two dimensions of isomorphism between the intellect and the world:

(a) an isomorphism in the real order
(b) an isomorphism in the logical order

I shall use the verb 'to picture' for the first of these 'dimensions' and the verb 'to signify' for the second. I shall argue that a confusion between *signifying* and *picturing* is the root of the idea that the intellect as *signifying* the world is the intellect as informed in a unique (or immaterial) way by the natures of things in the real order. [Footnote: "this same confusion is the source of some of the more obscure features of Wittgenstein's *Tractatus*".]

(BBK §32, in SPR: 50; in ISR: 218–19)

[We need to substitute] the schema

[natural-linguistic objects] O_1', O_2', ... O_n' make up a picture of [objects] O_1, O_2, ... O_n by virtue of such and such facts about O_1', O_2', ... O_n'

---

[3] Cf. TC, SM ch. 3, NAO ch. 5.

for the Tractarian schema

> Linguistic fact pictures non-linguistic fact.

> (...) The natural-linguistic objects, which, by virtue of standing in certain matter-of-factual relationships to one another and to these non-linguistic objects, constitute a picture of them in the desired sense, are the linguistic counterparts of non-linguistic *objects* (*not* facts) ... [I]t is a system of elementary *statements* (*qua* natural-linguistic objects) that is the picture....

> (TC: 215; NAO V §92: 139/118)

The basic idea of Sellarsian picturing is easy enough to understand in these formulations. Picturing is a relationship of causally founded co-ordination between two concrete collections of natural items. Items in one of these collections, so-called "natural-linguistic objects", fulfil two additional constraints: first, these items must lend themselves to use as material embodiments of the 'elementary' (empirical) statements of a language game L; second, they must exhibit the kind of uniformities that are produced once that game is played.

The simplicity of this solution is deceptive, however. Sellars's claim that the key to an adequate account of empirical knowledge, or more generally, of mind–reality connections, hinges on the proper appreciation of the Janus-faced character of language is a kind of pedagogical encouragement to probe this relation more systematically. In which sense can material items 'embody' the linguistic role of an empirical statement in a language game? Would they not have to be *either* material *or else* normative, in the sense in which the 'bishop' in a wooden chess game is either the bishop *or else* a piece of wood, but cannot be both at the same time? If the causal order and the normative order are as strictly diverse as EPM makes them out to be, how could there be anything that we can conceive as belonging to both 'orders' at the same time? In other words, how are we to understand the hyphen in Sellars's notion in "natural-linguistic objects"? Let us take a closer look.

2. Natural-Linguistic Objects

"Natural-linguistic objects" are those natural items that can be said to picture. They are not necessarily the written or oral expressions of a natural language: they may be the hand movements of sign language, rhythmic patterns of an acoustic code, machine states of a Turing machine, or neurophysiological states. In fact, they include any collection of material items embodying a normative system as long as "there is a relevant degree of similarity" (MEV §36: 331; in ISR: 288) between the functioning of these items in their system and the observation statements of a natural language. Importantly, the functioning of language is prior in the order of knowing, as the direction of elucidation goes from the functioning of written or uttered expressions in natural languages to the functioning of material signs in other normative systems. Thus a natural-linguistic object is a member of any collection of material items that we can take to be functional analogues of the observation statements of some natural language.[4]

But this does not imply that all natural-linguistic objects are 'linguistic' or 'normative' items in the sense of the 'fully articulated', explicit normativity exhibited by the languages we use to make candid observations, i.e., languages containing normative vocabulary and explicit inference rules. Material items that picture are *implicitly normative* items that merely function like those that are explicitly subject to certain formative and inferential rules. In Sellars's view the distinction between normative items and items that function like them—or, as I shall put it, items with 'high-grade' and 'low-grade' normativity—provides the pivotal point for a "demystification of the place of mind in nature" (MEV §37: 332; in ISR: 288). Before looking at the further implications of this distinction, let us first try to understand it in greater detail.

---

[4] Sellars expressly introduces an "extended interpretation of the dot-quoting device" to allow for inclusion of non-linguistic functional analogues (MEV §§76–7: 340; in ISR: 295–6).

2a: *Three Conditions for Low-Grade Normativity*

In MEV Sellars labels collections of material items that embody a functional analogue of the observational part of a natural language as "representational systems". Even though these are modeled on "animal representational systems" (MEV §6: 326; in ISR: 283), the term 'representational' unhappily resonates with the presuppositions of the classical Cartesian notion of representation. Thus I will instead speak here of 'orientation systems'.[5] There are three conditions for membership in an orientation system.

First, orientation systems are systems that guide an agent, machine, or organism; they are not tools that are used. Even though we often use statements of natural languages instrumentally, there is "a more basic dimension" of language "presupposed by communication", where utterances are neither speech acts nor even pragmatic routines. An orientation system must function in the way in which language functions when we are 'thinking-out-loud', when we engage in "candid, spontaneous, overt verbal behavior".[6] In 'thinking-out-loud', language serves "as a medium in which we think" (MEV §11: 327; in ISR: 283) and supports the cognitive orientation of speakers in an automatic fashion, by facilitating and blocking certain transitions relative to a cognitive position. Sellars elucidates this form of unreflected cognitive operation by means of comparisons with position-sensitive action selection in a robot that is programmed to generate a map of its environment and adjusts its behavior relative to the data on this map.

Second, the material items embodying an orientation system must function like propositions. The internal composition (the syntactic structure) of such a propositional object is irrelevant.

---

[5] On the notion of orientation as replacement for representation in a theory of cognition cf. Seibt 2005a.

[6] MEV §12: 327; in ISR: 284. More precisely, a normative system N is an orientation system only if the functions of N include the functions of natural language statements in 'thinking-out-loud'.

Sellars famously championed a *flatus voci* account of predication in which predicates merely provide materially different articulation contexts or, more generally, 'tokening environments' for names. But a natural-linguistic object must be something that can count as the embodiment of a proposition; it must have at least two different material features one of which can embody the function of unique positioning in spatio-temporal terms (traditionally construed as 'reference') and the other the function of positioning in a network of inferential relationships (traditionally construed as 'characterizing (something) as (being such-and-such)').[7]

Third, in order for a collection of material items to count as an embodiment of an orientation system, these items must exhibit uniformities corresponding to the tripartite rule set of a natural language, governing language entry, intra-linguistic transitions, and language departure moves. Ordinary maps are not embodiments of orientation systems since they do not document the inferences we draw from a map. Sequences of machine states in a Turing machine or sequences of neurophysiological states make better candidates for material embodiments of an orientation system in an organism, since one may find in these not only the uniformities reflecting

---

[7] Embodying the function of 'characterizing as' must not be construed as predication, however. The point of Sellars's "Jumblese"—a language where different style designs of names replace predicate expressions—is that "not only are the predicative expressions of a language dispensable, but the very *function* performed by predicates is dispensable" (NAO III §37: 59/51), i.e., with the idea that anything in the tokening environment of a name—whether separate expression or style of sign design—has, as such, a semantic function. There is, in other words, an important distinction to be drawn in Sellars's view between (i) the direct attribution of semantic functions to the material features of an item and (ii) the requirement that an item have two material features allowing for this item to be involved in two types of functioning in a certain game (cf. NAO 56ff and TTP). Note, though, that in some places in MEV Sellars unhelpfully employs the traditional philosophical idiom without scare quotes, obscuring the intended reinterpretation of the relevant terms. For example: "To have propositional form, a basic representational state must represent an *object* and represent it *as* of a certain character. In case of sophisticated [representational systems] we speak of a basic representational state as *referring to* an object and *characterizing it* as thus-and-so" (MEV §60: 336; in ISR: 292). Or again: "A basic representational event is an event which has two characters: one by virtue of which it represents an object in its environment (or itself); another by virtue of which it represents that object as being of a certain character" (MEV §72: 338; in ISR: 294).

rules of positioning but also the uniformities reflecting rules of transition.[8]

The last two requirements for something's being a picturing or natural-linguistic object deserve additional elaboration.

(2b) Propositional Form Without Propositions

In several places Sellars stresses that his *flatus vocis* account of predication provides the "crucial step" to a naturalist theory of mind (MEV §§38–9: 332; in ISR: 288–9); it is this part of his account of picturing that he characterizes as "the foundation of a correct account of meaning and truth" (NAO III §33: 58/50) and even as "Ariadne's thread to the labyrinth of metaphysics" (TTP §131: 314). If predicates are shown to provide no more than tokening environments for names, one no longer can hold there is a radical difference between linguistic and non-linguistic representation systems. The importance of "the falsity of this latter notion", i.e., of the assumption that there is such a difference, "can scarcely be overestimated" (MEV §72: 339; in ISR: 295). But why should it be so significant that only natural-linguistic *objects*, characterized and related, picture natural *objects*, characterized and related? Let us quickly consider the alternative of what Sellars calls 'standard semantics'. If a sentence (here taken to consist of subject expression, predicate expression and the copula) was said to picture a fact (here conceived of as a complex of a particular, a universal, and an exemplification nexus), picturing could not be said to be a causal *and* structure-preserving correlation—for what could then serve as the direct causal correlate of sentential predication, given that exemplification is a "nexus" or "tie" at best?[9] Criticizing the standard theory in semantics Sellars remarks laconically, "To put it bluntly, propositional form belongs only in the linguistic and conceptual orders" (NAO III §76: 70/61–2).

---

[8] This does not necessarily imply, however, that material embodiments of orientation systems must be temporally or even merely sequentially ordered—an interpreted formal system surely would do as well.

[9] Cf. TTP and NAO ch. 3.

But strictly speaking this remark is misleading as it stands. It is the *form of a judgment*, the form of 'this *is* a white cube', that does not belong into nature. What is in nature, both at the side of natural-linguistic objects and at the side of natural objects, are ontologically speaking non-composite items that *both* lend themselves to a double functionality of referring and characterizing that constitutes a 'dot-quote proposition', i.e., a proposition in its functional abstraction. In this purely functional sense of proposition, the material items 'this white cube' and 'this is a white cube' are both propositions. However, and this is the point of Jumblese, Sellars's illustration of a language without predicate expressions, *any* material item with the right material features is *potentially* a dot-quote proposition—in fact, a white cube itself is *potentially* also a dot-quote proposition! Propositionality is constituted by the way in which a material item functions within a linguistic community. Given that the two sets of material items correlated by picturing are supposed to be isomorphic, it is only for contingent reasons, or better, due to practical requirements, that only certain natural objects are used by humans with the double functionality characteristic of classical propositions. Thus Sellars's 'Ariadne's thread to the labyrinth of metaphysics' actually consists of two braids: (i) the idea that predicate expressions have no semantic function whatsoever but contribute as material items to the semantic functions of a sentence, and (ii) the idea that propositional form extends beyond predication and can be purely functionally defined.[10]

Briefly, then, the functional definition of propositions in terms of the double functionality of locating and characterizing performed by *one atomic* natural-linguistic object, the sentence, is the key

---

[10] Sellars's views on predication seem intimately connected with his discussion in SM and IKTE of Kant's famous 'Clue' in the first *Critique*, namely, the claim that "the same function which gives unity to the various representations *in a judgement* also gives unity to the mere synthesis of various representations *in one intuition*" (Kant A79; B104–5). As Sellars reconstructs the passage, the 'this-such' nexus in a conceptualized intuition, constituting experiential contents such as *this white cube*, and the predication in a judgment, constituting the content of empirical statements such as *this is a white cube*, involve the same cognitive functions, those characteristic of propositional form—the transition is one of "the same content" occurring "in explicitly propositional form" (SM I §11: 5).

to ensuring that natural-linguistic items can be said to stand in isomorphic or structure-preserving relationships to natural items, *and* belong entirely, not only partly, to the natural order. If predicates were anything else but the articulation contexts of names, if names could be articulated without an articulation context, if we were to allow for any compositionality of the semantic function of a sentence beyond the purely nominal distinction between referring and characterizing, we would need to postulate in nature a causal correlate for logical predication—in Sellars's view an absurdity—or give up on the attempt to ground empirical judgments in causal relations.

But there is a further benefit involved in the adoption of a radical *flatus voci* approach. Once propositional form is recognized as consisting in the double-functionality of an atomic natural-linguistic item, orientation systems might be embodied in material objects that differ in structure and complexity radically from sentences in natural or programming languages.[11]

(2c) Two Notions of Inferential Form

The third of the requirements mentioned above says that picturing natural-linguistic items should exhibit uniformities that reflect the tripartite rule system of a language.[12] There are two ways in which this requirement may be fulfilled. Sellars distinguishes

---

[11] This last point is stressed by Jay Rosenberg, who argues that Sellars's discussion of "animal representation systems" contains the answer to the question of whether and how theoretical statements of science can picture. Even if theoretical physics does not identify microphysical entities by means of proper names, Rosenberg argues, we can treat definite descriptions "from the point of view of their representational function, as 'simple signs'"(Rosenberg, 2007: 114). See also Sellars SM V §§24–6: 124. To flesh out Rosenberg's idea somewhat differently, the functional definition of propositionality allows us to claim that mathematical representations in science, despite their internal inferential complexity, can qualify as atomic natural-linguistic objects to the extent to which they can be shown to have the same double functionality as an atomic logical formula. In microphysics, for example, candidates for natural-linguistic objects might be a state vector in Hilbert space, representing the state of a single particle system and thus functioning like '$F(a)$', or a state vector in Fock space, representing the interaction of 'particles' in terms of a distribution of field quanta and thus arguably functioning like '$R^n(a \ldots a_n)$'.

[12] For some exegetical and technical difficulties with this requirement see Rosenberg 2007.

between Humean systems that exhibit uniformities reflecting inferences where quantified premises or conclusions remain implicit, and Aristotelian systems that exhibit uniformities embodying all steps of deductive and inductive inferences. A Humean orientation system does not use conjunction or negation signs but rather operates with what one might call *modes of presentation* that implicitly have the logical force of conjunction and negation—conjunction is the mode of co-presence, and negation is the mode of rejection (MEV §96: 343; in ISR: 299).[13] We can reconstruct the operation of a Humean orientation system—its transitional "associative propensities"—by *mentioning* logical operations, but "only by the confusion involved in what James called the Psychologist's Fallacy can we be taken to *ascribe* logical operations to the Humean [orientation system]" (MEV §101: 344; in ISR: 300).

On the other hand, human "thinking", Sellars insists, can only be understood on the model of Aristotelian orientation systems, which "contain ... items which function as do logical connectives and quantifiers, i.e. have logical expressions 'in their vocabularies' " (MEV §82: 341: in ISR: 296). Aristotelian orientation systems have two types of elements, atomic and "molecular", i.e., containing logical expressions, while this contrast does not make sense for a Humean orientation system: here all sentences are 'atomic', albeit presented in different (e.g., rejective or conjunctive) modes. This has an important consequence. While in a Humean orientation system *all* elements can be said to picture, in an Aristotelian system this holds only for the atomic elements, since the logical

---

[13] Remarkably, in MEV Sellars does not elaborate on the 'mode of presentation' that carries the logical force of existential quantification. While in SM he postulates that such "molecular" natural-linguistic objects picture in the sense that they "pick out sets of pictures within which they play no favourites" (SM V §11: 119), in MEV he merely associates transitional propensities ('triangle at x →~square at x') with universal quantification. The question of whether there is a specific mode of presentation associated with existential quantification, whether natural-linguistic objects with existential quantifier signs picture in the mode of negation (of a universal quantification), or whether they picture indeterminate, non-particular natural objects, raises deep systematic issues beyond the space of this paper.

expressions of these systems do not stand in one–one relations to natural objects.

The claim that something is a natural-linguistic object standing in a picturing relation thus is systematically ambiguous not only with respect to how propositional form is materially embodied (with or without predicate expressions), but also with respect to whether the inferential role it has is "pre-logical" or "logical." Presented with two material elements of a system, θ and ϕ, and a transition from θ to ϕ, we can take these elements to function like the natural-linguistic objects 'triangle/x_P' and 'circle/x_R' (in the modes 'presentation' (P) and 'rejection' (R)) of a Humean orientation system, directly connected by association, or to function like the natural-linguistic objects 'triangle there' and 'not-circle there' of an Aristotelian system connected by logical inference via an additional quantified premise (MEV §99: 344; in ISR: 299). It is important to see, however, that the latter interpretation depends on the former: the atomic sentences of Aristotelian orientation systems picture only because they have functional analogues in Humean systems. To be sure, it is Aristotelian, "logical [orientation systems]" that provide the elucidatory model for language "as the medium in which we think"; to restate, Sellars insists that the normativity of human thought or the "space of reasons" cannot be adequately captured by transition propensities of Humean orientation systems that merely "ape" reasoning. And yet, the 'representational' character of Aristotelian orientation systems derives by functional analogy from the 'representationality' of Humean orientation systems, where inferential role and propositional form remain implicit and all elements of the system can be said to be in one–one correlations with natural objects (MEV §§99,100, 344; in ISR: 299–300).

In sum, natural-linguistic objects or picturing items are, in the first instance, items with low-grade normativity: with implicit propositional form and implicit inferential roles, "pre-linguistic" (MEV §57: 336; in ISR: 292) items which function in certain central ways like linguistic entities. There is a curious epistemic interdependence between low-grade and high-grade normative items. It is only due to the functional likeness with observational sentences that certain material aspects of a cognitive system can be treated as *more* than natural objects—we need high-grade normative objects to recognize low-grade normative objects. On the other hand, it is only due to the isomorphic correlatedness of low-grade normative items that we can attribute any 'representationality' to our observational language.

Whether the low-grade normativity of 'natural-linguistic objects'—i.e., actually: 'natural-pre-linguistic objects'—establishes a coherent conception of such hyphenated entities shall concern us further below. Let us now turn to the other end of the picturing relationship and investigate those items that are said to get pictured.

3. Natural Objects and the Transcendental Role of Picturing

"Natural objects" are the causal antecedents of (functional analogues of) observation statements or perceptual judgments. But precisely what, in metaphysical and ontological terms, are "natural objects"? At first blush, Sellars's answer appears overly sparse. From explicit discussions of picturing (TC, BBK, SM ch. 3, NAO ch. 5) we can glean the following. (i) A natural object is an item that can be pictured. (ii) A pictured object is something mentioned in a scientific theory of picturing, i.e., a theory of human perception and the production of perceptual judgments (or of functional analogues of these in machines). (iii) Such a theory sets up a 'projection table' or "method of projection" (SM 135) correlating natural objects with natural-(pre)-linguistic objects that are (the functional analogues of) observation sentences. (iv) This correlation is a bijective structure-preserving mapping, which means that there are no structural differences between the entities correlated. (v) The correlation is causally established, possibly mediated by a complex interaction of causal processes past and present.

Upon inspection, however, we can see how these few characterizations suffice to develop, in the context of Sellars's discussion
of scientific realism, his answer to the problem of the metaphysical status of natural objects and their ontological features. Given
that natural objects are 'referents' of (actual and possible) scientific
theories of picturing, the question has shifted to the metaphysical
status of scientific objects: are natural objects *qua* scientific objects
real, and if so, in which sense?

Sellars's position on the reality of scientific objects would seem,
at first glance, to derive from his famous *scientia mensura* principle
in EPM (§42: in SPR: 173; in KMG: 253; in B: 83): "in the
dimension of describing and explaining the world, science is
the measure of all things, of what is that it is, and of what is
not, that it is not." But by itself this principle is neutral with
respect to any metaphysical commitments. We could take the
principle to speak about the domain of real existents in the sense of
unconceptualizable 'things-in-themselves' or at least in the sense
of extra-mental and mind-independent entities. But we might also
identify 'what there is' with the Kantian world of experience, a
domain of extra-mental but mind-dependent entities. All three
of these readings are compatible with what is actually at issue in
Sellars's invocation of the *scientia mensura* principle, namely, to
highlight that naturalism is a position that contains a parameter: as
science changes over time, so does the domain of natural entities
and—*vide* the debate about the mind-dependency of microphysical
entities—even their metaphysical status, the kind of reality we can
ascribe to them.

Sellars's explicit commitments to a "scientific realism" are equally
of limited use for any attempt to clarify the metaphysical status of
scientific objects. For scientific realism is not a *premise* in Sellars's
scheme. He introduces scientific realism as consisting of (a) a claim
about the representationality of theoretical terms, contrasting with
instrumentalism, and (b) a claim about the primacy of the scientific
description of the "world":

To take a realist stance towards scientific theories is to take seriously this role of theoretical language as providing a method of picturing the world.

(SM VI §57: 171)

Thus the Scientific Realist need only argue...that the language [of "physical theory"] could replace the common sense framework in all its roles, with the result that the idea that scientific theory enables a more adequate picturing of the world could be taken at its face value.

(SM V §90: 146)

Both of these claims depend on the notion of picturing already being in place. Thus we seem to move in a circle: in order to determine the metaphysical status of natural objects, i.e., of the entities that are said to get pictured, we need to investigate the role picturing is to play in Sellars's arguments for scientific realism. As shall become apparent presently, however, the notion of picturing at play in the latter context is the minimal conception of a causally established isomorphism between natural and natural-linguistic entities whose metaphysical status is unspecified, and thus no circularity arises. Let us then move on and clarify in which ways Sellars employs the notion of picturing to argue for a certain type of scientific realism, which in turn will enable us to determine the metaphysical status of the natural entities we picture with our observation statements.

Sellars's scientific realism is developed from within a philosophical program of analytical philosophy that takes its metaphysical bearings from Kant rather than from Hume, and thus centrally includes—in John McDowell's characterization—"the transcendental task...[of] entitling ourselves to see conceptual activity as directed toward a reality that is not a mere reflection of it."[14] In Sellars's view the 'transcendental task' can only be discharged via the naturalization of intentionality (or mental representation or primitive aboutness, respectively) by combining a functional

---

[14] McDowell 1998, 473.

account of mental content with a causal relationship replacing aboutness. The strategy becomes fully visibly only in SM, where Sellars supplies the first extended discussion of picturing. Even though Sellars highlights that picturing plays the key role in his solution to the transcendental task, the text leaves room for controversy about the structure of the underlying argument. John McDowell takes Sellars to establish the "objective purport" of observation statements by merely relying on the fact that picturing relationships are the content of a scientific theory, charges this move with "scientism", and concludes that "Sellars's attempt to be responsive to Kantian concerns goes astray in his idea that an appeal to science could do the transcendental job".[15]

In my view Sellars takes a different route in implementing 'the transcendental job'. In order to ground the "objective purport" of observation statements in McDowell's sense, i.e., in order to ensure that observation statements can be said to relate to a reality that is 'not a mere reflection of our conceptual activities', Sellars does indeed appeal to the fact that picturing relationships are part of empirical science, but this appeal does not involve or presuppose the scientistic trust in the representationality of scientific statements. To the contrary, the claim that the natural objects pictured by scientific statements are real entities is the conclusion of the argument, not a premise. Sellars has us realize that the conditions for the possibility of entitling oneself to a strong notion of empirical truth as correspondence to real items are surprisingly modest, once one has given up on the idea of primitive aboutness or that contents are directly related to items in reality. Let us review these conditions step by step.[16]

(1) There must be certain uniformities in sets of natural objects that can be viewed as an isomorphism between two sets of such natural objects.

---

[15] McDowell 1998, 467, 469n.
[16] The following is essentially a reconstruction of SM ch. 3, but for the first two steps see e.g., SRLG and NAO, ch. 5.

(2) We must be able to recognize that one of two isomorphic sets of the natural items, call it S, functions as a language. This means that S must be involved in further uniformities that we can consider as reflections of the tripartite rule system of a language or orientation system. In other words, we must be entitled to consider one set of the correlated natural objects as *natural-linguistic* objects.

(3) We must be able to associate the purely factual descriptions of isomorphic correlations of natural and natural-linguistic objects with the language entry rules (ought-to-bes) of an orientation system or language: "in thinking of pictures as correct or incorrect we are thinking of the uniformities involved as directly or indirectly subject to rules of criticism" (SM V §56: 136). For example, we must be able to associate (i) and (ii):

(i) *Projection table:* red objects (in standard conditions of observation for suitably prompted speakers) are followed by utterances of *this is red*.

(ii) *Language entry rule:* it ought to be that suitably prompted speakers of English in standard conditions of observation respond with a 'this is red' to red objects.

(4) We must be able to compare several such correlations of natural and natural-linguistic objects or projection tables. That is, from our position within one orientation system or language or, using here for convenience Sellars's generalization over languages, from within one "conceptual structure" we must be able to compare the language entry rules and thus the associated projection functions of several conceptual structures.[17] Such language- or conceptual-structure-internal comparisons of the functional set-ups of other languages or conceptual structures or orientation systems are possible due to our capacity of performing functional abstractions.

---

[17] More precisely one should speak here and in the following paragraphs not of languages or conceptual structures but rather of the empirical parts of these alone, of their so-called "world stories".

(5) We must be able to recognize that the differences in the functional set-ups of conceptual structures or orientation systems dovetail with differences in practical consequences. We must be able to recognize *that some conceptual structures or orientation systems support our navigational tasks—in a broad sense of this term—better than others*. Science is a type of interaction with our environment that serves the declared purpose of improving our navigational capacities by generating better orientation systems. Thus the fact that science improves our interaction with nature is the condition for the possibility of taking the mere *difference* in the set-up of projection systems generated by doing science as a *difference in practical adequacy*. In other words, Sellars's "scientism", in the sense of an unjustified premise, is very weak indeed—it consists merely in the observation that the conceptual structures or orientation systems produced by science can be considered as practically more adequate projections to the extent to which they improve our interaction with nature.[18] Sellars takes science to be a particular form of theory construction (i.e., a particular way of setting up orientation systems) that (i) includes a controlled interaction with nature, (ii) postulates theoretical entities, and (iii) *de facto* improves our navigational capacities and our interactions with nature.

(6) We must be able to translate differences in practical adequacy of orientation systems into differences of representational adequacy. We can't do this directly, since the fact that we can recognize practical differences of conceptual structures and their associated 'projection tables' or scientific accounts of perception, has, as such, no implications for their relationship to reality. For instance, the fact that a dot-quote 'this-particle-with-momentum-m' of conceptual structure CS_1 yields better navigational results than a dot-quote 'this-substance-with-impetus-i' of CS_2 has not, as

---

[18] A new scientific theory improves on our navigational capacities if relative to it there are fewer unexplained events and more predictions coming true, cf. SM §§30, 32: 126f; §56: 135; and §§70, 72: 140f.

such, any implications as to the greater representational adequacy of CS_I vis-à-vis reality—the isomorphism between the natural-linguistic objects of CS_I and the natural objects postulated by CS_I does not say anything about how (or that) the latter relates to reality. But assume that there is a scientific theory CS_P that ideally supports our navigational tasks, i.e., leaves nothing unexplained, nothing unpredicted, and all its predictions come out right.[19] The structure $<N>$ of natural objects in the 'domain' of the projection table of CS_P must then be isomorphic to reality—these objects and the natural-linguistic objects that picture them can be considered a structural repetition and thus a re-presentation of reality. But if, in the ideal limit of the development of science, natural objects can be viewed as stand-ins or representatives of real items, then we are entitled to view them as standing in the dimension of representativeness also before the development of science has reached its ideal limit. We may then speak of less-than-perfect orientation systems as being isomorphic to structures of natural objects that are themselves less-than-perfect proxies of real items.[20]

It is important to realize that Sellars's reference to Peirce does not amount to a switch to an 'external', non-transcendental point of view. Sellars writes:

Peirce himself fell into difficulty because, by not taking into account the dimension of 'picturing', he had no Archimedeian point outside the series of actual and possible beliefs in terms of which to define the ideal or limit to which members of this series might approximate.

(SM V §75: 142)

---

[19] That we can conceive of such an ideal conceptual structure imparting ideal navigational capacities is made possible by the observation of relative improvements of our navigational capacities; cf. Seibt 1990, 224ff.

[20] This line of argument would have appeared particularly motivated and attractive to a logical empiricist trying to accommodate a neo-Kantian structuralist account of reality, such as the author of *Der Logische Aufbau der Welt*, a work Sellars was well-familiar with and might have drawn some inspiration from, cf. Seibt 2000a.

This passage has been read as suggesting that picturing would supply us with such an Archimedeian standpoint.[21] But I think Sellars meant to point out something completely different: *given that there is no Archimedeian standpoint*, we cannot make sense of the limit of science in terms of a series of possible beliefs; however, there is another way to define that limit, namely, as the perfect map. The perfect map is a full proxy or replication, which allows us to treat the causal isomorphism of picturing as re-presentation and to view natural objects as described by imperfect maps as imperfect stand-ins of reality. The conceivability of an isomorphism between the ideal conceptual structure and reality does not imply that reality—neither now nor in the ideal limit of science—would be a 'mere reflection of our conceptual activities'. This is ensured by the requirement that picturing relationships are established in the course of doing empirical science, which is essentially interactive.

This concludes my brief reconstruction of Sellars's approach to the 'transcendental task'. In a nutshell, Sellars argues that we are entitled to a notion of empirical truth as correspondence to a reality that is 'not a mere reflection of our conceptual activities', since our claims about picturing relationships are gained by means of a reliable interactive method that in the ideal limit would generate a full structural duplicate of reality. Full re-presentationality of scientific statements in the ideal limit entitles us to assign to current scientific statements a certain degree of re-presentationality at least. Scientific realism does not figure as a premise in this argument, which assumes of science nothing more than the rather uncontroversial claim that the scientific method serves to optimize our navigational capacities. Rather, it is a consequence of this argument—and this is the answer to the question posed at the beginning of this section—that natural objects, scientific objects, are more or less perfect stand-ins (structural representatives) for real entities.

---

[21] Cf. Rosenberg 1975.

Of course, there is another and much shorter path to a transcendental argument in support of the "objective purport" of our conceptual activity:

> Whatever else language does, its central and essential function, the *sine qua non*, is to enable us to picture the world we live in.
>
> (TC: 213; NAO V §89: 137/117)[22]

If it could be shown that it is a condition for the possibility of any language that its observation statements stand in picturing relationships to real entities, Sellarsian scientific realism would not depend on any assumptions about empirical science, not even on the latter's characteristic practical features as a causal method for the improvement of our navigational capacities. As I will argue in the following final section, in his last writings Sellars embraces this shortcut to the transcendental task in the course of investigating the concrete implementation of picturing, setting intriguing pointers to a naturalist interpretation of linguistic normativity.

4. Picturing Happens (Partly) by Sensing

Picturing is said to be a "relation, indeed, a relation between two relational structures" (SM V §56: 135) and, following Wittgenstein, Sellars often specifies the logical properties of this relation in mathematical terms as "projection" and "isomorphism". But these characterizations of the inferential or logical properties of statements about picturing relationships do not imply that picturing belongs ontologically in the category of relations. In fact, Sellars's early illustrations of implemented picturing are mechanical non-linear process structures, physically implemented learning algorithms with feedback loops.[23] The decisive clues for the ontology of picturing, however, we find in Sellars's late writings from 1980/81, in BLM, MEV, and FMPP, where Sellars illustrates 'picturing' with the

---

[22] Reading 'reality' for Sellars's usage of "world" in the given context.
[23] NAO V §47ff: 123/106ff; BBK §§39–40: 53.

orientational capacities of biological systems—robots and rockets now give way to rats.[24] This is a significant change, since until then Sellars had used evolutionary explanations only as a "model" for an explanation of language acquisition by social conditioning, without considering the evolutionary explanation of language itself. In MEV Sellars takes that further step, with some hesitation.

> Such representational systems (RS) or cognitive map-makers, can be brought about by natural selection and transmitted genetically, as in the case of bees. Undoubtedly a primitive RS is also an innate endowment of human beings. The concept of innate abilities to be aware *of* something *as* something, and hence of pre-linguistic awarenesses is perfectly intelligible.
>
> (MEV §57: 336; in ISR: 292)

The causal relation of picturing is now for the first time further specified as a result of evolutionary reinforcement, and human languages are presented as deriving from the sophistication of animal orientation systems.

However, the evolutionary explanation of language offered here merely establishes that orientation systems can be thought of as 'innate' in that they can be thought of as serving some evolutionary function or other. Sellars does not argue here that the particular function that renders orientation systems an evolutionary advantage is the fact that they contain world-coordinated natural-(pre)-linguistic objects. In other words, these passages do not yet suffice to establish that the condition for the possibility of languages (or, more generally, orientation systems), the "condition *sine qua non*", is the 'representationality' or world-coordinatedness of their natural-(pre)-linguistic objects. In order to discharge the 'transcendental task' mentioned above, in order to show that our observation statements are related to a reality that is 'not merely a reflection of our conceptual activities', one must show that nothing

---

[24] But note that Sellars was deeply interested in stimulus–response learning already in the 1940s, and in his 1954 SRLG (in SPR: 326f; in ISR: 33f) he suggests that particular instances of pattern-governed behavior have a causal explanation in evolutionary terms.

else but 'representationality' is the feature why language is selected for in evolution.

This is a formidable assignment, since it will also not do to explain in evolutionary terms the existence of one-to-one correlations between sets of natural objects such that one of these *can be interpreted* as language. It will not do to argue that there are biological systems exhibiting behavior (such as the dance of the bees) to which we *can* apply the normative vocabulary that characterizes linguistic episodes.[25] Rather, what needs to be shown is that world-coordinatedness is the evolutionary condition for the possibility of a certain class of natural items that would not exist if they were not involved in normative functioning: that world-coordinatedness and the specific normative functioning of 'natural-(pre)-linguistic' objects are selected for in combination.

Briefly, the shortcut to the 'transcendental task' via the necessary 'representationality' of language requires an evolutionary argument for the "Janus-faced character" of language. Sellars himself nowhere supplies such an argument but, as I shall suggest in the remainder of this section, his process-ontological vision in the Carus Lectures (FMPP) prefigures the relevant foundational moves. Following the trajectories of FMPP we find in recent work on the naturalization of normativity observations and strategies that can be used for the purpose of developing an evolutionary argument for natural items which could not exist if they were not 'Janus-faced', i.e., both normative and world-coordinated.

---

[25] For such a 'merely ascriptive' approach compare, for instance, Ruth Millikan's account of naturalized intentionality:

The intentionality lies not in the function of the dance, but in the explanation of how the function is performed, in the principle involved. Roughly, the principle is mathematical isomorphism. Variations in possible bee dances to which worker bees are designed to respond correspond one-to-one to variations in possible location of nectar in such a way that being guided by the dances produces arrival at sites of nectar. Why is this intentionality? Because the dances display the characteristic trait of the intentional: namely, they can be wrong or false.

(Millikan 2003: 97)

To restate, as the label should have suggested all along, 'picturing' is implemented by a process, a process that—setting mechanical illustrations aside—is part of the complex interactivity of a biological species and its environment. But there are many varieties of process. In FMPP Sellars envisages a new categorial guise for both picturing and pictured entities in terms of a category of "absolute or pure processes", i.e., ways of happening without substratum. Such 'pure dynamics' we can, in first approximation, conceive of *in analogy to* the denotations of common sense sentences with 'dummy subjects', such as 'it is snowing', 'it is lightning', or 'it is hurting'. Within an ontology of pure processes, Sellars suggests, we could differentiate types of physical processes in terms of their dynamical context. We could distinguish between, on the one hand, so-called "physical-2" processes that constitute "what goes on in non-living things and insensate organisms"—for instance "what in a humorous vein we might refer to … as electronings and quarkings"—and, on the other hand, so-called "physical-1" processes that would be "the transposition of sensa into the framework of absolute process" such as "C#-ings" and "reddings" (Sellars FMPP §114f).[26]

The category of pure processes has two unusual features that are crucially significant for the interpretation of Sellars's account of picturing, and, also more generally it appears, for a successful approach to naturalist account of cognition. First, pure processes are non-particulars.[27] In traditional ontology 'particulars' are necessarily

---

[26] Sellars originally defined the distinction between physical-1 and physical-2 in CE:

> Physical-1: an event or entity is physical-1 if it belongs in the space-time network.
> Physical-2: an event or entity is physical-2 if it is definable in terms of theoretical primitives adequate to describe completely the actual states though not necessarily the potentialities of the universe before the appearance of life. (CE: 252)

[27] In the concluding paragraph of PSIM (quoted below) Sellars explicitly commits himself to "non-particulate items" but in FMPP Sellars obscures this feature by using the same label, "absolute process", for the category of non-particular items as well as for the model of that category, spatio-temporally localized 'C-sharpings from that corner now', which are particulars; see Seibt 2000b and 2007: 127ff. The interpretation of pure processes as

located in one determinate, bounded (and mostly topologically connected) spatio-temporal region. In contrast, pure processes exist in space and time in determinate or indeterminate locations. (Such indeterminately located individuals we usually make reference to when we reason about stuffs, as in 'the water in the Alps is getting warmer' or 'sodium chloride dissolves in water'.) While particulars are individuated in terms of their location, pure processes are individuated in terms of how they operate or function. (This is familiar from the individuation of activities: whether swimming differs from running, or combustion from electromagnetic radiation, depends on operational aspects.) As non-particular individuals, pure processes can play the role of a pre-conceptual sensory manifold that is indeterminately located in a region encompassing the organism and its environment.[28]

Second, processes combine and interact in ways that are quite different from the ways in which things may be aggregated or assembled. The theory of cognition has been hampered, Sellars claims, by a focus on causal structures that fit the interaction of things but not those of processes.

This sufficiency of mechanistic variables, combined with the almost tangible *thingishness* of physical objects and with an impact paradigm of causation made it difficult to conceive of a mode of causation in which the development of a system of material particles might be influenced by nonmaterial items, whether *states* of a 'mind' or Hobbesian *objects* (appearances).

(FMPP III §102: 83)

non-particular entities I offer here is inspired by the features of the basic category of the theory of 'general processes', which is a further development of Sellars's process-ontological intuitions, cf. e.g. Seibt 2005*b*, 2008.

[28] One of the trajectories that can be drawn out from FMPP thus leads from Sellars's discussion of the Kantian forms of intuition, space and time, in sensing (e.g., SM ch. 1) to recent arguments about the "embodied mind" and "non-trivial causal spread" in cognitive science, aiming to show that certain cognitive phenomena—e.g., sensing—'ain't in the head' but spread out over extra-neural (environmental) and neural processes which constitute these phenomena in combination, cf. e.g. Thelen/Smith 1994, Keijzer 1998, Wheeler/Clark 1999, Wheeler 2001.

That is to say, whereas the objects of contemporary neurophysiological theory are taken to consist of neurons, which consist of molecules, which consist of quarks... —all physical-2 objects—an ideal successor theory formulated in terms of absolute processes (both physical-2-ings and physical-1-ings [sensings]) might so constitute certain of its 'objects' (e.g., neurons in the visual cortex) that they had [physical-1-ings, sensings] as *ingredients*, differing in this respect from purely physical-2 structures.

(FMPP III §124: 86–7, my emphasis)

From the present vantage point, we can take Sellars here to grope at ideas of self-organization, downward causation, emergence, or complexity. While it might have seemed unduly speculative in 1981 to challenge the particularist billiard ball model of causation, today dynamic systems theory provides a respectable theoretical context to advance the claim that a certain activity is an 'ingredient' or emergent dynamics of another activity. Moreover, applying dynamic systems theory to the philosophy of mind, proponents of the so-called "dynamic hypothesis" in cognitive science have since worked out a strong scientific paradigm for anti-representationalist accounts of cognitive functions that explicitly confirm the Sellarsian notion of sensing as an ingredient or emergent dynamics of 'neuroning' just as metabolism is an emergent dynamics of the interaction of chemicals in a cell, or a virtual metronome an emergent dynamics of the swinging of linked pendulums.[29] It is important to note, however, that the mathematical description of emergent phenomena in dynamic systems theory to some extent obscures the ontological requirements for emergent causation, which Sellars was fully aware of and responded to in FMPP. Only pure processes or any other category of dynamic non-particular individuals affords a coherent description of emergence at the ontological level.[30] Only if processes are categorized as 'subjectless goings-on-thus-ly', the interaction of processes may, in the context

---

[29] Cf. in particular the seminal contributions by Van Gelder (e.g., 1995 and 1998), Thelen and Smith 1994, Wheeler 2005.

[30] Cf. Seibt 2008.

of certain process architectures, amount to a different way of going on, i.e., to the emergence of a 'new' process.

From these more general ontological observations let us now return to the interpretation of picturing. In FMPP Sellars suggests, quoting from PSIM, that in the context of a suitable process architecture the goings-on-thus-ly of physical processes constitute the going-on-thus-ly of sensing:

> [W]hen it comes to an adequate understanding of the relation of sensory consciousness to neurophysiological process, we must penetrate to the non-particulate foundation of the particulate image, and recognize that in this non-particulate image the qualities of sense are a dimension of natural process which occurs only in connection with those complex physical processes [which are currently categorized as the central nervous system].
>
> (PSIM, in SPR: 37; in ISR: 404−5)

The natural continuation of this line of thought would be to claim that under suitable conditions the going-on-thus-ly of sensing may go on in the ways that constitute the going-on-thus-ly of imagining and further of judging. Sellars does not explicitly add this further step in FMPP, but his discussion of sensing, imagining, and judging in SM and IKTE supplies sufficient pointers, I believe, for a process-based emergentist model of cognition that challenges the idea that there is a clear line between the physical, the sensory, and the conceptual way of going on of natural processes.[31] Moreover, the process-based model of cognition also precisely goes against the thought of a clear line of demarcation between the causal and the normative.[32] Rather, the suggestion is that there is a whole spectrum of ways of going on or functioning, and even though we can *contrast* the ends of the spectrum, i.e., the merely causal and the merely normative of the conceptual, there is a range of intermediate functioning between mere causes and proper reasons. Such intermediate functionings are causal processes with what we

---

[31] Cf. SM chs. 1 and 2, and IKTE II.   [32] As attributed to Sellars in McDowell 1998.

called above the 'low-grade' normativity of Humean orientation systems and degrees of normativity even lower than that.

It is here then, in the range of causal dynamics with various degrees of 'low-grade normativity' that we find the most suitable candidates for 'natural-linguistic objects', those curiously 'hyphenated' entities that in Sellars's scheme 'do the picturing'. Some of these dynamics also fulfil precisely the condition needed for our shortcut to the transcendental task. They occur only in normative contexts and their very occurrence entails their 'representationality' or world-coordinatedness. This at least is the core idea of the so-called "interactivist" interpretation of mental representation recently championed by theoretical biologists and cognitive scientists, a process-based theoretical model that fits Sellars's philosophy of mind particularly smoothly, as I want to sketch briefly in the following paragraphs.[33]

World-coordinatedness, or so proponents of interactivism argue, is only one type of natural normativity that begins already at the level of so-called self-maintaining systems, i.e., process configurations that exist far from the thermodynamic equilibrium and maintain their existence for a certain amount of time. The components of such process configurations presuppose each other; for example, to use the interactivists' canonical illustration, in a burning candle the main component processes, namely, melting of the wax, percolation of wax in the wick, combustion, air convection that adduces oxygen and carries away residues, all feed into each other. That one process in this configuration occurs (or fails to occur), is functional (or dysfunctional) for the existence of any other and the configuration as a whole, thus endowing the entire non-linear causal configuration with rudimentary normativity as a system of items that are functional for each other.[34] To be sure, the

---

[33] Cf. in particular Christensen/Bickhard 2002, Bickhard 2003, Bickhard 2008, Hooker 2008, Levine 2008.

[34] "A [far-from-equilibrium] system is autonomous (self-maintenant) if it interactively generates the conditions required for its existence ... contributions to autonomy are the

sense in which component processes of self-maintaining systems serve a function is far remote from the usual, 'intentional' account of function as fulfilling a certain purpose or design. But unlike regulatory cycles with positive or negative feedback in arbitrary natural processes, self-maintaining far-from-equilibrium systems cannot be described exhaustively in a purely causal idiom. While the increase or decrease of an existing process can be described as the causal effect of another, a richer dependence relation is necessary to describe a process configuration where all component processes depend in their very existence on each other. Thus the functionality of the components of self-maintaining systems is not a matter of ascription—the existence of a self-maintaining system is a functional norm put directly into nature.

Organisms are a more sophisticated type of such self-maintaining systems—they are "recursively self-maintenant" in that they can maintain the conditions for their self-maintenance by suitable interactions with their environment. To use again the standard illustration offered by interactivists, a bacterium, for example, has a chemical mechanism that causes the bacterium to swim if moving up a sugar gradient (environmental dynamics A) and to tumble if it is moving down a sugar gradient (environmental dynamics B). In other words, a bacterium-cum-environment is a process configuration P that includes a rudimentary version of an orientation system: an internal dynamics α that co-occurs with environmental dynamics A and engenders swimming and an internal dynamics β that co-occurs with environmental dynamics B and engenders tumbling. The normativity of these transitions is the functionality of self-maintenance: P could not persist without α and β which in turn are internally related to A and B—their very occurrence depends on their being functional for P, which they are only insofar as their occurrence

basic instances of *serving a function* ... the asymmetry functional/dysfunctional is derived in this model from the fundamental physical asymmetry between far-from-equilibrium and equilibrium systems" (Christensen/Bickhard 2002: 19).

presupposes the co-occurrence of A or B, respectively. The occurrence of α and β thus entails their 'representationality' or world-coordinatedness, and, vice versa, their world-coord-inatedness is also the warrant of their functionality or ('low-grade') normativity.[35]

Different types of organisms involve such basic 'representational dynamics' in different and often highly complex dynamics. Basic world-coordinated internal dynamics may get 'caught up' in the dynamics of Humean or even Aristotelian orientation systems. But in so far as the latter 'high-grade' normative ways of functioning are emergent on the occurrence of processes with less than 'low-grade' normativity and their 'built-in' world-coordinatedness, the very occurrence of an observation statement can be said to entail its rep-resentationality as the "sine qua non of language" in evolutionary terms.

5. Conclusion

The dimension of givenness that is under attack in EPM is the classical Cartesian conception of mental representations. Working towards a replacement account, Sellars postulates that episodes with cognitive content are *qua* "natural-linguistic objects" causal repre-sentatives of natural objects, correlated with the latter by a structure-preserving mapping. I highlighted that this relationship, called 'picturing', holds in the first instance only for natural-linguistic objects with "low-grade normativity", for pre-linguistic orienta-tion systems, and only derivatively for observational statements or linguistic orientation systems. The main purpose of picturing is to warrant "a dimension of givenness that is not in dispute", i.e., of ensuring the world-directedness or world-coordinatedness of ori-entation systems. I suggested that Sellars's final strategy here seems to be to claim that the causal representationality of languagings is entailed by their very existence and to argue for this claim in

---

[35] Cf. Bickhard 2003: 139ff.

evolutionary terms. Even though Sellars has not completed this argument, his process-ontological description of the cognition at the level of the "sensory-body problem" combines well with recent "anti-representational" descriptions of sensing and mental representation in cognitive science, and in particular within the so-called 'interactivist paradigm'. The particular interest of this combination lies in the fact that it shows us a way to leave the metaphor of the 'Janus-faced' character of language behind and approach the 'hyphenated nature' of "natural-linguistic" objects in a theoretically more coherent fashion. Once we adopt a process ontology we can integrate normativity into Sellars's naturalist scheme as modes of functioning, arranged in an emergent hierarchy, leading from mere causing to reasoning proper.

References

Bickhard, M. (2003) 'Process and Emergence: Normative Function and Representation', in: J. Seibt (ed.), *Processes: Analysis and Applications of Dynamic Categories*, Dordrecht: Kluwer, 121–55.

BonJour, L. (1973) 'Sellars on Truth and Picturing', *International Philosophical Quarterly* 13, 243–65.

Christensen, W. and Bickhard, M. (2002) 'The Process Dynamics of Normative Function', *The Monist*, 85, 3–28.

Keijzer, A. (1998) 'Doing Without Representations Which Specify What to Do', *Philosophical Psychology* 11, 269–302.

Margolis, J. (1976) 'On Picturing and Signifying', *Logique et Analyse* 10, 277–86.

McDowell, J. (1998) 'Having the World in View', *Journal of Philosophy* 95, 431–91.

Millikan, R. (2005) *Language: A Biological Model* (Oxford: Oxford University Press).

Rosenberg, J. (1975) 'The Elusiveness of Categories, the Archimedian Dilemma, and the Nature of Man: A Study in Sellarsian Metaphysics', in: H. N. Castañeda (ed.), *Action, Knowledge, and Reality: Essays in Honor of Wilfrid Sellars* (Indianapolis: Bobbs-Merrill).

Rosenberg, J. (2007) 'Sellarsian Picturing', in: *Fusing the Images* (Oxford: Oxford University Press, 104–27).

Seibt, J. (1990) *Properties as Processes. A Synoptic Study in Wilfrid Sellars' Nominalism* (Reseda: Ridgeview).

—— (2000*a*) 'Constitution Theory and Metaphysical Neutrality: A Lesson for Ontology?' *The Monist* 83, 161–83.

—— (2000*b*) 'Pure Processes and Projective Metaphysics', *Philosophical Studies* 101, 253–89.

—— (2005*a*) 'Kognitive Orientierung als epistemisches Abenteuer', in: W. Stegmaier (ed.), *Analyse und Orientierung*, 197–224.

—— (2005*b*) *General Process Theory*, Habilitationsschrift Universität Konstanz.

—— (2007) *Wilfrid Sellars. Moderne Klassiker, vol. 3*, Paderborn: Mentis.

—— (2008) 'Forms of Emergence in General Process Theory', *Synthese*, in print.

Sellars, W., BBK (1960) 'Being and Being Known', in SPR, 41–59.

—— CE (1956) 'The Concept of Emergence' (with Paul Meehl). In *Minnesota Studies in the Philosophy of Science*, vol. I, H. Feigl and M. Scriven (eds.) (Minneapolis, MN: University of Minnesota Press: 239–52).

—— FMPP (1981) Foundations for a Metaphysics of Pure Process—The Carus Lectures. *Monist* 64, 3–90.

—— IKTE (1987) 'The Role of Imagination in Kant's Theory of Experience', The Dotterer Lecture 1987, in *Categories: A Colloquium*, ed. Henry W. Johnstone (Pennsylvania: Pennsylviania State University Press, 231–45).

—— ISR (2007) *In the Space of Reasons: Selected Essays of Wilfrid Sellars* (Cambridge, MA: Harvard University Press).

—— NAO (1979/1996) *Naturalism and Ontology* (Atascadero: Ridgeview).

—— MEV (1981) 'Mental Events', *Philosophical Studies* 38: 325–45.

—— PSIM (1962) 'Philosophy and the Scientific Image of Man', in SPR, 1–41.

—— SCE (1934) *Substance, Change, and Events.* Master's thesis, University of Buffalo, The Sellars Webpage, http://www.ditext.com/sellars/, hrsg. von A. Chrucky.

—— SM (1965) *Science and Metaphysics: Variations on Kantian Themes* (London: Routledge & Kegan Paul).

—— SPR (1963) *Science, Perception and Reality* (London: Routledge & Kegan Paul).

—— SRLG (1954) 'Some Reflections on Language Games', in SPR, 321–59.

—— TC (1962) 'Truth and Correspondence', in SPR, 197–225.

—— TTP (1985) Towards a Theory of Predication. *How Things Are*, hrsg. von Bogen, J. and T. McGuire (Dordrecht: D. Reidel, 285–322).

Thelen, E. and Smith, B. (1994) *A Dynamic Systems Approach to the Development of Cognition and Action* (Cambridge: MIT Press).

Wheeler, M. and Clark, A. (1999) 'Genic Representation: Reconciling Content and Causal Complexity', *British Journal for the Philosophy of Science* 51, 103–35.

—————— (2001) 'Two Threats to Representation', *Synthese* 129, 211–31.

10

On Sellars's Two Images
of the World

Jay F. Rosenberg

Professor Bruce Aune once chose Sellars's distinction between the
manifest and the scientific images as a point of entry into the rich
and complex Sellarsian philosophy, comparing Sellars's two images
with Hume's "two systems of ideas" in a useful and revealing way.[1]
There can be no question that Sellars saw himself as a contributor
to the broad dialectical tradition which, since the beginning of the
modern period, has been centrally occupied with understanding the
place of the "new science" within a comprehensive and systematic
philosophical worldview. As useful as the comparison with Hume
is, however, it is also importantly limited. Its limitations begin to
emerge when we recall that Hume, in the last analysis, was prepared
to adopt a skeptical attitude with respect to both the "popular"
and the "philosophical" or "corpuscular" systems of thought,
calling into question the (metaphysical) categories of substance and
causation which, in an important sense, were common to them. In
contrast, Sellars is ultimately unwilling to adopt a skeptical attitude
toward either of his "images". It will repay our efforts to discover
why this is so.

[1] Aune's contribution to a Symposium on the Philosophy of Wilfrid Sellars at the
Eighty-seventh Annual Meeting of the American Philosophical Association, published in
The Journal of Philosophy, 87 (Oct. 1990): 537–45.

To frame the issue more sharply, we can begin by noting that Aune asks why, given that it is scientifically obsolete, the manifest image still deserves serious philosophical attention, and there is nowadays no shortage of philosophers who are inclined to conclude that it does not and would enthusiastically echo the Quinean sentiment that "philosophy of science is philosophy enough". But the most significant challenges to Sellars's views surely come from the other direction, from advocates of the "perennial philosophy" who endorse the manifest image as real and understand the discourse of science as conceptually dependent upon it,[2] or from radically historicist "post-modern" thinkers who hold that all discourses are created equal and eschew normative epistemology entirely.[3]

The traditional bite of a challenge from this direction, as Sellars recognizes and Aune rightly stresses, is that persons are essentially beings who conceive of themselves in terms of the categories of the manifest image, as knowers and doers in a world of causally-interacting spatio-temporal sensible objects.[4] (Post-modernists, of course, tend to reject the idea that persons are "essentially" anything, and to stress making and doing at the expense of finding and knowing. It is unclear, however, to what extent, if any, they would be prepared to endorse the prima facie paradoxical idea, which appears to be a consequence of such a repudiation of

---

[2] For example, E. M. Adams, "The Scientific and the Humanistic Images of Man-in-the-World", *Man and World*, 4 (1971): 174–92. Bas van Fraassen's fictionalist "constructive empiricism" belongs in this category as well. See his "Wilfrid Sellars on Scientific Realism", *Dialogue*, 14 (1975): 606–16, and *The Scientific Image* (Oxford: Oxford University Press, 1980).

[3] Paradigmatically, Richard Rorty, e.g., in *Philosophy and the Mirror of Nature* (Princeton, NJ: Princeton University Press, 1979), and *Contingency, Irony, and Solidarity* (Cambridge and New York: Cambridge University Press, 1989).

[4] Sellars: "[Man] is *essentially* that being which conceives of itself *in terms of the image which the perennial philosophy refines and endorses.*" "Philosophy and the Scientific Image of Man", in *Frontiers of Science and Philosophy*, Robert Colodny, ed. (Pittsburgh, PA: University of Pittsburgh Press, 1962): 35–78. [Reprinted in *Science, Perception, and Reality*, [SPR] (New York: Routledge & Kegan Paul, 1963, reissued Atascadero, CA: Ridgeview Publishing, 1991): 1–40, and in *In the Space of Reasons*, [ISR] eds. Kevin Scharp and Robert Brandom (Cambridge, MA: Harvard University Press, 2007): 369–408.] Henceforth PSIM. The quote is at SPR: 8; ISR: 376.

essences, that there could be persons who did not, or even could not, think of themselves as persons at all.) To put the point more revealingly, at least in part, persons are constituted by a reflexive self-understanding of their own subjectivity, and Humean worries regarding the reality of "external objects" can arise only for such subjective, apperceptive consciousnesses, i.e., for beings who are conceptually equipped with a distinction between (the one objective) "external" and (their own subjective) "internal" worlds in the first place. What is "manifest" can be manifest only to some such subjectivity. It is this person-constitutive role that gives Sellars's "manifest image", in contrast to Hume's "popular system of thought", an inescapable philosophical moment.

The scientific image, in contrast, purports to be objective through and through. Natural science knows only one world. Its language is deliberately non-indexical and a-perspectival; its causality is non-teleological; its temporality is a time without tense; and it recognizes no distinction between "internal" and "external" beyond that of mere spatial enclosure, the separation of an "interior" from an "exterior". The true challenge posed by the scientific image is thus that, taken seriously, it appears to leave no room for subjectivity and, hence, has no place for persons, that is, for us.[5] Much of Sellars's philosophical work can be understood as an attempt to show how the person-constitutive categories of the manifest image might be reconciled with or coherently added to the scientific image to produce a "stereoscopic" or "synoptic" image.[6] In light of these considerations, however, the question

---

[5] "[My concern] is with the question, 'In what sense, and to what extent, does the manifest image of man-in-the-world survive the attempt to unite this image in one field of intellectual vision with man as conceived in terms of the postulated objects of scientific theory?' The bite to this question lies … in the fact that man is that being which conceives of itself in terms of the manifest image. To the extent that the manifest does not survive in the synoptic view, to that extent man himself would not survive" (PSIM, 54; in SPR, 18; in ISR: 386).

[6] For a fuller discussion, see my "Fusing the Images", *Journal for General Philosophy of Science* (*Zeitschrift für Allgemeine Erkenntnistheorie*), 21, 1990; reprinted in Jay F. Rosenberg, *Wilfrid Sellars: Fusing the Images* (Oxford and New York: Oxford University Press, 2007), pp. 8–32.

of why philosophy should take the scientific image seriously in the first place surely becomes increasingly acute. The scientific image, Sellars tells us, emerges from the exercise of a certain kind of postulational theoretical reasoning. The distinction between the two images is thus *au fond* epistemological, and, at least initially, it is not clear why such a distinction should have significant ontological consequences at all, much less give rise to a global philosophical challenge to our own self-conception and self-understanding.

These questions can be answered, if at all, only by bringing into sharper focus just what sort of postulational theoretical reasoning demarcates the scientific from the manifest image, for the application of postulational reasoning *per se* carries with it no profound philosophical consequences. As Aune insightfully points out, there is nothing problematic about positing, e.g., microbes, and we should recall, too, that the (sensory and intentional) states of persons postulated by Sellars's own mythical genius Jones are central ingredients of the manifest image.

Aune goes on to suggest that what is criterial for the scientific image are postulations of entities that are "incompatible with the ultimate reality of manifest objects". While this remark is surely right as far as it goes, I can't help but think that it raises more questions than it answers. At the very least, we should want to know what it is about some scientific theoretical posits but not others that generates a philosophical tension with the manifest image. Even more significantly, however, we need to ask with what epistemic authority natural science could possibly challenge the ultimate reality of manifest entities. For epistemic authority presupposes epistemic norms; norms exist only immanently in the activities of persons; and persons, as we have seen, are constituted by the manifest image. The Sellarsian texts indeed provide points of entry for explorations of both of these questions, but a properly extensive, detailed, and illuminating discussion is notoriously lacking. Such difficult matters will occupy me for the balance of these remarks, although I do not pretend that I will be able to begin to deal adequately with any of them.

To get a rough and provisional handle on the first of our questions, it will be useful to recall Sellars's discussion of the basic objects of the manifest image. The ontology of any conceptual framework, Sellars reminds us, is a hierarchical structure of dependencies, and that of the manifest image is no exception. Its basic objects, he tells us, include "persons, animals, lower forms of life, and 'merely material' things, like rivers and stones". An entity is "basic", in this intra-framework sense, just in case it is neither a modification of nor system of any other, even more basic, entities. The short answer to our first question is that intra-framework theoretical posits—postulations of new relationships, properties, states, or further instances of a framework's basic entities—although ontologically commissive, are, in the relevant sense, philosophically innocuous. Only inter-framework theoretical posits are philosophically problematic. Both Aune's microbes and Jones's thoughts and sensations are postulations which remain within the manifest image. Microbes are just additional basic objects (i.e., plants or animals, although extremely small ones), and thoughts and sensations are introduced as states of basic objects (namely, persons).

A theoretical posit represents a challenge to a conceptual framework, in contrast, when it purports to tell us from what elements the framework's basic entities are constituted, that is, when it is ostensibly a story about "more basic" entities out of which those entities are composed. The idioms here are characteristically mereological,[7] but it is one of Sellars's more startling theses that such mereological idioms cannot be taken literally in this context. As he puts it, it cannot be the case that "manifest objects are identical with systems of imperceptible particles in the simple sense in which a forest is identical with a number of trees" (PSIM, in SPR: 26; in ISR: 394). When we look for Sellars's explanation of why this is so, what we find are his notoriously opaque discussions of a tension between the "ultimate homogeneity" of sensory contents

---

[7] But this is also the point at which talk of "reduction" and "theoretical identity" comes into play.

and the "gappiness" or "graininess" of the scientific image. I'm not convinced that those discussions have yet been properly understood and appreciated,[8] and this is not the appropriate forum for a fresh attempt.[9] Be that as it may, however, Aune is surely right to observe that brusque attempts simply to dismiss the philosophical significance of such Sellarsian considerations by relegating phenomenological continuities to the domain of "mere appearance" remain utterly impotent, absent good reasons to believe that apparent continuities can be adequately understood and explained without invoking actual ones.

Given, then, that postulational theoretical reasoning can in this way not only refine but also in principle challenge a conceptual framework which, as Sellars put it, purports to be a complete picture of man in the world, there remains the question of how earnestly one must or should regard such an ostensible challenge. Here the text of "Philosophy and the Scientific Image of Man" is initially less helpful, and it will be useful to begin with an evidently simpler question: What epistemic authority do the methods of natural science command within the manifest image?

The surprising answer is that, already within the manifest image, the epistemology of natural science is arguably best understood in Sellarsian terms as a systematic working out of an ontological dialectic of appearance vs. reality. Natural science, that is, systematically exploits a method for discovering a "reality" which "underlies" and "gives rise to" empirical "appearances". This is, of course, hardly the occasion for a detailed exposition and defense of a ("convergent realist") normative epistemology for natural science developed along the indicated lines (a project I have attempted to

---

[8] Here I do not intend to exclude my own previous interpretive attempts, e.g., "The Place of Color in the Scheme of Things: A Roadmap to Sellars' Carus Lectures", *The Monist*, 65 (1982): 315–35; reprinted in Rosenberg, *Wilfrid Sellars: Fusing the Images*.

[9] One place to begin such a fresh attempt would be by a consideration of the classical and kinetic theories of gases. From the perspective of the classical theory, a gas is a continuous homogeneous compressible fluid and, using the term 'gas' with those implications, one can make straightforward sense of the claim that a gas cannot be identical with a system of discrete incompressible Newtonian particles (i.e., molecules) in the simple sense in which a forest is identical with a number of trees.

carry through, at least in part, elsewhere[10]). Here, I must content myself with a brief elucidation of the principal elements of such a picture.

A proper Sellarsian understanding of the epistemology of natural science turns on appreciating the relationships between two motifs. The first is that the fundamental business of a natural science, its epistemic *raison d'etre*, is to conceptually equip us to explain phenomena; the second, that what (conceptually) connects the ontological categories of "appearance" and "reality" is precisely an explanatory 'because'. If reality is something that "underlies" or "gives rise to" appearances, then a fortiori it is necessarily something that explains them as well: Things will seem as they do because things are as they are.

Both these motifs describe cognitive constraints at the interface of two (partial) world-stories. In particular, both physical (empirical) phenomena and (speaking loosely) the circumstances or states of affairs invoked in aid of explaining them are epistemically present to inquiring subjects only by way of judgments (propositions) framed in terms drawn from one or another inferentially-integrated system of descriptive predicates. An epistemological account of natural science must consequently undertake, *inter alia*, to devise and defend a principled story about the inferential (and perhaps other) relationships that (should) obtain between such descriptive systems when propositions framed in their terms are (properly considered to be) related as explanandum and explanans.

The contentive concepts in terms of which a description of phenomena (explananda) is drawn may already be elements of a quantitatively-precise, theoretically-articulated world-story, within which phenomena are representable by assignments of numerical values to parametric properties, themselves in turn thought of both as observationally accessible to measurement and as confirmably subsumable under inductively-lawful mathematical relationships.

[10] See, for example, "Coupling, Retheoretization, and the Correspondence Principle", *Synthese*, 45 (1980): 351–85, and "Comparing the Incommensurable: Another Look at Convergent Realism", *Philosophical Studies*, 54 (1988): 163–93.

They may also, however, belong to a purely qualitative, early, "pre-theoretical", and even quite crude and rudimentary descriptive phenomenology of nature. Thus the explananda falling within the scope of, for example, Newtonian astronomy encompass the Keplerian equations of planetary motion and the concomitant numerical observational measurements (e.g., Tycho Brahe's) which they closely fit, but also the "pre-theoretical" qualitative phenomenology of "fixed" stars, a "rising" and "setting" sun, "wandering" planets, and a "waxing" and "waning" moon.

Systematic reflection on this and similar examples reminds us that, epistemologically considered, natural science lays claim to be a progressive and, at the level of explananda, in some sense also a cumulative enterprise. We learn, too, that the theoretical positing of micro-entities, of which macro-entities are ontologically composed, although itself clearly one mode of implementation of the fundamental explanatory strategy of scientific epistemology, does not belong to its essence. The basic epistemological moment of natural-scientific explanation is already exhibited in, e.g., the transition from the geocentric (Ptolemaic) to the heliocentric (Copernican) cosmological world-story. In any event, however, natural science progresses by constructing new stories, i.e., new theories, which not only improve upon their predecessors but also supersede them.

Natural science manages to pull off this trick of progressively cumulating over phenomena while at the same time methodically abandoning its successive commitments to the systems of contentive concepts, in terms of which those phenomena are initially described precisely, by adopting a "realist" self-understanding according to which the fundamental import of an explanatory theory is ontological. Phenomena are "saved" by being systematically relegated to the category of appearance and their prior (theoretical) representations, correlatively, to the language of "seeming". In short, the 'because' of theoretical explanation and the ontological 'because' of being and seeming are understood as one. *Sub specie* Ptolemaic theory, it is because the sun actually orbits a spherical earth that it apparently rises and sets; *sub specie* Copernican theory, it is because the turning spherical earth actually orbits a central sun that the sun (Ptolemaically) appears to orbit a stationary spherical earth.

Thus understood, the aim of theorizing is not to model a steadily growing family of observations (measurements) over some conceptually-privileged phenomenal domain by a series of equations successively yielding an ever more accurate mathematical fit but rather to explain observations and measurements by telling ontologically-committal stories about what it is that is being observed or measured and thereby also, *inter alia*, about in what (physical interactions) its being observed or measured consequently consists. Successive theories over a given phenomenal domain do not "meet" only in the original phenomena. Since the nature of the phenomena to be explained is ontologically reinterpreted under successive theoretical conceptualizations, a successor theory explains the phenomena ostensibly explained by its predecessor only as appearances, by supplying conceptual resources for giving an account of the pragmatic meta-phenomena of that predecessor's actual explanatory failures and apparent explanatory successes. The former correspond to explanatory anomalies, i.e., breakdowns of intra-theoretical explanatory strategies, whose emergence (characteristically at extremes of measurement) intimates a need to pass beyond extant theory; the latter, to the degree of purely mathematical (and, thus conceived, ontologically neutral) descriptive fit between measured and theoretically-computed values exhibited by the predecessor's "observational base" of "inductive" confirmations.

The moral we should carry away from these (admittedly drastically schematic) considerations is that, already within the manifest image, the epistemic authority of the method of theoretical postulation is sufficient to underwrite ontologically significant conclusions. And when we bring this observation together with our earlier remarks regarding basic entities, we can finally see that the manifest image contains, so to speak, the epistemic seeds of its own ontological destruction. For nothing exempts the descriptive predicates covering the framework's *basic* entities from such relegation to the language of seeming if there are good enough theoretical, i.e., explanatory, reasons for doing so, provided that "the appearances" are properly and adequately "saved".[11] And this sets the stage for two closing remarks, both highlighting aspects of Sellars's rich "two images" story which Professor Aune's insightful comments have perhaps underemphasized.

First, it is important to see that part of "saving the appearances" in this instance is preserving the definitive role of persons as both the subjects and the sources of norms. Thus what Sellars envisions is not the wholesale replacement of the manifest by the scientific image *tout court*, but rather the development of a "stereoscopic" or "synoptic" image in which the abandonment of the manifest image framework concept of (sensible) "corporeal substance", which arguably provides (via spatio-temporal continuity) the sole principles of unity and identity for empirical persons, does not entail the ultimate loss of persons as unitary single subjects of multiple logical, semantic, and epistemic predicates.

[If] the human body is a system of particles, the body cannot be the subject of thinking and feeling, unless thinking and feeling are capable of interpretation as complex interactions of physical particles; unless, that is to say, the manifest framework of man as one being, a person, capable of doing radically different kinds of things can be replaced without loss of descriptive and explanatory power by a postulational image in which he is a complex of physical particles, and all his activities a matter of the particles changing in state and relationship.

(PSIM, 66; in SPR: 29; in ISR: 397)

Secondly, however, it is crucial to recognize that, on Sellars's view, the very existence of any normative order at all can ultimately be explanatorily accommodated only within a mature scientific

[11] Left tacit in this discussion is the important role of models and commentaries in analogical concept formation, a proper appreciation of which is crucial to understanding how a global (ostensibly "complete") conceptual framework can, as it were, "grow" new categorial concepts, i.e., concepts of kinds of entities of which it can make sense to suppose that the framework's (old) basic entities are (merely) appearances.

image. Thus there is another, deeper, sense in which the manifest image already contains the seeds of its own destruction. Within the manifest image, the existence of any normative order at all appears as a radical discontinuity.

[Anything] which can properly be called conceptual thinking can occur only within a framework of conceptual thinking in terms of which it can be criticized, supported, refuted, in short, evaluated.... In this sense a diversified conceptual framework is a whole which, however sketchy, is prior to its parts, and cannot be construed as a coming together of parts which are already conceptual in character. The conclusion is difficult to avoid that the transition from preconceptual patterns of behavior to conceptual thinking was a holistic one, a jump to a level of awareness which is irreducibly new....

(PSIM, 43; in SPR: 6; in ISR: 374)

In the nineteenth century, the long-standing philosophical proclivity to respond to this perceived discontinuity with Platonic stories of "intelligible essences" and "illumination" ("grasping Forms") began to give way to a growing recognition of the essentially social character of norms and the consequent ineliminable role of the group as mediating between the "brute" causality of the physical world and the presence in individuals of the framework of conceptual thinking. Nevertheless, claims Sellars, the manifest image did not thereby acquire explanatory resources adequate to account for and defuse its own ostensible "emergentism". The manifest image was now

... construed as containing a conception of itself as a group phenomenon, the group mediating between the individual and the intelligible order. But any attempt to explain this mediation within the framework of the manifest image was bound to fail, for the manifest image contains the resources for such an attempt only in the sense that it provides the foundation on which scientific theory can build an explanatory framework....

It is in the scientific image of man-in-the-world that we begin to see the main outlines of the way in which man came to have an image of himself-in-the-world. For we begin to see this [as] a matter of evolutionary development as a group phenomenon, a process which is illustrated at a simpler level by the evolutionary development which explains the correspondence between the dancing of a worker bee and the location, relative to the sun, of the flower from which he comes. This correspondence, like the relation between man's "original" image and the world, is incapable of explanation in terms of a direct conditioning impact of the environment on the individual as such.

(PSIM, 54; in SPR: 17–18; in ISR: 385–6)

Scientific discourse, Sellars wrote thirty-five years ago,[12] is "a continuation of a dimension of discourse which has been present in human discourse from the very beginning" (EPM §41, in SPR: 172; in KMG: 252; in B: 81–2). In consequence, we have seen, the scientific picture of the world can legitimately lay claim to the epistemic authority to replace the world-picture of even a philosophically refined commonsense. The problem of understanding the relationship between the conceptual and the natural orders, of making intelligible the intelligibility of the encountered world, has been a standing challenge to human discourses, if not from the very beginning, then at least since the emergence of our perennial traditions of self-conscious philosophical reflection in ancient Greece, traditions which have perennially responded to this challenge by reifying the intelligible in an ontology of irreducibly abstract or intentional entities. Sellars's striking contention, we now see, is that only a scientific world-picture which indeed exercises its prerogative to supersede the descriptive ontologies of everyday

---

[12] "Empiricism and the Philosophy of Mind," (Presented at the University of London in Special Lectures in Philosophy for 1956 under the title "The Myth of the Given: Three Lectures on Empiricism and the Philosophy of Mind"), in *Minnesota Studies in the Philosophy of Science*, vol. I, eds. Herbert Feigl and Michael Scriven (Minneapolis: University of Minnesota Press, 1956): 253–329. Reprinted with additional footnotes in *Science, Perception and Reality* (London: Routledge & Kegan Paul, 1963), re-issued by Ridgeview Publishing Company in 1991. [SPR] Published separately as *Empiricism and the Philosophy of Mind: with an Introduction by Richard Rorty and a Study Guide by Robert Brandom*, ed. Robert Brandom (Cambridge, MA: Harvard University Press, 1997). [B] Also reprinted in W. deVries and T. Triplett, *Knowledge, Mind, and the Given: A Reading of Sellars' "Empiricism and the Philosophy of Mind"* (Cambridge, MA: Hackett Publishing, 2000) [KMG]. Cited in the text as EPM, page references to SPR, KMG, and B editions.

life can finally supply resources for explanatorily accommodating the very existence of the manifest image, i.e., for properly locating the normative conceptual order within the causal order of (a categorially homogeneous) nature.

To be sure, it is not obvious whether this is so, but the claim is unquestionably as important as it is provocative. Coming properly to terms with it will be an indispensable part of our efforts fully to appreciate and to appropriate as our own the many insights encompassed in Sellars's story of the two images. One can hardly agree enthusiastically enough with Professor Aune's conclusion that this remains a philosophical project well worthy of our continued attention.

References

Adams, E. M., "The Scientific and the Humanistic Images of Man-in-the-World", *Man and World* 4 (1971): 174–92.

Aune, Bruce, "Sellars's Two Images of the World", *The Journal of Philosophy* 87 (Oct., 1990): 537–45.

Rorty, Richard, *Philosophy and the Mirror of Nature* (Princeton, NJ: Princeton University Press, 1979).

—— *Contingency, Irony, and Solidarity* (Cambridge and New York: Cambridge University Press, 1989).

Rosenberg, Jay F., 'Coupling, Retheoretization, and the Correspondence Principle", *Synthese* 45 (1980): 351–85.

—— "The Place of Color in the Scheme of Things: A Roadmap to Sellars' Carus Lectures", *The Monist* 65 (1982): 315–35.

—— "Comparing the Incommensurable: Another Look at Convergent Realism", *Philosophical Studies* 54 (1988): 163–93.

—— "Fusing the Images", *Journal for General Philosophy of Science* (*Zeitschrift für Allgemeine Erkenntnistheorie*) 21 (1990): 3–25.

—— *Wilfrid Sellars: Fusing the Images* (Oxford and New York: Oxford University Press, 2007).

Sellars, Wilfrid S., "Empiricism and the Philosophy of Mind", (Presented at the University of London in Special Lectures in Philosophy for 1956 under the title "The Myth of the Given: Three Lectures on Empiricism and the Philosophy of Mind"), in *Minnesota Studies in the Philosophy of Science*, vol. I, eds. Herbert Feigl and Michael Scriven (Minneapolis: University of Minnesota Press, 1956): 253–329. Reprinted with additional footnotes in *Science, Perception and Reality* (London: Routledge & Kegan Paul, 1963), re-issued by Ridgeview Publishing Company in 1991. [SPR] Published separately as *Empiricism and the Philosophy of Mind: with an Introduction by Richard Rorty and a Study Guide by Robert Brandom*, ed. Robert Brandom (Cambridge, MA: Harvard University Press, 1997). [B] Also reprinted in W. deVries and T. Triplett, *Knowledge, Mind, and the Given: A Reading of Sellars' "Empiricism and the Philosophy of Mind"* (Cambridge, MA: Hackett Publishing, 2000) [KMG]. Cited in the text as EPM.

—— "Philosophy and the Scientific Image of Man", in *Frontiers of Science and Philosophy*, ed. Robert Colodny (Pittsburgh, PA: University of Pittsburgh Press, 1962): 35–78. Reprinted in *Science, Perception, and Reality*, [SPR] (New York: Routledge & Kegan Paul, 1963, reissued Atascadero, CA: Ridgeview Publishing, 1991): 1–40, and in *In the Space of Reasons*, [ISR] eds. Kevin Scharp and Robert Brandom (Cambridge, MA: Harvard University Press, 2007): 369–408. Henceforth PSIM.

van Fraassen, Bas, "Wilfrid Sellars on Scientific Realism", *Dialogue* 14 (1975): 606–16.

—— *The Scientific Image* (Oxford: Oxford University Press, 1980).

Index